# Get a
# Freelance
# Life

# Get a
# Freelance
# Life

## mediabistro.com's

### Insider Guide to Freelance Writing

# MARGIT FEURY RAGLAND

Foreword by Laurel Touby, founder of mediabistro.com

 THREE RIVERS PRESS • NEW YORK

Grateful acknowledgment is made to the following for
permission to reprint previously published material:

**Sierra Club:** *Sierra Magazine's Writers Guidelines.*
Reprinted by permission of *Sierra Magazine.*

**The Society of Professional Journalists:** *The Society of Professional Journalists
Code of Ethics.* Copyright © 2005 by Society of Professional Journalists.
Reprinted by permission of the Society of Professional Journalists,
3909 N. Meridan St., Indianapolis, IN 46208, www.spj.org.

Library of Congress Cataloging-in-Publication Data
Ragland, Margit Feury.
Get a freelance life : mediabistro.com's insider guide to freelance writing /
Margit Feury Ragland.—1st ed.
Includes index.
1. Freelance journalism.   2. Authorship.   I. Title.
PN4784.F76R34 2006
808'.02—dc22        2005028944

ISBN-10: 0-307-23803-2

ISBN-13: 978-0-307-23803-0

Printed in the United States of America

*Design by Lynne Amft*

10 9 8 7 6 5 4 3 2 1

First Edition

*To Gar, then Burke, and finally Elroy:*
*my true companions during the writing of this book*
*on Koontz Farm in rural West Virginia.*

# Contents

# MIND YOUR OWN BUSINESS

15. Manage Your Finances   *219*

    Running Your Freelancing Business

16. Affordable Health Insurance   *232*

    It's Hard to Find Affordable Health Coverage as a Freelancer, but It's Not Impossible

17. Taming Your Taxes   *235*

    Tax Time Is Very Different for Freelancers Than for Employees

18. Invest More in Yourself   *244*

    Bring Your Business to the Next Level

19. Boost Your Bucks   *250*

    Strategies for Increasing Your Income

20. Conclusion   *273*

21. Resources   *274*

    Lingo   280
    Acknowledgments   294    Index   297

I'll never forget the moment I decided to try my hand at journalism.

While I had worked on my college newspaper as a reporter, the fact that my father had been a professional newspaper journalist had somehow been more intimidating to me than encouraging, and I had ended up in advertising. But when my friend Adrian Nicole LeBlanc started writing investigative pieces for the *Village Voice*, that got me thinking that maybe this was something I could do, too. As Adrian put it, "This is the only work I can think of where I am paid for my curiosity."

That was the clincher.

Over the next couple of years, I managed to score a staff job at (now defunct) *Working Woman* magazine in New York City, develop a specialty in business writing, land my first freelance assignment, and contribute to magazines as varied as *Cosmopolitan* and *New York*. I went back on staff once more, at *Business Week,* thinking that security was the most important thing for me, but quit when I realized that creative control was even more valuable. I then took a plum gig as a contributing editor at *Glamour* magazine because it offered me the chance to freelance again.

While working for *Glamour,* a friend and I started a series of Press Club–style cocktail parties that would later become the crux of the mediabistro.com Web site and business. The first party in the East Village of New York drew a mere ten people. That's how many contacts my friend and I had in the media business. Those original attendees were mostly editors and writers who sought the companionship of like-minded people. They paid for their own drinks and I put on a feather boa (they couldn't miss the hostess that way) and introduced guests around to each other. The parties quickly grew, and before I knew it, I had 20,000 of the media world's top talent on my e-mail list. I regularly helped people get full-time jobs and freelance gigs—and some even hooked up romantically.

By 1997, guests who were attending the parties began asking me why I didn't have a Web site where they could meet up virtually 24/7. That year, I started a community site to help journalists from all over the world reach out to each other. Today, the site, www.mediabistro. com, is *the* hot spot for media people to meet, get gigs (both freelance and full-time), find specialized writing, editing, and other types of classes, and generally share resources. Mediabistro.com's Bulletin Board is a popular online watering hole for full-time as well as aspiring writers who muse on topics ranging from "What's your dream job in media?" to "How do freelancers really pay the bills?" We also added original interviews with editors, experienced award-winning writers, best-selling novelists and agents, and a wide range of journalistic tools to help media professionals manage the work process and do their jobs better. The site logs 450,000 unique visitors per month, from top media professionals to aspiring journalists.

When I first started freelance writing, I would never have trusted any book to tell me how to be a freelancer. Because I had worked on the "other side" as a magazine editor, I knew that landing an assignment from a major national newspaper or magazine was rarely a straightforward endeavor. Rather, it was often a tortuous path of dead ends and near misses. Many a fine pitch letter didn't get the writer an assignment, many experienced writers were passed up for friends of the editor-in-chief, and many a piece was assigned and killed for apparently no reason. It didn't seem like there were any real "lessons" to be taught, short of making friends with editors who could give you work!

It would have been great to be able to consult with someone

skilled in handling the kinds of sticky situations I was encountering. Beyond the constant grinding rejection from too-busy editors, there were practical matters I didn't know how to deal with, such as what to do when your assigning editor has been ousted (and no one returns calls), how to decode an editor who can't communicate her wishes, or how to get paid when a magazine is going under.

That's one reason why we at mediabistro.com decided to produce a book on freelance writing. With all the many freelancing books on the shelves, there is still a tremendous need for practical guidance and mentoring. I was once on a panel at an industry event discussing "making it as a freelance writer," and I was besieged with requests from attendees that stretched via e-mail months after the event was over. In fact, every day I receive e-mail from people facing age-old freelance dilemmas. Our *MBToolbox* Blog was created to help freelancers solve some of these problems. It's at www.mbtoolbox.com and our blog editor is barely able to keep up with demand from writers with thorny questions. But, where mbtoolbox.com is a random assortment of questions and answers that users pose on the fly, this book tackles the whole wild and woolly world of freelancing and helps you make sense of the entire spectrum.

Another reason we decided to write this book was to provide our readers with the type of access to top editors and writers that mediabistro.com uniquely serves. That's why we included "Insider Guide" to freelance writing in the subtitle of the book, because it's not just about the basics, but about how to really get a leg up in this insular world. I could have used a book like this not only when I was starting out, but throughout my freelance career. I'm proud to be able to offer it to you and I truly hope that it will make your path to happiness and success as a freelancer a little bit clearer. You deserve to be paid well (and on time) for *your* curiosity, too.

*—Laurel Touby*

PART I

Are You Ready to
Be Free?

# 1

# Is Freelancing Right for You?

Things to Consider Before Taking the
Plunge

So you want to be a freelance writer. Welcome to the club. There are many wannabe freelancers out there but only a limited number of talented, dedicated, motivated, hardworking, and successful freelance writers. It's not that it's an impossible goal; it's that freelance writing is hard and demanding work—although potentially very rewarding. It's doable, *if* you're cut out for it. Here are eleven questions to ask yourself before deciding whether freelancing is right for you.

## 1. Do you like being alone?

Working at home is certainly a luxury—you can sleep in, work in your pj's, take a break when the sun is out, or meet friends for a long lunch. But it can also be lonely. There's nobody standing at the water-cooler (or at your fridge) waiting to discuss last night's reality-TV program. There's nobody to vent to after an editor asks you for the third rewrite of a piece that was a bore from the beginning. And you have only yourself to rely on when trying to come up with a catchy headline.

The good news is that many writers have developed creative techniques to deal with this isolation: heading to a coffee shop every morning for a cup of joe, the newspaper, and some conversation; weekly meetings with different editors; a class at a nearby college; regularly scheduled lunches; volunteering a few hours a week; or even partaking in online discussion groups.

**Loneliness will kick in, so be sure you can handle it. And have a plan to nip at least some of it in the bud.**

## 2. Where are you now?

If you've been working as an accountant for the past fifteen years, even if you're very proud of what you publish in your diary each night, it's probably not yet time to jump ship for a full-time freelancing career. That's okay—the great thing about freelancing is that you can start doing it while you're still doing something else. You can slowly but consistently start accumulating writing samples (known as clips) and establishing connections; this lays the groundwork for a freelancing career.

On the other hand, if you've been getting published fairly regularly (let's say once or twice a month) in a few different publications that pay at least decently (around $1 a word), you might be in a better spot to make a go of it.

But you'll need to continue to work your connections correctly and leverage what you've already been doing. And you'll need to be realistic. If you've been employed as the restaurant reviewer at a community newspaper for the past two years, don't expect to quit and jump right into freelance travel writing.

And before you say *hasta la vista* to your boss, work to keep a relationship—and even better, a freelance income—with your current employer, if you can. This is key. The benefits of having a steady gig set up before you set out on your own are great.

And don't be afraid to ask yourself some of those dreaded interview questions, such as "Where do you want to be in five years?"

---

### WHEN TO MAKE THE MOVE

"There's never really a completely safe time to start a business. It's always a risk. But one good way of going about things is to start your business while you are still employed. If you're a staff writer, start building a client list of freelance assignments. Yes, it's tiring to have a full-time job and then work on the side, but it sure beats not being able to pay your rent. Once you get a list of clients, you can use this as leverage to get more and more clients."

—*Duy Linh Tu, founder and creative director of Resolution Seven, LLC. Duy is a writer, videographer, motion graphics designer, and photographer and he teaches new media at the Columbia University Graduate School of Journalism.*

---

(Possible answer: Working regularly with around ten different publications, writing at least four articles a month, or bringing in at least 5K a month.) If you are planning on embarking on a solo career, you'd better be able to answer that question for yourself.

**You can't just call yourself a freelancer and expect assignments to roll in. Know where you are and where you want to be, and map out a reasonable plan to get from A to B.**

### 3. Can you afford it?

Don't get fed up with your boss and decide that today is the day to go it on your own. Unless you have a few regular well-paying gigs already set up or a handful of folks just itching to buy your work, chances are you can't go freelance cold turkey—you can't afford it! It takes some seed money—not to mention preparation and prior thought—to take the giant leap into a writing career.

Obviously, the amount of steady freelance income you need before

**BEFORE YOU QUIT**

"If you are contemplating leaving your full-time job to go freelance, make sure you have some 'cushion' to protect yourself. It generally takes a bit of time to get paid when you first start up in the freelance business, anywhere from three weeks to six months once you complete a job. So make sure you have about three to four months of living expenses saved up in the bank, and then another $500 to $2,000 on hand for all the start-up costs of your new business, such as accountant and lawyer fees, a computer, business cards, office supplies, a cell phone, a second phone line, and more."

—*Howard Samuels, CPA MST, managing partner in S&C LLP, a NYC-based Certified Public Accounting firm specializing in tax for small businesses and individuals*

"My advice is: First, trim the fat. Get rid of cable TV (you won't have time to watch anyway), get rid of your gym membership (go run in the park), get rid of whatever you really, really don't need in your life. Then, create a realistic budget. You'll be surprised at how much you were spending before on things that were not absolutely necessary. Once you get enough work to be able to support about 75 percent of that amount, take the plunge, quit your job, and start your business."

—*Duy Linh Tu*

quitting your day job depends on your financial needs. You shouldn't go solo without first looking at your monthly expenses and comparing that to how much you can realistically bring in each month. (There's more on setting up a budget in Chapter 15.) If you're unable to analyze your budget on your own, set up a meeting with an accountant and have a chat to gauge whether you can really afford to take this big step.

In addition, remember that even if you get $4,000 worth of assignments in the first month of freelancing full-time, there's no telling when you will be paid. For instance, if your contract says you'll be paid "upon publication," you won't get a check in the mail until the month when your article appears in the publication—which could be months and months after the piece was first assigned.

As we mentioned before, if you can set up a regular freelance gig with your current employer (especially if you're already working in publishing), you will be a step ahead of the game.

**Assignments take some time to start rolling in—checks take even longer. Develop a financial plan before making any rash decisions.**

### 4. Are you flexible?

Few freelance writers have a regular schedule. Chances are you won't have, say, one article due every Tuesday at noon. The experts you want to interview are seldom available when it's most convenient for you. And editors often call needing quick turnaround on a piece—seemingly invariably on a week you've set up as your "nice and easy" week. When you have a huge project due on a Thursday for publication A, chances are great that on Wednesday morning your editor from publication B will call needing a revise of the piece you handed in three weeks earlier, and she'll need that revise ASAP. Somehow, you have to make it all work.

**The freelancer's life can be unpredictable. You'll have to develop a schedule that works for you, but one that allows unexpected changes to your plan.**

### 5. Can you stick to a budget?

The term *biweekly paycheck* is unknown to freelancers. Waiting to get paid can be even harder than waiting for an assignment. And when that nice, big check does arrive, it'll look large . . . until you remember it might need to carry you for a good long while (and that you'll have to pay taxes on it; as freelance income, nothing's been withheld).

So if you're not good with numbers, you'll need to find someone who is, quick. (There's more on this in Chapter 15.) Freelancers need to be aware of all necessary expenses, monitor spending closely, map out a budget plan long in advance, and act as an accountant on nearly a daily basis.

**Freelancers don't have regular paychecks. You need to have a budget that builds in a cushion for slow months and late checks, and you need to be able to monitor it and abide by it.**

## 6. Are you organized?

If you miss deadlines, misplace interview notes, or hand in sloppy work, chances are you're not going to get many repeat assignments. Freelance writers are often juggling multiple projects at any one time and, except for a lucky few, act as their own secretaries and mailroom workers and benefits experts and supply clerks. As well as monitoring your own budget, you have to manage your own daily schedule, all your interview notes, all your fact-checking materials, all your sources' contact information, all of your due dates, and on and on. It can be daunting, but you must stay on top of everything.

**A freelance career will work out only if you can stay highly organized.**

## 7. Can you separate work and life?

Working out of your own home can quickly overwhelm you, becoming far more than a nine-to-five, Monday-through-Friday job. Sure, the more you work, the more money you'll bring in. But there's a breaking point, and you need the self-control not to get pulled toward it.

The nice thing about freelancing is that you can work all weekend if you have no plans, or burn the midnight oil for days at a time and then take a completely worry-free three-week vacation. Problems begin to arise when you find yourself spending every waking moment in front of your computer. You think about going to the gym, but then you can't stop thinking about that looming deadline. Your family is heading out for a picnic in the park, but you just brainstormed a better lead for that assignment due next week. Eventually, all work and no play becomes too much. You need to keep a good balance between your work life and the rest of your life.

**You must be able to develop methods to enforce a relatively normal work schedule.**

### 8. Can you be your own boss?

Many people look at the life of a freelancer as heavenly. No one to report to, no one making you get approval before taking action, no time-consuming, nonproductive staff meetings. People expect that will add up to an easy, no-stress work life. It doesn't.

Bosses keep you motivated. Bosses require you to get things done. Bosses pay rent on the office and make sure you have a paycheck. When you're on your own, it's all your problem.

If the phone hasn't rung in three weeks, and the rejection letters are filling your in-box, you may not have someone to report to, but a whole different type of worry sets in. Will I be able to pay my rent or mortgage next month? Will the star source for my article ever call me back? Will that check ever come? Will I ever get another assignment?

And even when things are moving along nicely, nobody else is going to be there to tell you to sit down at your computer by 9 a.m. And nobody is going to know if you take a 5-minute—or

50-minute—coffee break, except you. Many former freelancers are no longer because they couldn't tear themselves away from *Regis and Kelly* in the morning or get off the phone with friends all afternoon. You must remember that you are your own boss, and you alone are responsible for your paycheck. That's great, but if you can't whip yourself into action, there's only one person who is going to be responsible for your failure. There is no way to pass the buck when you are a freelance writer making it on your own. You have to be able to get the job done.

**You have to work hard and be self-disciplined, or a freelance career will never work out.**

### 9. Can you sell yourself?

You want to be a writer, not a salesman. But freelance writers must also do quite a bit of self-promotion to be successful. It's often said that some of the most successful writers are not necessarily the most talented ones, but those who are able to get their names out there and into the hands of editors doing the assigning.

Does this mean that a shy individual can never make it freelancing? Certainly not. How creative you are is probably more important than how outgoing another writer is. But you've still got to get that creativity and those ideas into editors' hands, and you need to do it in a way that's neither too reticent or too chest thumping.

If you can find the right words to describe your talents and your brilliant story ideas, then you will be well on your way to a successful career. Walking the fine line of self-promotion is of utmost importance.

**Every freelancer is a salesman, too. Get used to it, and learn to do it well.**

## 10. Can you say no, and can you handle it when someone else says no to you?

Because freelance work can be so unpredictable, many freelancers are eager to take any projects that come along. But if you do that, you may end up with more work than you can handle—and you'll be doing nobody any good if you are scrambling to finish assignments and not doing a thorough job on the work you hand in. Editors will stop calling you with more assignments. You have to know when to say no, to have the confidence that work will come when you need it and therefore the discipline not to accept projects you really shouldn't.

The opposite is also true—there'll be times when you'll be doing all that you can to find work but nothing seems to pan out. Even very established writers have ideas they absolutely love but just can't sell. In this business, rejection letters are the norm. Get used to them. Eventually you'll be able to find a place for most ideas, and if not, sometimes you need to leave an idea behind and move on to something new.

**You need to be able to deal with the ebb and flow of assignments. Don't take on too much just because you can, and don't be too worried when editors aren't biting—there's always something new for you to try pitching.**

## 11. Do you have many interests?

Sure, some writers become rich and famous writing about the same topic day after day, week after week. But, in general, that's rare. You'll need to be open to everything that's going on around you; it's all a potential story. The writers with the best story ideas are the writers who are full of curiosity. They see things in the world worth investigating and worth talking about. Then they put those observations down on paper, dig a little deeper, talk to the experts, and inform themselves as they inform the world around them.

**You have to be open and curious about the world around you, or else you'll never be able to find enough ideas for pitches.**

After reading through the above questions, analyze how you feel. Maybe you really are ready to enter the full-time world of freelance writing. Or perhaps it's time to take your part-time freelancing up a notch. Or maybe you just need to sit down and churn out your first query letter. Whichever it is, this book will lead you on the journey.

## 2

# Invest in Yourself

The Bare Necessities for a Successful
Freelancer

Launching a freelance writing career is like starting any new business: it takes money to make money. The nice thing is you don't need a storefront or a fully stocked warehouse to start this company. Not literally, at least. The storefront you need is a way to sell yourself—the ability to compose a flawless pitch letter, some decent clips, and perhaps a vibrant Web site or an intriguing résumé. And instead of a warehouse, you need a mind stuffed with brilliant ideas and a fully operational office in which to execute them.

## The Basics of a Freelancer's Résumé

While the pitch letter—also called a query—is of utmost importance in launching a freelance career (more on that in Part III), an appropriately tailored résumé can get you noticed.

As a freelancer, you aren't out to land a full-time job. So details about your education and even past employment are not as important on your freelance résumé as information about your writing experience.

Of course, that advice comes with a caveat. If you're looking to pitch beauty stories and you've worked in a trendy spa for the past four years, definitely highlight that work background. If you're pitching travel pieces about Italy and you spent the previous six months traveling through Tuscany, showcase that experience. And if you want to write health pieces and you just finished medical school, by all means play up your education.

If you have no published clips and no related experience—and, really, even if you do—your résumé and query letter must read like beautiful prose; otherwise they're destined for an editor's recycling bin. And as a beginner you'll need to work a little harder on your résumé to illustrate that you are well rounded and interested in the world around you. But that may be enough to conquer the lack of experience and clips—as long as it comes with a great story idea, of course.

Remember these key tips when creating your freelancing résumé:
- Keep it relatively simple and straightforward. Nothing too fancy or flowery, unless you're hoping to pitch a gardening story to *Martha Stewart Living*. Use a clean font, in an easy-to-read size. Go with traditional, white or off-white résumé paper.
- You might want to skip the "objective" (it's not necessary to say, "I'm hoping to obtain some freelance writing assignments") and instead consider including three or four bullet points illustrating why an editor should toss some assignments your way. For example, mention your nutrition background if you want to develop diet plans for women's magazines. Or play up your ability to meet tight deadlines, even if it's in an entirely different line of work. If you've worked as a physician's assistant, bring to the forefront your ability to interview people and get them to reveal personal information quickly and accurately—that's a valuable skill for an investigative reporter.
- Keep it fresh. Because freelancers are often involved in many small projects at once, it's important to keep your résumé updated. For instance, if you have an article in a publication currently on the newsstand, be sure that fact is featured prominently on your résumé. If you are just finishing up two or three assignments that

are scheduled for future issues of a publication, you might not want to reveal the title or specific topic of the article, but you can state the assigning publication. For example, under your list of recent work, you can write "*Family Circle:* How-to article to appear in upcoming issue." If you know the actual issue when the piece will run, list the issue date. Once that date arrives, update your résumé to list the exact title of the article and verify the issue.

- Consider creating several different résumés if you plan to write on different topics for different kinds of publications. One version might focus on your background in finance and another on your culinary expertise. Tailoring your sales pitch always helps you close the deal.

- Be sure to use strong, action words—it sells you better, and it shows you can write. Instead of saying you're "good at making things sound exciting," describe yourself as a "prolific writer." Instead of saying you'll "hand in error-free assignments," talk about yourself as "meticulous."

## How a Résumé Can Help

A great résumé can show your expertise and credibility in a certain field—and help you get a gig—even if you have little experience pitching publications. For example, if you are a shopping addict, allude to that when pitching women's publications. "The most important thing to remember when introducing yourself is to highlight any expertise you have in scouting out home, fashion, or beauty goods," says Karen Catchpole, deputy editor at *Shop Etc.* "Send a résumé and a letter explaining any relevant experience or expertise in the world of shopping and, if possible, clips that do the same. . . ." One freelancer sent in clips and a résumé and referred to herself as a 'product junkie.'" That "beauty-obsessed" writer's work appeared in a recent issue.

Here are some sample résumés from established freelancers:

# SAMPLE RÉSUMÉ #1

## ROBIN DONOVAN  robin@robindonovan.com

IN A NUTSHELL
- Creative and versatile food writer with articles in *Cooking Light, Fitness, San Jose Mercury News, Seattle Post-Intelligencer, Las Vegas Sun*, Amazon.com, Sallys-Place.com, *Vine, San Francisco Chronicle*'s SFGate.com, and other publications.
- Published cookbook author—my first book, *Campfire Cuisine: Eating Well in the Great Outdoors*, is published by Quirk Books.
- Skilled at developing inventive original recipes.
- Knowledgeable and passionate about food, cooking, and the culinary industry.
- Proven ability to produce quality work on deadline.
- 16 years of experience in the publishing business, including: • Writing • Reporting • Content Development • Marketing Communications.

WHAT I'VE BEEN DOING ALL THESE YEARS
- Writing my first cookbook—*Campfire Cuisine: Eating Well in the Great Outdoors.*
- Writing feature articles for magazines, newspapers, and Web sites on topics ranging from the clandestine world of wild mushroom hunters to the health benefits of honey and the worldwide revival of ancient varieties of rice.
- Developing original, inventive, diligently tested recipes.
- Researching and reporting on food industry trends and current events—developing and maintaining industry contacts, interviewing experts, and conducting field, Internet, and library research.
- Writing cookbook and restaurant reviews for magazines, newspapers, and Web sites.
- Writing marketing copy for Web sites, book jackets, catalogs, print advertisements, brochures, and other materials.
- Planning and executing Internet marketing campaigns, including Web promotion, direct e-mail, content placement and syndication, pay-per-click advertising campaigns, search engine optimization, and more.

WHERE I'VE BEEN
Freelance Writer 2000–present
Berrett-Koehler Publishers, San Francisco Sr. Online Marketing Manager.
  1999–present
Senior Promotion Manager, 1998-1999
Promotion Manager, 1994-1998
Hunter House, Publishers, Alameda, CA Promotion & Publicity Manager,
  1992–1994
China Books & Periodicals, San Francisco Publicist, 1991–1992
*Southern Exposure Magazine,* Durham, NC Reporter/Editorial Assistant,
  1990–1991
Butterfield Associates, Emeryville, CA Publicity Assistant, 1988–1990

WHERE I LEARNED THE BASICS
UC Santa Cruz, BA Psychology with honors, Phi Beta Kappa Honor
  Society, 1988.

REFERENCES AND WRITING SAMPLES FURNISHED ON REQUEST

## SAMPLE RÉSUMÉ #2

### KRISTEN KEMP

XX XXXXXX Street
Hoboken, NJ 07030
(917) XXX-XXX
kristen@kristenkemp.com

FREELANCE EXPERIENCE
**Books**
*Breakfast at Bloomingdale's,* teen novel (Scholastic, 2006)
*The Dating Diaries,* teen novel (Scholastic/Push 2004)
*Healthy Sexuality: Your Guide to Sex and Your Body,* teen nonfiction
  (Scholastic, 2004)

(continued)

*Vulvodynia: A Survivor's Guide*, adult nonfiction (New Harbinger Press, 2002)
*I Will Survive*, teen novel (Scholastic/Push, 2002)
*Genny in a Bottle*, series of four preteen novels (Scholastic, 2001)
*Strut Your Stuff*, preteen nonfiction (Scholastic, 2001)
*Who Are You Really?*, preteen nonfiction personality quizzes (Scholastic, 2000)
*2 Grrrls Guide to Friendship*, children's nonfiction (Scholastic, 2000)
*2 Grrrls Guide to Style*, children's nonfiction (Scholastic, 2000)
*Bands We Love*, unauthorized biography (Scholastic, 2000)
*B*Witched: Backstage Pass*, unauthorized biography (Scholastic, 1999)
*Jewel: Pieces of a Dream*, unauthorized biography (Simon & Schuster, 1998)

MAGAZINES AND NEWSPAPERS
*The Advocate, AARP, Cosmogirl!, Cosmopolitan, First For Women, Girls' Life, Glamour, Honey, Investor's Business Daily, Ladies' Home Journal, Mademoiselle, Marie Claire, Men's Health, Modern Bride, My Generation, The New York Daily News, Parenting, Redbook, Self, Seventeen, Stuff, 'Teen, 'Teen's All About You, Twist, YM*

MAGAZINE EDITING/CONTRIBUTIONS
Contributing editor for *Girls' Life* (October 2002–present)
Freelance health editor for *Modern Bride* (February–April 2005)
Freelance senior editor for *Cosmogirl!* (August–October 2004)
Contributing editor for *YM* (May 2000–May 2002)
Freelance senior editor for *YM* (August–September 2000)
Freelance entertainment editor for *YM* (December, 1999)

SPEAKING
New York is Book Country; Indiana University School of Journalism classes; New York University Graduate Journalism School classes; New School journalism classes; New York Presswomen's Association panelist; high, middle, and elementary school classes; ED2010; mediabistro.com

TEACHING

The Woodhull Institute co-instructor, 3-day intensive on Non-Fiction
Writing (November 2004–present)

mediabistro instructor, 8-week courses on Basic Journalism (May 2004–
present)

mediabistro instructor, 8-week courses on Writing for Women's
Magazines (May 2004–present)

mediabistro instructor, 12-week courses on Writing the Young Adult
Novel (May 2003–present)

TELEVISION

*Sally Jesse Raphael Show* / *Philly After Midnight* / Showtime's *Penn &
Teller: Bullshit*

STAFF EXPERIENCE

*First For Women,* Editor-at-Large (March 2002–September 2002)
Assigned, edited and generated real life, sex, and relationship copy;
managed our staff's service editors and writers; wrote and edited
various health columns.

*Cosmopolitan,* Associate Editor (October 1998–October 1999)
Edited columns and articles; wrote sex and relationship features, careers columns, and quizzes; researched sex Q&A column; generated
ideas and story outlines.

*Twist,* Staff Writer (May 1997–October 1998)
Edited quizzes, real life stories, entertainment copy and comic strip;
wrote cover features, columns, quizzes and entertainment pieces;
did emergency rewrites; researched and generated ideas.

*Girls' Life,* Assistant Editor (August 1996–May 1997)
Edited, wrote, and assigned in the following departments: features,
horoscopes, news bits, celebrity interviews, and movies; generated
ideas; handled queries and correspondence.

*New Albany Tribune,* Reporter (January 1995–September 1995)
Wrote general interest and feature stories; produced six articles
per week.

EDUCATION

Indiana University, Bachelor of Arts in Journalism, 1996

## Now It's Time to Start Promoting Yourself

As a freelancer, you're not just a writer; you're also your own marketing and public relations firm. The only person who will be promoting your work will be *you*.

**Clips:** A good place to start is with your writing samples. If you don't currently have any, get writing—for your neighborhood flyer, your church newsletter, your office news alert, your local gossip bulletin, whatever. At this point, don't worry so much if you're not getting paid. The important thing is, you're going to need published samples of your work in order to get assignments from more established, well-paying publications. (More on clips in Chapter 7.)

### HOW I GOT MY FIRST CLIP

"I didn't study journalism, so I didn't know where to start when I wanted to be a journalist. I was living in D.C. and working at a bar. One day I bicycled to the office of a free weekly, the *City Paper*. It was in some poor, sketchy neighborhood. I went in and said I want to talk to the editor. The staff was so amused that I showed up without an appointment that I actually got to see the editor. He wrote a phone number on a piece of paper and said, 'Call this guy and ask him how the city cable contract was awarded, and write an article about it.' I just had no idea—clueless, just totally clueless. But the city cable contract was awarded in a sort of sleazy way, and there was a lot of corruption in D.C. at the time, and I thought, Well, I don't know what I'm doing but I'll just concentrate hard enough and find out the answer. I think that's true—you know I have no idea how to repair a car engine but I feel like if I sat down with a shop book and a bunch of tools, I would eventually—maybe it would take months or years—but eventually I'd figure engines out. And that's sort of my approach to journalism."

—*Sebastian Junger, author of* The Perfect Storm, *is a national magazine award-winning journalist who writes for numerous publications, including* Outside, American Heritage, *and* Men's Journal.

"I was living in Chicago and at the time there was a new alternative weekly called *New City*. I just started doing music reviews—without even talking to anybody there, and just started sending them in. I did that for a couple of weeks, probably sent in two or three different pieces. Eventually they actually liked one of them, ran it, and paid me $30.

"I don't know if there's a plan [for other freelancers] there, except to just set the bar relatively low for that first piece. That led to another piece, and like I said I was getting paid $30, which probably works out to be 5 cents a word. You have to be somewhat fearless and not be afraid of rejection and humiliation. Because the odds are that at least at the beginning you're going to get a lot of rejection and have to believe in your writing. Just kind of stick with it and keep plugging away until you get a break because I think that's basically it. You have to have enough faith in your stuff and set somewhat realistic goals. Don't think that a month after you get out of j-school you're going to be pitching stories to the *New Yorker*. Try to find something [a publication] that kind of speaks to your sensibilities that also seems attainable, whether it's a weekly or a monthly or whatever. A lot of alternative weeklies can give you that first opportunity."

> —*Steve Rodrick is a contributing editor at* New York *and a writer-at-large for* Los
>   Angeles Magazine. *He was previously a contributing editor at* George, ESPN,
>   *and* Men's Journal.

"My first clip was in high school. My first paid clip: I had been writing record reviews and concert reviews for my college paper, and around that time I decided I wanted to become what was then known as a 'rock critic.' So at one point I tried to get tickets to see the Rolling Stones, so that I could cover it for the college newspaper. And the tickets were sold out, so I tried to get in touch with their PR person, and I failed. I didn't get in to see the Stones. So I wrote a piece called 'Exile on 34th Street,' and I don't think I even knew what a spec piece was, I just wrote the story and sent it in to my favorite rock magazine, called *Crawdaddy*. And they wrote me back and said that they couldn't use that piece, but would I be willing to write a record review? It was the first Doors album after Jim Morrison died. I don't remember the name.

(continued)

"For someone just starting out, I'd tell them to first find a publication where the bar for entry is not set high. Find the equivalent of the $25 record review. Get your stuff in print *somewhere*. I always tell my interns, go to a newsstand and just spend an hour there staring at the magazines and newspapers there. Spend enough time to figure out which ones you're suited for. You just start climbing the ladder. You build. Each clip is a rung in the ladder, and clips are your calling card."

—*Michael Gross, a contributing editor of* Travel + Leisure, *has worked as a columnist for the* New York Times, GQ, Tatler, Town & Country, *and the* Daily News; *and was a contributing editor of* New York *and of* Talk; *was a senior writer at* Esquire; *and was a senior editor at* George. *His latest book,* 740 Park, *is the inside story of New York's richest, most prestigious, and most secretive cooperative apartment building.*

Once you've got some clips, display them in the best possible light. If you are going to send these writing samples to editors in the mail, don't simply photocopy them in black and white. Spend the extra dime for color copies. Even if your only clip is a six-line piece in your local podunk paper, make it look good. Get creative: reproduce the cover of the edition of the paper the article appeared in and plop your piece in the center. That doesn't mean you should doctor the cover so that it appears you had a cover story when you didn't. But you should make it look as attractive and substantial as possible—you don't want to send six tiny little lines in the middle of a blank sheet of white paper.

## THE PLUSES AND MINUSES OF WRITING ON SPEC

You may encounter an editor who requests you send in an article "on spec." Basically, this means the editor will not decide whether to purchase the piece until after he has read the article. Whether you should in fact write an article "on spec" is often debated among freelancers. Below, two writers offer their opinions.

"I think it's fine to write on spec if that's your only option. But to me 'on spec' means that you've written a proposal and gotten an editor interested; that editor's just reluctant to offer you a contract and commit to covering your expenses. The first article I wrote for the *New York Times* travel section was on spec, after pitching other ideas unsuccessfully. But now the editor helped focus my topic into one that could run, and with her guidance I was able to write something that did. Thereafter I was only offered contracted assignments. So writing on spec can be a great foot in the door. But that's only ideal if you can't get in your whole body."

—*James Sturz, author of the novel* Sasso *and more than sixty articles in newspapers and magazines including* Travel + Leisure, The New York Times Magazine, The New Republic, *the* Boston Globe, Men's Health, *and* Glamour

"Don't write on spec. Too often, you wind up unpublished, unpaid, and asking yourself, What was it all for? If someone wants you to write on spec, why not instead say, 'I don't write on spec, and I believe I can deliver on this assignment. If you're not satisfied with my article, I'll be happy to do a rewrite. If it still doesn't work out, we can agree on a kill fee.' "

—*Miranda Spencer, freelance writer and editorial consultant based in Philadelphia*

**Blogging:** You can also create a blog and start "marketing" it (by sending the link around) to friends, family, coworkers, industry colleagues, and anyone who'll read it. Make sure it's based on something you're passionate about, so you'll be able to consistently make two to six blog posts a day. If you build enough traffic, get linked to other bloggers and start to get buzz, this can be a great way to get recognized by a major media company. Brian Stelter, the editor of TVNewser.com, is a perfect example of this approach. He started a blog from his dorm room in college in 2004 and soon gained a following among top news producers, anchors, and other television executives. Within a few months, the *New York Times* had written a glowing article about the blog and Stelter got a job offer from mediabistro.com, where he works today.

**A Web site:** Another great way to present your clips and yourself is with a well-designed Web site. While you can go all out and hire a designer to produce something really flashy, with today's technology you can easily—and inexpensively—put together your own straightforward but highly functional site. Mediabistro.com offers two options for writers who want an easy-to-use Web site for their clips. If you join AvantGuild ($49/year), you can upload clips and other information to your own home page. For an additional fee, you can join Freelance Marketplace (FM), which allows you to upload content to your own ready-made Web page that is part of a database searchable by editors and others looking to hire freelancers. Go to www.mediabistro.com/avantguild and www.mediabistro.com/fm, respectively, for more information on these two services. To see some examples of freelancers making use of the FM Web sites, check out these links:

- http://www.mediabistro.com/insideguide/fmsample1
- http://www.mediabistro.com/insideguide/fmsample2
- http://www.mediabistro.com/insideguide/fmsample3

However you decide to set up your Web site, the point is to have one organized location where editors can easily view your (constantly updated) résumé, find your contact information, and read your clips via links to the published articles. If some of your clips are from print-only publications, you can scan them as images and include them on the site. It's often easier for an editor to click over to your clips than to receive a sheaf of paper in the mail (there's less paperwork cluttering up his office, and everything's available at the touch of a mouse). Even better, with a Web site you can always make sure your best and latest clips are highlighted.

Here you will find some sample Web sites from established freelancers:

ALISON STEIN WELLNER, Author and Journalist

alison@wellner.bi

Home
On Business
On Health
On Trends/Culture
Books

**Welcome.** I'm **Alison Stein Wellner**, an award-winning journalist and author, specializing in stories about trends, health, business, and culture. I'm currently a Contributing Editor at *Inc.* magazine, and formerly Editor-at-Large at *American Demographics* magazine. Every month, you'll find my byline in the nation's most respected publications.

**Credits.** **[Magazines and Newspapers]** American Archaeology. American Demographics. AmericanStyle. Boston Magazine. BusinessWeek. The Chicago Tribune. The Christian Science Monitor. The Chronicle of Philanthropy. Continental. Crain's NY Business. Fast Company. Glamour. HR Magazine. Inc. Ladies' Home Journal. Men's Health. Psychology Today. Sierra Magazine. The Washington Post. Working Mother. Workforce Management. Yankee. And others. **[Books]** Best of Health: The Demographics of Health Care Consumers. (New Strategist, 2000). Americans at Play: The Demographics of Outdoor Recreation and Travel. (New Strategist 1997). And others. **[Awards]** National Press Foundation Fellowship. *New York Times* Fellowship. And others.

**What's New.** I'm pleased to announce the launch of my new blog, **A Curious Mind**. That's where I'll post updates on new articles, share the story behind the story of pieces I've published, and otherwise spread the word on the latest in my writing life.

This website will continue on as my online portfolio, a place where I'll showcase and archive my favorite work. Please navigate by using the menu at the left.

Contact me: alison@wellner.biz

*(c) 2005. Do not reproduce anything on this site without my permission.*

Updated: August 2005.

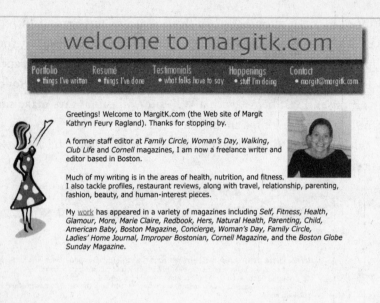

# welcome to margitk.com

| Portfolio | Resumé | Testimonials | Happenings | Contact |
|---|---|---|---|---|
| • things I've written | • things I've done | • what folks have to say | • stuff I'm doing | • margit@margitk.com |

Greetings! Welcome to MargitK.com (the Web site of Margit Kathryn Feury Ragland). Thanks for stopping by.

A former staff editor at *Family Circle, Woman's Day, Walking, Club Life* and *Cornell* magazines, I am now a freelance writer and editor based in Boston.

Much of my writing is in the areas of health, nutrition, and fitness. I also tackle profiles, restaurant reviews, along with travel, relationship, parenting, fashion, beauty, and human-interest pieces.

My work has appeared in a variety of magazines including *Self, Fitness, Health, Glamour, More, Marie Claire, Redbook, Hers, Natural Health, Parenting, Child, American Baby, Boston Magazine, Concierge, Woman's Day, Family Circle, Ladies' Home Journal, Improper Bostonian, Cornell Magazine,* and the *Boston Globe Sunday Magazine.*

HOME | PORTFOLIO | RESUME | TESTIMONIALS | HAPPENINGS | CONTACT

# Greg Beaubien

### Professional/Personal Overview

During 17 years of professional experience, I have been a feature writer for top newspapers and national magazines, a book writer, business ghostwriter, speechwriter and media relations expert. My specialties include real estate, architecture, health and international business and travel. I am looking for executive ghostwriting projects, book contracts and opportunities to write columns and essays for magazines, newspapers or websites.

### Work Samples

#### Writing

**Travel + Leisure Magazine**
Chicago Catches a Wave. When summer cooks Chicago, chill in style aboard an armada of new sightseeing vessels sailing from the revamped Navy Pier. The Windy, a four-masted schooner, launches her first full season this month. For a wilder ride, chop waves on the bright yellow speedboat Seadog. Or voy

**Audubon Magazine**
Hazard Lights. What to do about mercury in some popular shoes. Kids think they're cool: tennis shoes with little red lights blinking in the heels. But mercury fires the glow, about a gram of it in each pair of shoes. The manufacturer, L.A. Gear—which markets them under the names L.A. Lights and My Li

**The Empathy Effect: Build Your Business-And Your Wealth-by Putting Yourself in Other People's Shoes**
I conceptualized and ghostwrote this autobiographical business book for entrepreneur Tom Ward. The Empathy Effect is available on Amazon.com. (Click book title for link.)

#### Media Relations

**Donald Trump Press Conference**
I ran media relations and site recommendations for this press conference for Donald Trump in downtown Chicago, Oct. 28, 2004. Held to kick off demolition of the Chicago Sun-Times Building, which Trump is replacing with a 90-story condo tower, the press conference generated global coverage, including

### Contact Info

Greg Beaubien
Chicago, IL
USA

**E-Mail:** gregbeaubien@msn.com

Greg Beaubien is a Chicago-based writer and media-relations consultant.

## Q&A: LIFE ON THE WEB WITH MELODY REED

*Melody Reed teaches digital photography at the City University of New York and Web design at the Pratt Association of Graphic Communication.*

**Q. Does a freelance writer need to know HTML to set up their own Web site?**

A. Not necessarily, but it would help. Programs, such as Dreamweaver, are available that enable relatively easy creation of Web sites without using fancy HTML code. With Dreamweaver, a person can build a page and view it exactly as it will appear on a Web page. But it helps to have a basic understanding of how the underlying language, HTML, works. That way if you have a problem in Dreamweaver, you can go into the code window and at least have a clue of what to look for. It gives the writer a certain amount of independence and confidence.

**Q. What makes a good domain name for a freelancer?**

A. A good domain name should take into consideration the goal or function of what the writer wants to accomplish, i.e., what type of writing they do. For example, for a mystery writer a title such as mystery_ novels.com is descriptive and therefore functional and easy to find if someone does a search for that topic. You want to use your name only if you have a known name, i.e., melodyreed.com. I use my name only because my site is geared toward my students, who of course know my name. However, I also have a second domain name, melodysmediamix. com, to reach the audience of my cable TV show by the same name.

**Q. Where should a freelancer go to secure a name?**

A. There are many places to go for a domain name. If you type in "domain name" in Google, you will find pages of listings. You can shop by price. I used the first listing for myself, Godaddy.com.

**Q. How does a writer go about setting up an e-mail address that comes right to them . . . not a Yahoo or Hotmail address?**

A. By registering with a Web server company to get space to post your Web site, you will also get the opportunity to use your domain name for your e-mail, i.e., anything@melodyreed.com. The advantage of having anything as a prefix is that I can give different people different e-mails depending on the situation. Some of the places that give you domain names will also host your site and provide you with e-mail. Go-daddy is one place that does it all.

**Q. Should a freelancer put their résumé on their site?**

A. I feel that there should be an "About Me" section where one can put a generalized summary of their accomplishments, and perhaps drop a few significant names or company names. If this interests the right person, he or she will be in touch for the details. I wouldn't put it all out there [in a résumé] for the general public. Just post a teaser.

**Business cards:** It's also a good idea to produce a stack of business cards. Of course you'll want to hand them out if you meet an editor in person, but it's also smart to send one along with every pitch letter you send out. Best possible scenario—you end up in an editor's Rolodex, filed under "talented writers."

Your business card is often the first thing an editor will see (along with your résumé and clips, if you have them). You want that first impression to be good. A high-end, beautifully executed business card on heavy 80- to 100-pound card stock says "I care about how I present myself, I take myself and my work seriously, this is not just a part-time sideline. I have invested in this." You wouldn't wear jeans to an interview. Consider every business card distributed as an "interview" on 2" x 3½" paper.

Invest in an original design, if your budget permits. And, always include your Web address on your business card.

You can go high-end with professionally designed cards, or you can go low-end by printing them out from your home computer on serrated business-card forms available at any office-supply store. In the middle price range, it's easy and inexpensive to have a personalized card designed from a template at a stationery store or quick printer.

Here are a few sample cards.

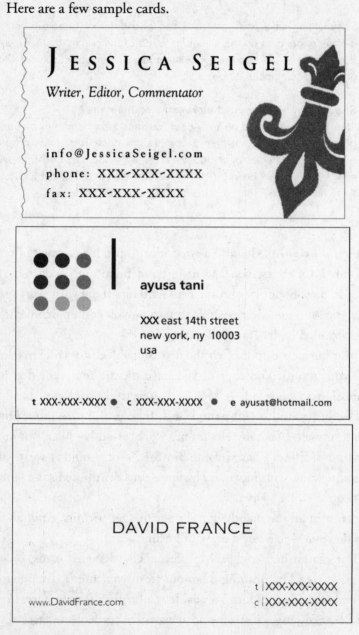

*David France card: Courtesy of Susan Burdick (burdick1s@aol.com)*

## Develop Your Personal Business Plan

Don't worry that you don't have an MBA; a freelancer's business plan doesn't need to be a formal document. But freelancing *is* a business, and it's a good idea to plan out how your business will succeed. Write down your major goals—be it a target income each month or a certain number of assignments every year. Create a time line for reaching mini-goals along the way—perhaps getting your first small assignment in the next three weeks, getting an assignment that pays more

---

### THE BUSINESS PLAN

"Don't freak out about writing your business plan. Unless you're getting investors, a business plan is merely a guide or road map to keep your business on course. Here are some tips:

1. Just sit down and do it. It's much easier to write a business plan than to actually run a business.
2. Think about where you want to be in five or ten years. If you cannot answer that question, then you need to step back and think of whether you really want to start a business, or if you just want to get out of your current situation.
3. Don't limit yourself ahead of time, and just as important, don't let someone else set your goals for you. Shoot for the stars. There will be plenty of people to tell you that you can't do it. And there will be even more people who will want to define what a successful business is for you. Don't lose sight of why you started freelancing in the first place.
4. Carefully identify what you want to do. This means, if you are an editor and you want to continue to do hands-on editing, as well as writing, figure that into your plan. Perhaps you can hire others (or plan to in the future) to do some of the parts you don't have much interest in—keeping track of expenses, transcribing your notes, and the like."

*—Duy Linh Tu, founder and the creative director of Resolution Seven, LLC. Duy is a writer, videographer, motion graphics designer, and photographer, and teaches new media at the Columbia University Graduate School of Journalism.*

than a certain amount (say $500), getting the three clips you already
have into a presentable form by the end of the week, asking for
more money on your next assignment, or sending out one query letter every other day. Map out the publications you want to write
for and any contacts you might have out in the publishing world.
Keep this plan close at hand, and refer to it, edit it, and update it
frequently.

## You'll Work Best in a Functional Office

There's always the dreamy vision of writers who show up at Starbucks
at eleven, down an espresso, and pound out thirty-five pages of spectacular prose, then meet a friend for a late lunch. Real life, of course,
is rarely like a dreamy vision. The picture may be a little more like
this: The writer rolls over at 4 a.m. and starts worrying about the
two-thousand-word piece due in thirty-six hours. After tossing and
turning for an hour, she gets out of bed, plops herself in front of the
computer, and tries, over and over, to come up with a lede. Nothing
comes and the computer's keys remain still. Come 8 a.m., the writer
gets on the phone, makes countless calls trying to get a killer quote,
and continuously gets thrown into voice mails with "out of the office
till next week" messages.

The chaos of a place like Starbucks won't make things any easier.
All writers need a functional, quiet, and productive place to practice
their craft. When you're starting out in the freelance world, you might
be able to use your kitchen table for two hours two nights a week,
after the kids go to bed, to work on some fun short pieces for the PTA
newsletter. But as your workload begins to increase, you'll need an office or designated office space solely dedicated to your writing.

**A separate spot:** Your office must be a quiet place away from
the rest of your life. If you live alone in a studio apartment, it can be
simply a desk in the corner. But if you have kids and pets running

around your home, you need a place where you can go and close the door—maybe a home office, an extra bedroom, the basement, or a small rented office in a building downtown.

**Furniture:** You'll do no good as a freelancer with a strained back. Get a real desk and a comfortable, ergonomic chair. If other family members use your "writing computer" during the day, lay claim to at least a drawer in the desk and one shelf on the bookcase for your writing materials. And be sure you have proper lighting. Your work will suffer if your eyes are tired and strained.

**Computer:** Think about whether a laptop or desktop works better for you. Desktops are typically less expensive, but what if you need to travel? Many publications use Macintosh computers, as they are basically considered more user friendly when it comes to the design and layout of magazines. But as a writer, you really need little more than a word processing program such as Microsoft Word, so either a Mac or a PC should get the job done.

Be sure to suck it up and pay the extra money for insurance and

---

## BADIMPRESSION@YAHOO.COM

"Perhaps it sounds harsh, but it's true, I don't look so highly upon pitches coming from a Yahoo, Hotmail, AOL (or the like) e-mail account. It just doesn't look professional. Take the time to set up an e-mail account under your own domain name. Or set up your name or your 'company' name (it could just be your soon-to-be company name!) with a recognizable, esteemed domain like FitnessWritingInc@earthlink.net. That will sound more professional arriving in an editor's e-mail box than larryspinks18967@hotmail.com."

—*Douglas Imbrogno, editor of the online arts and entertainment magazine thegazz.com, for the* Charleston Gazette *in West Virginia* troubleshooting care on your computer, unless you happen to be a computer geek on the side. A freelancer without a working computer is worthless.

In addition, find some way to back up your computer. Whether you invest in a flash drive, zip drive, discs, CDs, DVDs, or something else, set up a system for saving your data on a very regular basis. Editors have little sympathy for writers who lose their notes, e-mail database, or entire piece in a computer crash.

And dial-up is pretty much archaic for the freelance writer. If you are going to be doing research online (and what writer doesn't), you are going to be wasting lots of time (and therefore money) waiting for pages to load. If you have not already, treat yourself to a high-speed connection. It will be more than well worth it.

**Communication:** If you're trying to be a professional, you should have a professional phone line. Get a line—and maybe even a fax line—dedicated to your freelance-writing business. It's just not professional for editors, or interview subjects, to call you and get a voice mail taking messages for Joe, Dick, Harry, and Spot. Some freelancers use their cell phone as their office line, which is fine, but just be sure you always have a clear line. Fuzzy connections do not make for good interviews.

Use a headset when on the phone with editors and when conducting interviews. This way you have your hands free to take notes—either on paper or directly into your computer. Plus, you avoid a sore neck!

When on vacation, most freelancers don't have an assistant on hand to take messages, so change your phone message to let people know you are unavailable and when you will be returning. Or do what most freelancers do so they never miss out on an assignment—check your messages regularly, even while on vacation.

It's also a good idea to invest in a fax machine, a copier, and perhaps even a scanner. They now come three-in-one at very reasonable prices.

## A PEEK INSIDE A SUCCESSFUL FREELANCER'S OFFICE

My core items are a 15" PowerBook and a Dutch-made Technivorm Mocca-master coffeemaker, which brews coffee at 200 degrees Fahrenheit, which is 15 degrees hotter than traditional drip units. For the freelancer, coffee is crucial.

Then here's the rest.

- Two AirPort Extreme Base Stations, for wireless connectivity throughout my apartment.
- Brother MFC-8420 Multifunction Copier. It's a 600 dpi black-and-white laser printer that's also my fax machine, scanner, and copier. For color or portable printing, I also have a Canon i80 but I barely use it.
- I have an Olympus DS-330 digital voice recorder for live or telephone interviews (I keep it plugged into the phone as a default). I also have a foot-pedal attachment for transcribing interviews on my computer and a special earplug for recording cell-phone conversations.
- My cell phone is an old-model tri-band Nokia through T-Mobile. It's nothing to look at, but it works in every foreign country I've ever visited.
- For land phones, I have 5.8 "Gigarange Supreme" Panasonic, which is a two-line desk station with remote hand units. Each unit has a speakerphone, keypad, and call waiting with ID. I also pay for a monthly package from Verizon that includes call forwarding and "distinctive ringing," which gives me a "third" phone number for the fax, although I only have two actual lines. Why two lines at all? My wife works at home, too. We can't share one.
- I have headsets for both phones and cell phone, but I rarely use them.
- Two years ago I bought a really nice Open Up desk chair from Knoll. It has lumbar support, a headrest, armrests, and lets me work easily with my feet on my desk and my laptop in my lap, which is my favorite position. My desk is also from Knoll. I bought it at an antiques fair.
- My digital camera is a Sony DSC-TI, tiny and wonderful and already out of date.
- Sometimes I write about scuba, so my equipment includes an underwater slate for taking notes, too.

  —*James Sturz is the author of the novel* Sasso *and has written for more than sixty newspapers and magazines.*

If you think it will help you with your reporting, consider investing in a transcribing machine and/or some type of recording device.

**Storage:** Set up a filing system for organizing assignment letters,
contracts, research materials, invoices, receipts, and more. Purchase a
file cabinet—there are attractive wooden and wicker ones nowadays.
Categorize materials into sections by publication, and then further
divide them into file folders by assignment. Nothing's worse than
being unable to find the research material you need when an editor is
clamoring for a change on a piece. And come tax time, you'll be very
glad you organized all your receipts and invoices.

**Finances:** Consider purchasing a computer program (or at least a
notebook or ledger) that keeps track of expenses, payments, and the
like, especially for tax purposes. When your freelance career is just
getting under way (say when you have a few assignments under your
belt), make an appointment with an accountant who works with individuals or small businesses to lay the groundwork for how you
should deal with your finances. If may seem costly up front, but being
organized and understanding the dollars and cents of a freelancer's
life early on will save you time and money in the long run. (See
Chapter 15 for more on finances.)

All business-related expenses can be written off on taxes,
so you'll want to keep records of all costs that are in any
way related to a particular story or anything you purchase
to help your freelancing work. Having a separate bank account (with a separate credit card) for your freelancing
expenses will make tracking your business-related expenditures a lot easier.

**Reference:** Start a library of reference books that will help you in
your work. Obviously a dictionary and a thesaurus are important. So

are style manuals and books on key areas of interest. If you are focusing on a specific beat, start reading journals and trade magazines targeted at that specific niche. For instance, if you want to write nutrition articles, you probably want to subscribe to the *Journal of the American Dietetic Association.* Also, subscribe to the magazines and newspapers you want to write for, both to get a feel for their voices and to make sure you're not pitching something they've already done. And read major newspapers, not only to keep up on the news but also to help generate your own story ideas. Don't ignore your area's small, local papers, either; smaller publications are where you'll find out-of-the-ordinary ideas that not every other writer and editor is pitching.

You may consider subscribing to some of the big research services—such as LexisNexis or Factiva. While they are costly, if you use them regularly, it may be worth it. Also, these services do offer some less expensive à la carte services that may fulfill your needs—especially when first starting out. Otherwise, a trip to your local library when you need hard-to-get information may suffice.

Joining professional organizations, such as mediabistro.com's Avant-Guild, will provide you access to the inside scoop on freelance jobs, tips on pitching articles, discounts on classes, help with your résumé, and other benefits that will undoubtedly support your freelance career.

## Get Organized

As well as being writer, creative director, PR person, marketing manager, and office designer, you also have to be your own secretary. Right from the start, keep track of your every expense. Keep that receipt for a box of pencils from Staples. Make note of your rent payment. Track those magazines you buy at the airport kiosk. All are now business expenses and can be written off when you file your taxes. This is important for freelancers to be reminded of, again and again.

No matter how great your memory, write down everything.

Develop a system for notating phone calls made and phone calls received. It can be as simple as a notebook of calls or a database on your computer calendar. Create a method for scheduling phone interviews and noting article due dates. Again, work with a method that is easy for you to follow—if that means a paper calendar, fine. Or if a computerized or PDA device is better for you, go with that.

It's very helpful to invest in ACT! or another contact management system to keep track of the sources you interview for each article. That way, the next time you write an article on a similar subject for a different publication, you won't have to remember the name of the person you interviewed. Be sure to get one that allows you to make multiple categories for each source.

For example, you might add these categories to the record of the management guru you interviewed for an *Inc.* magazine article you wrote in December 2005 titled "How to Recruit and Retain Disabled Workers."

> Client: *Inc.* magazine
> Subject 1: Disabilities
> Subject 2: Management
> Subject 3: Small Business
> Date published: December 2005

**BOOKS EVERY FREELANCER SHOULD HAVE ON THE SHELF**

1. A dictionary (although www.dictionary.com may do the trick for both your dictionary and thesaurus needs)
2. A thesaurus
3. *The Elements of Style*
4. *The Writer's Handbook*
5. *The Writer's Market*
6. *The Chicago Manual of Style* or *AP Stylebook*
7. This book!

## Q&A: A DAY IN THE LIFE . . . OF A FREELANCER

**Q. How much time do you spend drumming up business?**

A. "I probably spend my time fifty-fifty between working on assignments and querying."

> —Jillian Lewis, a freelance writer in New York City who held staff positions at magazines in Sydney, Australia, and New York before launching into a life of flexible hours

A. "When you first start out as a freelancer, you have to do a lot of pitching and marketing of yourself, but over time the editors start coming to you, and so querying begins to occupy a smaller amount of your time. It's all about networking and getting your name out there. Once you prove to people that you can do the work by pitching a viable idea, they will start coming to you."

> —John Loecke, a freelance writer and interior designer living in New York. He is a frequent contributor to House Beautiful, Country Living, and Better Homes and Gardens.

**Q. Are you a nine-to-fiver?**

A. "I definitely take advantage of my freelance schedule—especially if I don't have any pressing assignments due. What's the point of freelancing if you don't remember one of the reasons you got into it in the first place—flexible hours!! I'm an early riser and will sometimes work from 7 a.m. to 10 a.m., then I'll busy myself with personal activities for a few hours, then I'll come back to my desk from about 2 p.m. to 6 p.m. Of course, if I have a ton of assignments due at the same time, I'll spend all day at my desk and sometimes a few hours on a Sunday afternoon. I also check my e-mail regularly, and will often reply to editors or interview subjects late at night."

> —Jillian Lewis

A. "I'm a nine-to-fiver when I can be. (I just finished a grad degree and work part-time at a university right now so it's hard.) But I do feel like I write best in the mornings and late evenings. I also find that I write best in busy, noisy coffee shops . . . so I try to get my reporting done during

(continued)

the day—and write when I have big blocks of time without interviews. It's relaxing."

—*Nicci Micco, former staffer at* Self, More, *and* YM, *is now a contributing editor at* Self. *She also writes for* More, All You, Cooking Light, *and* Men's Health *from her home in Burlington, Vermont.*

A. "My days are incredibly variable. I have built my business on the concept of diversity—that is, I don't depend on one type of media for my revenue. Right now, I am working on a radio documentary series, a commissioned book, an individual coaching project related to a different book, a magazine article, and of course teaching. I try to allocate the majority of each day to one project, also allowing time for marketing and business development. It's important to keep up with billing and collections, because the bank doesn't cut any slack on late mortgage payments!

"I catch up with whatever e-mail I can during the first half hour of the day. Then I might spend the morning doing phone interviews. The afternoon might be more interviews, writing time, a meeting, or rewriting or going over proofs on a different story.

"I try to always take a lunch break and get up and walk around now and then just to refresh my brain. If I feel stuck, I go outside and look at the birds and the sea (I live and work near the Pacific Ocean), or sometimes I stand on my head. It really works—all that blood to the brain is excellent. If I have taught the night before or worked late, I don't mind taking a nap. It's much better than staring at my computer, eating chocolate, and wishing I was taking a nap."

—*Sally Lehrman writes about health, medicine, and science policy for* Scientific American, Nature, Health, *the* Washington Post, *Salon.com, the DNA Files, and other publications and sites.*

A. "In a way, I'm always working: looking for ideas, reading, thinking about leads, or actually writing. But it often doesn't feel like work. Or if it is work, it's often being done in a pleasant cubicle-free place, like home or at a breezy cafe in Santa Monica. I also work at a place called The Office, which is full of screenwriters, journalists, and the occasional celeb (Brooke Shields) or the occasional celeb-journalist (Bernie

Weinraub). My writing and reporting generally starts at eight or nine and I go till four. The days are usually punctuated with run-around time with my two-year-old, Sebastian, and lunch with my wife, Ruth. At night, I might respond to e-mails or do some reading."

—*David Hochman, freelance writer for the* New York Times, TV Guide, Forbes, Playboy, Esquire, Money, Entertainment Weekly, Men's Journal, *and many other publications. His first freelance piece was an essay for* Newsday *on the day his home phone number got crossed with a phone sex line.*

Pay close attention to your own calendar. Pencil in work hours, lunch hours, appointments, interviews, gym hours, intermediate deadlines leading up to big deadlines, and, if you must, schedule in sleeping hours—and adhere to them, even if a big assignment is breathing down your neck. You're running your own business, and even if it's only a part-time gig, make sure you run it as professionally as you possibly can.

## Finding the (Part) Time

There are plenty of freelancer writers out there who hold regular nine-to-five gigs with steady pay and benefits. But they have their secret lives, too—when they return home to their personal computers and their rewarding moonlighting careers. How do they do it?

Claire Zulkey, author of *MBToolbox,* mediabistro.com's resource blog for writers and journalists, discussed this issue on the site with other part-timers. (Identities have been withheld to protect their real jobs!)

"My employer knows that I am a writer, but a few years ago expressed some concern that I don't have enough time to work and freelance. I felt that I did, but decided that he didn't need to know this and since then have kept my freelancing on the quiet.

"How do I do it? Much of it is circumstantial. My job doesn't take that much time to complete, so I have free time to work during the day. I have my own office (with a door), so people aren't popping up behind me, seeing me working on various projects. I don't work with that many people, so not that many people know what I'm up to at any given moment (unlike at my old job, where I'd keep some random work-related Quark document on my desktop so I could automatically switch to that when people walked by my cubicle, which was often, as it was next to the bathrooms). And above all, I get my day-job work done first so that my butt is covered.

"Working full-time can be a blessing and a curse. You don't have as much time to work on other freelance projects that you might like—in fact, you might not have much time at all. On the other hand, it's nice to have steady income and benefits."

*—Claire Zulkey's work has also been on NPR, at Second City, and in the Chicago Tribune, Modern Bride, and ElleGirl.*

"I am a full-time technical writer but am trying to develop a freelance business so that I can 'retire' from the nine-to-five and work from home. I am getting there slowly, laying groundwork and writing at home twenty hours a week or so. I try not to do too much of my 'own thing' during work hours, but usually have something that I can work on during lunch, or times when I need a break. I occasionally do some research while I am at work as well. I try to give these people forty hours a week and not take advantage of the situation, but when it is slow, I will work on a piece rather than just surf the Net like everyone else does! I have a nice office set up at home and it is ready to be occupied by a full-time freelance writer. I am going to make this happen."

*—Part-time freelancer #1*

"When I worked at a full-time job, I would especially check my e-mail at work only so that when I got back home, all I really had to do was reply to the important ones, and actually write. I'd also return calls to clients in my five-minute breaks from my cell phone. That would ensure that they could talk to me in office hours, and I didn't have a backlog of phone calls to take care of when I got home. I also hear that there are a couple of software packages that let you create two desktops, letting you switch between the two, so that no one else can see what else you've been working on."

—*Part-time freelancer #2*

"I work full-time while I freelance. Luckily, I have a 'results-oriented' supervisor, so as long as my 'work' work is done, she doesn't much care what I do the rest of the time. That motivates me (usually!) to get my 'work' work done as quickly as possible, which leaves the remainder of the day for writing. The department director isn't quite as generous, however, so I do resort to some tricks. I am supposed to be working on a big Web site redesign, but it's an onerous project that I'm having trouble getting motivated to work on, so I usually have Dreamweaver minimized on my screen, and whenever the director heads in my direction, I quickly maximize that window and squint at it, as if I'm beavering away on page design. Another thing I do is keep my desktop littered with papers. That way, I can always pick one up and appear to be studying it (frowning is an excellent way to keep people at bay because they're loath to interrupt you), while in reality I'm pondering how to restructure a sentence in my feature article that's due today.

"Phantom meetings are another way to carve writing time out of a regular job. I'm a middle manager, so none of my superiors truly knows how many committees and task forces I belong to. If I'm really feeling stressed about a deadline, I just grab my Handspring and say, 'I forgot I have that Network Implementation Task Force meeting today. I'll be back in a couple of hours.' Throwing in technical jargon (even nonsensical stuff) is one good way to avoid being questioned about these issues. Our director isn't too technically literate, so I usually add something like, 'We're discussing the rollout of the new stasis alleviation platform which will impact our hub and router configuration, so I plan to be really involved with this committee in order to make sure they don't screw up our computers.' I have also been known to come down with a sudden illness when I was on deadline. Not so often as to show a pattern, but often enough to keep my editors happy."

—*Part-time freelancer #3*

"For the most part, the only things I ever do at work are those that require a high-speed connection (usually sending and receiving large file attachments). Otherwise, the day job gets full attention during work hours. I'd never have the degree of peace and quiet I like to have for writing anyway, so it's not much trouble to keep them separate. Of course, my job usually requires me to work up to sixty-hour weeks now and then, so I don't feel at all bad about skimming a little time for my own work. On average, they're still making out quite well for what I'm being paid."

—*Part-time freelancer #4*

3

# Invest in Others

.......................................................................................................................

"Self-Employed and Overjoyed" is a phrase we kicked around while working on a title for this book. After all, many successful freelance writers are indeed self-employed and thrilled with the independence and freedom. But that's also a misconception about the full-time freelance life: even without official work hours and a hectoring supervisor, you're still not completely independent. There won't be a boss sitting you down for agonizing annual reviews, but your performance will nevertheless be judged constantly—probably by more people than you imagine. Despite what it might seem, a freelance writing career is not for a recluse. You need to work with other people and *for* other people. To a large degree, especially when you're starting out, connections are what can make or break a freelance career.

## Be Smart if You Decide to Leave a Full-Time Position

When launching out on your own, the best, smartest, and easiest thing to do is to leverage the connections you already have. As a new freelancer, you may feel suddenly independent, but it is certainly not the time to burn any bridges.

If you're resigning from a current job, approach your employer with a positive, upbeat attitude. Tell your boss all of the reasons you are so fond of working for the company, and explain that it's not that you want to leave your current position but rather that you're yearning to officially kick off your own freelance writing career.

If you work in publishing, you should investigate opportunities to keep a regular gig with your current employer as you go freelance. Have three or four proposals at the ready that illustrate how you could still work for the company on a regular contractual basis or just when needed. If you are writing, suggest continuing to write for the company in some capacity—maybe they need a recurring monthly column, or someone to help on editing for a few days per month at close time. Or if any of the tasks you currently do could easily be done remotely, ask to keep that work. For instance, if you copyedit the op-ed page of your paper every Wednesday, offer to continue to do so.

Even if you work in another industry, it's a good idea to see if there are any areas where someone with writing ability is needed. Perhaps the company has been thinking of publishing a monthly newsletter for some time, but it just hasn't come to fruition. Volunteer to pull it together. If the company communicates with the general public, offer to write advertising materials or other literature that is mailed out to potential clients or customers. If the company is looking to boost its exposure in the community, suggest that you write articles about new endeavors or spectacular employees in local newspapers. The company may even pay you a fee for pitching article ideas out into the community—for instance, if you can illustrate that you are sending out five query letters a month related to promoting work that the business is doing, they may pay you a set fee for doing so. In a way, you are volunteering to be a freelance public relations person for the company. If the company already has a PR or media department, go to those departments and offer up your services.

Your main goal is to continue to have some steady income, if possible. Even if it's just $1,000 a month to write two articles for the company Web site, it's a starting point. And it can't hurt to try; even if you can't keep any ties to your employer, you're planting seeds to help your future career—you never know when the company will need a fresh voice for a new project.

One thing you might want to avoid is getting locked into a binding contract that allows you to write for only one company and nobody else. Some editors who leave staff jobs get the chance to continue writing a column for their former employers. But they may be asked to sign a contract that forbids them from writing about the same topic or a similar one for any other publication. In this case, the writer needs to weigh the pros and cons. For example, let's say you're a nutrition expert, and you were planning to write about nutrition for a variety of publications. A $10,000 contract to write ten stories a year for one magazine, with a prohibition against writing for other magazines, may well hurt more than help—sure, it gives you a reliable check, but you might well be giving up another $50,000 in nutrition assignments from other publications. Then you'd be a nutrition expert stuck pitching other publications with totally different ideas, about which you don't really have expertise, because that's all that's still allowed for you. A limiting contract could hurt your finances and your visibility and networking opportunities as well.

## Maintain Connections—It's Essential

If you already work in publishing, when you leave your employer you don't want to lose any of the contacts you've made. It is a small world generally, and the publishing world is much, much smaller. People know people, and chances are someone you worked with once—even if you kind of hated working with them way back when—will one day end up as an editor at a magazine you're just itching to write for.

So make a point to leave everywhere on a positive note. Write resignation letters that praise all the good things about the company and people you are leaving. And return to your former places of employment often just to say hello and keep in touch. Send holiday cards—and birthday cards if you can—to keep your name positively in people's minds.

That's a good idea even if you don't work in publishing. You never know: your boss at the law firm may very well be married to—or college friends with, or next-door neighbor to—the executive editor of the next big magazine to hit the newsstands.

## Revive Old Connections

Did you work for your school newspaper or college magazine or have a six-month internship in publishing when you were fresh out of school? Get online and find that up-and-coming editor (no matter how nerdy he was back then) who supervised you and used to rip apart your attempts at newswriting. You'll be surprised at where people you worked with in the past ended up, so search them out and send an e-mail of hello. You never know who is looking for new writers—in most cases, all editors are looking for new talent all the time.

Be bold when contacting someone, but don't be obnoxious. Mention how much you're freelancing (whether full-time or part-time), talk about some recent writing work you've done, and then perhaps include just a link to your Web site or a few of your clips. You might not want to ask for work right off the bat. Instead, wait and see if you get a response. If you do, and your old connection mentions the type of work she assigns, then you should probably respond with a couple of ideas that would be appropriate for that person. It's a bad idea to just ask straight out for an assignment of any kind—it makes you sound desperate and not very focused.

## Making New Connections

Get out there and start meeting people. There are writing and journalism workshops, classes, cocktail parties, and networking events all over the country for people working in the media. Check mediabistro.com (and—fine, if you must—the other organizations listed in Chapter 21) for happenings in your area.

Instead of looking at fellow freelance writers as your competition, view them as resources. You can keep one another informed about new publications and writing opportunities in your area, share experts and sources, perhaps collaborate on big projects, give each other some of your workload if one of you gets too busy, help one another brainstorm story ideas, and perhaps spend some time together to avoid the loneliness of freelancing. If you can't find a local writers' group in your area to join, start your own.

You are a writer. Introduce yourself to people as such. You don't need a degree or some board approval to call yourself a writer. You don't even need to have been published. Just be prepared for the follow-up questions. If you say you are a writer, the response is bound to be "Wow, what do you write about?" Go ahead and assign yourself a beat. You can be specific, but keep it open as well. "I primarily write articles on parenting, but I'm also interested in food and general lifestyle topics." For all you know, the person you are chatting with knows somebody (or is somebody) who works at a magazine or newspaper, and maybe they'll be able to help you make a connection.

Remember that six degrees of separation is a very real and very helpful part of today's society. Tell everyone you can that you're launching your freelance writing career. Whenever anyone responds by saying they know someone in publishing, have your reporter's notebook handy, and write down the person's name and the connection. Follow up on all these leads. Send an e-mail, pop a letter in the mail, or call the contact to say hello. Even better is to come up with an amazing article idea that is perfect for this new contact. Instead of just sending a "here-I-am" note, you'll get much more mileage from sending a beautifully crafted pitch letter that also mentions the person you have in common. In this case, act quickly, while interactions and connections are fresh in people's minds. (More on pitch letters in Chapter 8.)

Keep in mind, though, that getting your foot in the door requires you to be aggressive but not rude. You have to be opportunistic but avoid being a leech. A letter or e-mail with a couple of follow-up phone calls is appropriate. Daily phone calls or repeated e-mails when you don't receive a response are not. And remember that editors, like everyone in the world, are busy people. So maybe you want to wait two months after trying to make contact with an editor and then make one final attempt at outreach. If you still don't get a response, move on.

---

### KEEP UP WITH COWORKERS

"I used to be the assistant editor at a magazine in Boston. When another company bought the magazine and moved it to a different city, several of my coworkers and I found ourselves suddenly thrust into the freelance life. We decided that since we were used to brainstorming ideas, offering encouragement, and sharing constructive criticism together that we should meet regularly to do the same thing as freelancers. Plus, we knew we'd need the socializing. Thus, our little group was born. We lost one member to a full-time job, but the other three of us still meet about once a month at a fun restaurant downtown to catch up, fine-tune pitches, and share ideas and contacts. Our friendship and our freelance careers have benefited tremendously—we stay involved in each others' lives, the pitch feedback is invaluable, and we've been able to recommend each other for projects we were too busy to take on ourselves."

—*Julia Maranan, a Boston-area freelance writer and editor*

PART II

# Prepare

4

# Finding the Great Idea

It's All About the Story Idea, So Know How to
Find Good Ones

If you're serious enough about freelancing to be reading this book, then you're probably serious enough about freelancing that you have some idea of what you want to write about. If not, now's the time to focus. Many aspiring writers are at one end of the spectrum or the other: either they have one extremely broad subject they want to tackle, or they have one very specific idea that they think can be developed into a spectacular article that everyone across the globe will be clamoring to read. One writer, for example, might want to write about all sorts of consumer technology, new and old, computers and televisions and stereos and cell phones, hardware and software, for business and for pleasure. Another might yearn to break the story of the top-secret, superfantastic, lightweight next-generation laptop that functions as a computer and also a television and a radio and a PDA and a telephone and an iPod and a GPS and a hair dryer and also makes really great fries. Neither is the right approach. Instead, you must choose a topic area—something specific, but not too hyperspecific—and work to establish yourself in that zone.

Early on in your freelance career, and on a regular basis thereafter, you need to think about just what type of writing motivates you most. Not only will it be much easier to make yourself settle down in front of the computer and start making those phone calls when you're working on a topic you love, but establishing a specific area of expertise is also an effective way to market yourself and get more work.

## Explore the Right Type of Writing for You

Plenty of people—young mothers at home with their children, guys watching *Monday Night Football,* tourists traipsing across the globe— think to themselves, "I could write an article about this," whether the topic is rearing children, the perfect pass, or a great, unknown restaurant in Paris. Unfortunately—or perhaps fortunately, for us professional writers—not everyone really is a parenting expert, sportswriter, or cultured travel correspondent, no matter what they may think of their own talent. Spending three days in Cancun does not make you an expert on Mexico any more than changing six diapers makes you a pediatrician. To be a successful writer, you have to know the topic, yes, but you also have to develop sources, content, and real expertise. That's why it's important to pinpoint what type of writing will work best for you. Here's where to start.

### What do you read?

Do you remember that grade-school teacher who pushed you to read more and more? "The more reading you do, the better writer you'll become," she'd say day after day. She was right, even if it didn't make sense to you then. You'd be hard-pressed to find an author on the bestseller list who does not have a home full of floor-to-ceiling bookshelves, or a magazine writer without piles of glossies stacked in her office, next to her bed, and alongside her bathtub.

So what do *you* read? Do you spend all day Sunday with the *New York Times,* or do you spend Friday nights curled up with a new self-help book? Do you run to the mailbox every Thursday looking for your *People* magazine, or do you dash there every Monday, prepared to spend a long night with *The New Yorker*? Take out a notepad. Write down a list of the publications you enjoy reading the most. Expand upon this list by jotting down the types of articles that you always seem to be drawn to in those mags. Chances are your greatest success will come from writing about topics that interest you most. Refer to and add to this list often.

After reading some of your favorite articles, ask yourself whether there are questions the piece raised in your mind that remained unanswered. Those points just might make your next article. For instance, back in 2005, there was a plane crash in Greece where initial speculation (in all of the published reports and on TV news) was that there had been a loss of cabin pressure that caused the pilots and passengers to lose consciousness before the plane actually crashed. Yes, these reports addressed people's nagging question: Did anyone on board experience any pain? (The reports said probably not, because they probably lost consciousness within seconds.) But not one article or news bite in the days immediately following the crash addressed this question: What about those darn air masks that they tell us about every time we board a plane? Why wouldn't the passengers have had them on? The reports implied that maybe there wasn't time. So does this mean you won't have time to put on your own mask, before helping your child with theirs? Ding-ding: a new story idea.

### What are your interests?

Just because you watch football all weekend doesn't mean you have the talent to be a *Sports Illustrated* columnist. But when a topic interests you, you're more likely to ask all the right questions and get to the real juicy details of a certain subject.

It's time to write another list. Jot down the things that intrigue you the most. What are your hobbies? How do you spend most of your free time? What do you most often find yourself pondering? These are things you'll be well suited to write about.

### Do you have previous expertise?

A great many successful freelancers had other careers before going into writing. Countless nutritionists have left behind hospitals and patients to write for women's magazines. There are horticulturists who've left the greenhouses and chefs who've stepped out of the kitchen only to plop down in front of their computers and launch exciting new careers.

What did you study in school? In what areas do you have the most experience? Focusing on where you already excel will increase your chances of landing an assignment. At the same time, though, be aware that many editors shy away from the doctor who promises an in-depth piece on new breast cancer research or the computer programmer pitching a piece on the most user-friendly software. Why? Those who know a subject inside and out often talk above the heads of the common reader, using difficult-to-understand technical jargon or simply assuming a base of background knowledge most readers don't have. So when pitching a story to a potential editor, make clear that you have a wealth of knowledge on a topic but be sure to underscore that you know how to write with a style that readers will understand.

### Are you going in cold?

What if you want to write about a field totally unrelated to the work you've been doing or where you have experience? For instance, let's say you've been a marketing executive but you love reading nutrition articles, and that's what you want to write. Is there any way for you to break into that market?

Obviously it will be harder for you to make the leap into nutrition writing than it would be for a registered dietician who has fifteen years of experience counseling clients on healthy eating. But it's not impossible. Look for story ideas that can help you bridge the gap in your background. For instance, maybe you can start by writing a piece about how to market to potential clients for a publication that goes out to nutritionists. Or flip it around, and pitch a story to a local paper about how marketing by fast-food chains positively or negatively affects our eating habits. After you have a few marketing/ nutrition pieces under your belt, it will be far easier to convince an editor to assign you a straight nutrition piece.

### Where's there a need?

Let's say your background is in human resources, but your ultimate goal is to write about decorating. Yet you keep coming across a listing on a local job board asking for someone who can write hip articles about workplace issues. Should you hold out and continue trying to pitch decorating ideas to the home section of your local paper and to Martha Stewart? If you are just starting out, it's probably a good idea to focus on what you know you're good at, rather than head straight for your dream writing gigs. If the market has a need, filling that need will get you some good clips that can help move you to your ultimate goal. Write a few of those workplace issue pieces, if that's what there's a market for—and especially if that's your background— and do a terrific job on them. Then start to mold that bridge—pitch a decorating idea on how a simple office cubicle can still reflect your inner style!

## Generating Ideas

You've narrowed down the field a bit and you have some idea of the kind of stories you'd like to write. Now it's time to get down to the story idea itself. The first step is just to generate a bunch of

ideas—maybe they'll be good, maybe they'll be bad, but you can figure that out later.

### What are your friends' and neighbors' interests?

Listen to what people are talking about at dinner parties, in line at
the grocery store, and over the backyard fence. If it's on people's
minds, chances are it could somehow be developed into a story. All
too often freelancers kick themselves when they open a magazine and
see a feature story about a topic they remember discussing at a family
meal a few months earlier.

### What piques your interest?

What have you liked lately? If you need some help here, ask yourself
these questions:

- Do you have a new favorite hobby, TV show, book, type of music?
- What are your pet peeves?
- What makes you really angry?
- What things in the world do you really wish you could change?
- What people, places, and ideas are in the news at the moment?
- Are there events coming up in the next six months or in the next
  year that are sure to be newsworthy and that you can get a jump
  on now?
- What's new in your city?
- What's new in your immediate neighborhood?
- What's new with your family?
- Is your generation, ethnic group, or racial group facing changes,
  hardships, or freedoms that have not been addressed in the past?

And remember, always carry a small notebook with you, so you
are ready to jot down thoughts and ideas.

If you need a little more inspiration, troll the Internet for intriguing or offbeat organizations, people, and events. Always peruse your local newsletters and newspapers to
catch anything that might be happening under the national radar.

### Who and what do you have access to?

The unfortunate adage "It's not what you know but who you
know" comes into play frequently for freelance writers. It helps you
get assignments when you know editors, but it also helps you get
story ideas and sources. And having access to exciting interview subjects is a great asset. This is not to say that Ben Affleck has to be your
best bud (although that would be helpful). Rather, look at whom you
know and where you have connections. Perhaps your uppity next-
door neighbor teaches etiquette to young children—that might make
a fun story for a parenting magazine. Is the owner of your favorite exotic spice shop opening two more locations in other cities and offering his extremely hard-to-find products online? Might make a nice
piece for an in-flight magazine.

At the end of each day, take a moment to think through the last
twenty-four hours, the conversations you had and the conversations
you overheard, the things you saw and the things that raised questions in your mind. Write them all down. All can be fodder for a successful piece. Over time you will start to notice the seeds of story
ideas in your everyday activities, as soon as they happen. You may
have to go home and dig before you come up with the larger story,
but that's the fun part.

As you are reporting a story, listen closely when you are interviewing sources. They may comment on other projects they are working on or something else one of their colleagues is researching. Many writers get ideas for their next piece while preparing their current assignment.

Writers are always at work, even when it doesn't seem like it. When you're at a cocktail party and hear an interesting story about something a friend of a friend is up to, make a mental note to follow up. Writers who break new stories are often snoops at heart, and they are not afraid to ask to be put in touch with their mail carrier's uncle's dog walker.

## Developing the Idea

Now you've got some possibilities. But which of these are likely to actually get an editor's interest and turn into a publishable story? Apart

### OLD STORIES, NEW TRICKS

"Old stories are redone all the time; the trick is making them feel new. Find a new study that will be coming out in three months, and hook it to that. Find a new person who is taking the story in a new and unique direction."

—*Doug Most, editor,* Boston Globe Sunday Magazine

"Read, read, read. Read the pub that you're pitching and notice how the editors are retooling old story ideas in new ways. And don't be afraid to copy an idea you've seen elsewhere and apply it to fresh subject matter."

—*Jennifer Tanaka, a senior editor at* Chicago *magazine and previous technology staff writer for* Newsweek from your own intuition, and asking some friends what they think of your idea, there are some basic things to consider when developing a story idea.

### Newsworthiness

Write down your idea and a few sentences that expand upon it. Then take a look at what you've written. Does it convey information that people want or need to know? Is it entertaining? Does it introduce readers to a new idea, a new experience, a new place, or an interesting new person? Is the idea creative, original, fun, fresh, and relevant? Is it opinionated or controversial? Does it contain tension and conflict, or express a point of view?

If the idea strikes you as too tired, think about how to use that old topic as a jumping point to something new. Do you want to write about breast cancer, but think everything that can be said has already been said? Start doing some hunting by contacting researchers on the forefront of breast cancer research. Find out if anything new is happening. Talk to friends and ask if they've any friends with breast cancer who've had especially unusual experiences. A fresh angle or new perspective can invigorate even the most overplayed story.

### What does an editor need?

Editors are always looking ahead. They constantly have to be scheduling pieces for future issues and filling holes when pieces don't pan out. So put yourself in the mind of an editor, and think about lead time. Most national monthly magazines work at least three months ahead of time. So in the summer, editors are already working on their fall issues, and they are beginning to schedule and assign stories for their holiday issues. Come winter, it's time to be thinking about spring and even summer. In addition, most magazines have editorial calendars, some of which are available to freelance writers. Go to the magazine's Web site or put a call in to an editorial assistant at the

## DEVELOPING IDEAS FROM PUBLIC RELATIONS FOLKS

Many editors complain about PR people. They're always calling trying to pitch story ideas. They don't understand what the editors are looking for or what's appropriate for the publication. Writers, too, often screen their phone calls, to be sure they don't get stuck on the line with someone trying to get an article written about their oh-so-wonderful client, their state-of-the-art new product, their up-and-coming nobody who is without a doubt going to be the next somebody.

But, all the clichés aside, publicity people often really do have some great new information to impart. Cozying up to the right people on the inside track may let you in on what's happening before other freelancers even have an inkling that anything is going on. For instance, in press releases PR people are notorious for overhyping "new information" to be announced at an upcoming press conference. If you're friendly with a certain publicist, she may let you know when the information is really newsworthy and interesting. In addition, she may send you the tidbit just a little ahead of time so you can start pitching the publications sooner than other freelancers.

Over time, and with experience, you'll begin to realize which PR people are legit and helpful and which are just out to sell you a story without a backbone. PR people affiliated with well-established firms, as well as those working with universities, major stars, and the real movers and shakers (experts) in the fields you cover are most apt to bring you reliable information.

In order to start receiving e-mails, as well as news and press releases from these PR people, simply put in some phone calls to firms or representatives that work in the areas in which you are interested. Or do some hunting on the Internet. For example, if you want to write about new products for children, go to the Toys "R" Us Web site and see if they have a section for the media or the press. You may be able to sign up for their media releases right on their site. Go directly to manufacturer's sites—Google Bugaboo strollers and see if their site has information for the press. Or get the main number for the company and call and ask to be connected to the media or marketing department. Introduce yourself as a writer and ask to be added to their mailing list.

You can make some phone calls and quickly get yourself on the media mailing list of associations, universities, nonprofits, book publishers, and other groups and societies in your areas of interest. Also ask other free-lancers about PR folks they like working with, and hopefully they'll be willing to share their contacts with you.

You can find PR firms by specialty in directories of PR professionals, such as www.odwyerPR.com. After you're connected to your particular beat, be aware that you're going to be receiving the same press releases as other freelancers—and editors—who write about that topic. For example, if you write about beauty and get a news release on a new Bobbi Brown product, you should assume the editors at *Allure, Elle,* and *Vogue* received that same release. So you either have to act fast when you come across a great idea or, better yet, come up with a creative angle that makes the idea more interesting, informative, and exciting. Sure, everyone knows about the new Bobbi Brown concealer debuting in the fall, but perhaps you can look at how that Bobbi Brown product can work for someone whose entire beauty regimen has always been with another line of cosmetics.

Many writers develop close relationships with PR people, to the degree that they not only listen to their pitches but also take the time to work together and develop late-breaking news into publishable story ideas. If you've found a great PR person to work with, milk it. Ask him to lunch and let him throw ideas at you. Nurture the relationship. It's a win-win. Often, as a writer, you will need to turn to the PR people when you are looking for the perfect subject to interview for a story, or when you need one final quote to bring your 3,000-word piece to a tidy little close. And they get their clients some press—their ultimate goal. Don't forget, if they tip you off on some news, or new product, or whatever, let them know if you use that information in the story. That's how they show their client that they are doing their job!

magazine and see if he or she can provide you with an editorial calendar. These calendars map out upcoming issues far in advance. For instance, a woman's health magazine may do a special section on heart health in February and breast health in October. Parenting magazines will likely address back-to-school topics in the fall. Fashion magazines revolve around seasonal styles, while travel magazines take you to the Caribbean and to the slopes in the winter and to Europe and honeymoon destinations in the summer. Your article on a state-of-the-art umbrella is probably not going to grab an editor's attention unless you are pitching it to run in a springtime issue—even though we all know it rains in months other than April. Maximize your chances for success, and work on the right idea at the right time.

---

### EDITORIAL CALENDARS

Many magazines suggest that writers contact an editor, or go to the publication Web site, to access the magazine's editorial calendar. Writers who do so will learn that some publications have detailed calendars, while others are rather minimal. You can find a basic rundown of magazine's editorial calendars on mediabistro.com if you are an AvantGuild member. Following are three examples, one from *Stuff* magazine, one from *Business 2.0*, and the third a taste of mediabistro.com's calendar sampling.

**STUFF** THE MAGAZINE EDITORIAL CALENDAR

| | |
|---|---|
| January: | The World's Best *Stuff* |
| February: | The Love Issue |
| March: | The Spring Fashion Issue |
| April: | The Music Issue |
| May: | The Best of Design and Style |
| June: | Summer Fun |
| July: | Summer Movie Preview |
| August: | Summer of Music |
| September: | The Fall Fashion Issue |
| October: | TV World |
| November: | Cars! Cars! Cars! |
| December: | The Ultimate Holiday Gift Guide |

**BUSINESS 2.0** 2005 EDITORIAL CALENDAR

| | |
|---|---|
| Jan/Feb: | The Smart List |
| March: | Get Paid What You're Worth/The Road Warrior's Guide to Business Travel |

| | |
|---|---|
| April: | The First Annual Bottom Line Design Awards |
| May: | Wiring the Future/Do This. Get Rich |
| June: | The 100 Fastest-Growing Tech Companies |
| July: | A New Generation of Leaders: The Under-40 Executives You Need to Know |
| August: | Special Global Issue: The Best Business Ideas in the World |
| September: | Working Smart to Live Well/The Third Annual Underground Guide to Business Schools/How to Score 5 Million Bucks |
| October: | Seven Business Breakthroughs That Will Change Everything/Car Tech |
| November: | The Next Boom Towns: Cities That Work |
| December: | How to Succeed Next in 2006/Wi-Fi Survival Guide/The Gadget Guide |

**Special Sections**

| | |
|---|---|
| July: | Ringing Up ROI |
| September: | The Savvy Traveler |
| October: | Diversity |
| November: | Hybrids Hit the Road |
| December: | Holiday Wish List |

SAMPLE OF EDITORIAL CALENDARS ON MEDIABISTRO.COM

| | |
|---|---|
| January: | *Sports Illustrated* nba/nhl Midseason Reports |
| February: | *Essence:* The Passion Issue/Celebrating Black History |
| March: | *Bon Appetit:* The Annual Kitchen Issue |
| April: | *Travel + Leisure:* Annual America Issue |
| May: | *Maxim:* The Maxim Hot 100 |
| June: | *Popular Science:* Annual Best of What's Next |
| July: | *New York:* Cheap Eats |
| August: | *Self:* Annual Fitness Issue |
| September: | *Ellegirl:* Fall Fashion |
| October: | *Travel + Leisure:* Annual Style Issue |
| November: | *Men's Journal:* The Best Issue |
| December: | *Time:* Person of the Year |

As you're brainstorming, beware of the dreaded idea drought. It's horrible, but it happens. So be prepared. Start a folder or a notepad devoted to random ideas. Even if you can't think of a way to mold them into a firm story idea at the moment, things could be different when you revisit an idea in a few days, weeks, or even months. Some writers schedule time just to brainstorm and develop little ideas into concrete proposals. Maybe it's every Wednesday afternoon, or the first Thursday of the month—whatever works for you to find some time in your calendar for story development.

---

### TIMING IS EVERYTHING

"If you don't have a specific idea, feel free to e-mail editors an introductory letter saying you'd like to write for them and requesting the editorial calendar so that you can pitch ideas for upcoming issues."

—Nerve *editor-in-chief Michael Martin*

"The thing that a lot of freelancers miss with us is timing; they're not thinking about our editorial calendar. They may be very much on point, and it may be a good piece, but by the time it [appears in the magazine], no one will be talking about it."

—Foreign Policy *managing editor William J. Dobson*

5

# Oh, the Places You'll Pitch

I t is wise to think about what type of publications you want to target for your great idea and how to go about approaching them before you start merely pitching to some of your favorites. There are
thousands of publications to write for, with new ones starting every
day. There are magazines about politics, pets, and playboys. There
are national newspapers and small-town newspapers and expatriate
papers around the world. There are Web publications for most any
special niches, from weddings to sports cars to flower arranging. And
you'll find newsletters for members of different professions, for resi-
dents of many towns and villages, for all sorts of associations, and
for a variety of hobbyists. If you have a good understanding of what
venues are out there, you can pitch your story ideas to just the right
publication—and increase your chances of success.

> Many freelancers spend time each week in bookstores
> and at newsstands familiarizing themselves with what's be-
> ing sold (including what new publications are out there)
> and what's hot.

When it comes to magazines, "general interest" is the label used to describe a broad category of publications that are intended for a large audience. Many, such as *Reader's Digest* and *Parade,* cover a wide variety of different subjects. Other general-interest publications are based on current news, such as *Newsweek* and *Time.* Magazines like *Us Weekly* and *People* report almost solely on current celebrity news.

Apart from general-interest titles, many magazines focus on one general subject but still intend to reach a wide group of people. Examples include *Vogue* (focusing on fashion), *Car and Driver* (targeting readers interested in automobiles), *Sports Illustrated* (meant for sports buffs), and *New York* (directed at those connected to life in the Big Apple). There are dozens of *categories* of nonfiction magazines— let alone the thousands of individual magazines—and here are some of them: agriculture, alternative, animals, architecture, automotive, aviation, business, career development, computers, education, entertainment, environment, finance, fitness, food, gardening, gay and lesbian, health, hobbies, home, in-flight, men's, parenting, regional, science, seniors, sports, teens, travel, women, and wine. (Plus, there are also categories of fiction and poetry magazines.)

Additionally, nearly 1,500 daily newspapers are published in the United States, plus thousands of weekly community papers and alternative papers. And they're all always in need of writers. Of course we're all familiar with the big players like the *New York Times,* the *Wall Street Journal, USA Today*, and others. But don't overlook your smaller local publications. In New York, for instance, the borough of Queens alone has sixteen weekly newspapers, including the *Forest Hills Ledger* and the *Jamaica Times*. In western North Carolina, in the area surrounding the not-so-big town of Asheville, you'll find at least six weekly papers, including the *Haywood County News, Black Mountain News, Asheville Daily Planet, Asheville Global Report,* the *Asheville Tribune,* and *Mountain Xpress.*

Take a look at your local newsstand and those stacks of freebie journals and papers in your local supermarket or favorite coffee shop. There are countless venues looking for writers.

## Assess the Marketplace

Not everything is open to freelancers, however. Let's say an entertainment magazine has two movie-related articles per week, one that's a review and one that's news-based. If you notice that the same movie critic (listed on the masthead, the page typically found near the front of the publication where the magazine's staff is listed) always writes the reviews and the same reporter (also on the masthead) always covers the news, then your pitch to review Nicole Kidman's next film isn't going anywhere. Staffers write those pieces, and there probably isn't a budget to pay freelancers for that section. Before you try to pitch a publication, you've got to know whether they even accept the sort of article you're pitching.

One of the easiest ways is to call the publication and ask. Try to reach an editorial assistant. They can usually tell you which sections are written by freelancers and the right editor to pitch.

If no one will answer your call or phone you back, you can also use your own investigative skills to determine what is freelance written. Start by getting familiar with magazine mastheads. Why? You will see on some a list of "contributing writers" or "staff writers."

Don't try to get the editor-in-chief on the phone. Your attempt will fail, at best. If, by some amazing, out-of-the-ordinary chance, you do get a top editor on the phone, odds are she won't be particularly happy to be answering questions about what's available for freelancers.

Chances are pretty good that magazines that include "writers" on the masthead are written largely by people either on the publication's staff or in an already-established group of freelancers. These publications are, for the most part, much harder for new freelancers to break into than publications with no writers on staff. For example, weeklies such as *Time* and *People* work with such quick turnaround times that much of their content is written by staff members. It would be almost logistically impossible for those magazines to assign their articles to freelancers on a weekly basis (however, they assign certain types of stories to non–staff members).

Another place to check is the contributors page, if there is one. Also found in the front of most magazines, the contributors page often contains pictures and short bios of some of the writers in that publication. By reading the contributors page you can get a good idea if that magazine hires freelancers to do some of the writing. For instance, *Vanity Fair* often has several pages dedicated to its "contributors," but that does not mean they hire lots of new freelancers. Read a few of the contributors' descriptions and you'll see that many of them are labeled *Vanity Fair* "contributing writers" or "contributing editors." This means they write for the magazine on a regular basis, may have a contract to write a certain number of pieces each year, and may even have an office at the magazine and collect a regular salary from the publication. But if you glance at a copy of *Organic Style*, on the other hand, you are more likely to see a contributor described specifically as a "freelance writer" who lives and works in a city anywhere across the country. Magazines like that are easier to break into than are the big boys like *Vanity Fair.*

And one more way to get a feel for how much of a magazine is freelance written is to look at the actual articles in a magazine. For instance, at the end of an article in *Child* magazine the author often gets a quick bio: "Margit Feury Ragland is a freelance writer based in

Boston, Mass." Another trick: if the author has a byline at the top but no bio at the end of the piece, do a quick cross-reference between the byline on that article and the name on the masthead. Not a good sign if they match. You may see that all of the beauty stories in issue after issue of a magazine are written by people listed on the masthead as beauty or fashion editors—which means the magazine is probably not taking freelance submissions for that section.

## Start Small and Then Grow

While you may dream of writing for the big magazines—titles you typically read—you're very unlikely to break into major national mags at the start of your career. For instance, if you have never been published before, take your ideas to smaller local publications first— perhaps your neighborhood newspaper or a city mag. Newsletters published by organizations are often looking for writers.

If you don't currently have any clips, don't be afraid of writing a few articles for free. It will be worth it to have some published clips that will help you get your first paying gig.

Some people focus solely on getting an article in a national publication, even if it's just a two-line blurb in a news section, or a letter to the editor. The thinking is that getting your name in a big publication in any form will be a great entry point into freelancing for similar titles. But most assigning editors will tell you they're much more impressed by a person with a handful of well-researched and well-written articles in a little unknown, small-town paper than with a small article in a major publication.

The small piece doesn't give you a chance to show off your writing and reporting chops, and, even worse, editors know that the small piece for the national pub was likely reworked by three different editors. Your big takeout in the *Podunk Post* or *Office Oracle* probably

## Q&A: CLIPS FROM BIG AND LITTLE GUYS
## WITH LAURA CONAWAY

Laura Conaway is executive editor of the *Village Voice*.

**Q. If I'm going to send you some clips, would you rather see a short thing I've written for the *New York Times* or for the *Village Voice* (the gold standard of alt-weekly), or would you rather see a big, interesting feature that I did for something smaller, but that you really got into?**
A. If you can write in English—if you have something that shows me that you have written in English at some time in your life, send it. That's good.

**Q. So you don't care what the clip is.**
A. I don't care. Why should I care? I came from nowhere.

underwent little, if any, editing or rewriting. Editors would rather see what you can do than see what big name you can drop.

After you've broken into the smaller-circulation publications, you can start planning your move to the big leagues. Take those travel pieces you wrote for your local paper and consider pitching an idea to a larger travel magazine. Pull together clips from your PTA newsletter, and use that piece on how your school district is making school lunches healthier to develop a bigger pitch to a parenting magazine.

There is always the question of what to do if you have a huge idea before you have a decent set of clips. Should you waste it on a small-town newsletter or should you shoot for the big guns? If you have a strong feeling that yours is a breathtakingly terrific idea, go ahead and launch it off to your dream magazine. But be aware that your chances of getting published—maybe even your chances of hearing back—are slim. Still, a great idea is a great idea, and there's always the chance your pitch just might make an editor stop in his tracks and

## BIG IN NAME OR BIG IN CONTENT?

"When I was an editor, I liked to see both clips from small pubs and from the big names. Editors know it is hard to break into freelancing for big publications and we always recommend starting with small items—it gives us the chance to see what you're like to work with and if you can come up with appropriate ideas. Sending a longer piece from a local paper is proof that you're capable of researching and writing more than two hundred words, which is good to know, but is probably still not going to get you a long assignment off the bat."

> —*Jillian Lewis, a freelance writer in New York City who held staff positions at magazines in Sydney, Australia, and New York before launching into a life of flexible hours*

"Occasionally, good clips from a zine or alt-weekly that show a lively combination of knowledge and style will catch my eye."

> —*Alan Light, former editor in chief,* Tracks

"Often I'll get a pitch on a travel narrative, but all the clips are about gear. It's very hard to know if someone has the narrative voice based on even very well reported pieces about sunblock."

> —*Brad Wieners, executive editor,* National Geographic Adventure

take notice of you. Then, if you don't hear back from an editor in a few weeks, even after you follow up by phone or e-mail, you can always pitch your piece elsewhere. Remember that even if you end up writing that fab piece for just your local paper, the result may still be a great clip that can help bring your freelancing career to the next level.

## A Look at the Newsstand

It's impossible to make blanket statements about what parts of newspapers and magazines freelancers write and what parts staff members always write. Every publication must be looked at on a case-by-case basis. Here is a sampling of daily, weekly, and monthly titles, along with a bit of insight into what's open to freelancers and what's strictly off-limits.

### Dailies and Weeklies

Much of the content in daily and weekly publications is written in-house. These publications work on such tight schedules that there is not much leeway for assigning out—and then editing—timely pieces. That said, there are some select sections of these publications that are open to freelancers.

#### Entertainment Weekly

This magazine's editors are inundated with pitches from writers— and from nonwriters who think they are blessed with some out-of-the-ordinary pop-culture wisdom. Most will never get an assignment. For the most part, the only time freelancers are used is when they have an "in" or access to some information that nobody on the mag's big staff does. And that is rare. The only place where freelancers may have a chance is in the front-of-the-book section, "News & Notes," which features a mix of fundamentals and fluff each week. The "Style Sheet" section, which follows "News & Notes," occasionally accepts chart pitches from freelancers. Nearly everything else in the magazine—features, reviews, roundups—is written in-house.

#### LA Times Weekend Calendar

Appearing in the *LA Times* each Thursday, the Weekend Calendar has freelancers producing about half the content. As with all pitches to newspapers, make sure your great idea hasn't already been covered in another section of the paper. "Here and Now," the Weekend Calendar's 700-word opener, is almost always freelanced, although it's usually written by an experienced writer and submitted in full. If you want to take a stab at it, be sure your piece has a distinct voice and relates broadly to Southern California. "Up Front: Pop Music" is also assigned out, but a time hook is crucial: performers must either be performing live in the week after publication or, if it's a slow concert week, releasing an album. The 600-650 word "Getting Personal" column (also called "Tell" and formerly known as "Single in the City") is most often pitched to by freelancers. A winning pitch avoids clichés about men and women and doesn't involve speed dating or online dating. It quickly states the theme, includes insightful, funny anecdotal support, and sums things up in a nut graf. "With the Kids" is written by freelancers half of the time. All freelanced arts pitches should focus on a smaller show at a place not typically reviewed by the *Times*. In addition to information about the artist, include a description of the space, creation, or setup. Stories about major shows in theaters, museums, and galleries tend to stay in-house or go to the publication's freelance stable. In addition, all reviews are off-limits, as regular freelancers take those slots. Cover features tend to be written by staff, but freelancers are urged to try pitching a broad topic with wide appeal and clear depth of reporting.

### Newsweek

Obviously well known for covering world events and politics, *Newsweek* is written mostly in-house. Aspiring freelancers may have a chance pitching a service piece to the "Tip Sheet" lifestyle section that resides in the back of the magazine. Designed slightly differently than most magazines, since the news dominates this pub, the "Tip Sheet" contains as many as fifteen to twenty relatively short (about 150 words) items per week—covering health, technology, travel, style, food, and personal finance. The only other possibly freelance-friendly area of *Newsweek* is "My Turn," the reader-submitted personal essays that run in the front of the book. It's important to note that these are personal essays, not op-ed pieces.

### The New York Times "City" Section

Writers hoping to break into the *New York Times* often start with the
"City" section, which is traditionally fertile ground for freelancers.
The caveat: ideas must have something unique to say about the New
York experience. Avoid pitching to the columns "FYI" (a Q&A on a
topic of the day), "Restaurants," "Wine," or "Bending Elbows" (the
bar column), as all are written by a small staff of full-time freelancers.
A better bet is the "Neighborhood Reports" column.

### Time Out Chicago

Chicago is the second U.S. city—after New York—to gets its own
weekly *Time Out* publication. Since it is a local book (the term *book*
is used interchangeably with *magazine*), local writers naturally have
the best chance at getting in. This publication is split up into sections, such as "Eat Out," "Drink Up," "Chill Out," and "Check Out"
(devoted to restaurants, bars, wellness, and shopping, respectively).
Freelancers will have the best luck pitching an opener (the short
pieces that open each of these sections). For out-of-towners who are
interested in acquiring clips at a city pub, the reviews section (music
and books) might be a place to get a foot in the door.

About 75 percent of *Time Out Chicago*'s articles are about national artists who are performing in Chicago that week. The remainder are about Chicago artists. CD reviews are pegged to release dates

and include national artists as well. Once you make inroads by writing some openers or reviews, you have a better chance of getting to work on larger features in the magazine.

### The Village Voice

While every section, in every issue, contains a sizable amount of free-lance work, the country's first and largest alternative newsweekly is a tough nut for a freelancer to crack. Why? The music editor alone already has more than a hundred freelancers who write for him on a regular basis. So to get your pitch accepted, it must be about something totally out of the ordinary. Any typical article or review will already be assigned to one of the regular contributors.

### The Wall Street Journal's Weekend Journal

Staff reporters write the hard news of almost all newspapers. The feature sections are the better bet for freelancers. Even that business-man's bible, the *Wall Street Journal,* has a lighter side with the *Weekend Journal,* which runs every Friday, and the Saturday *Weekend Edition.* As with most publications, freelancers should start small, pitching to "Takeoffs & Landings," a travel column that sometimes uses freelance contributions, and "Details," a short column that usually covers home, design, and décor.

### Web Sites

Here's some scoop on a few Web sites that are open to freelancers.

### The Knot

Best known for its wedding Web site, *The Knot* also puts out a national magazine, along with regional publications, making the opportunities for freelancers great. Freelancers write much of *The Knot* material. You can pitch general features, as well as anything

---

### ALL PUBS ARE NOT THE SAME

"A lot of people think, 'Oh, this is a travel story, so I can pitch it to
the *New York Times, Travel + Leisure, Condé Nast Traveler,* and *National
Geographic Traveler,*' but the fact is, we're all different."

—Travel + Leisure *features editor Nathan Lump*

---

for the "Real Weddings" column. The editors look for pieces that can
include a couple of super-service-friendly sidebars. ("Service" in publications refers to content that provides practical information, resources, and advice on a particular subject.) So pitch those along with
your main idea. Also frequently assigned are travel pieces and stories
that draw from a writer's specific skill or interest, such as food, music,
or photography.

### Salon

This left-leaning online magazine of news and culture freelances out
about half its content. No one section is easier than another to break
into, although most film, television, and music reviews are written
in-house. The editors are always looking for story ideas that are ahead
of the curve.

### Slate

The most pitchable part of this daily online magazine is the
culture department. While articles in this section cover television,
movies, books, art, architecture, design, fashion, and food, don't
pitch a review, for this webzine is driven by ideas, not trends. A
freelancer's best bet is with the column "Culturebox." Here you'll
find ideas constructed around a specific argument or pieces meant to
really make people think.

### Monthlies

Monthly publications rely much more heavily on freelance writers than dailies or weeklies. Even so, there are often sections that are off-limits to freelancers, and that can vary from publication to publication. Some compose the entire front of the book in-house, because this section is newsy and must be extremely timely (so again no time to farm out pieces to freelancers). Since front-of-book items are relatively short, many publications do use this as a place to try out new writers—they're not putting a lot at stake when they assign something to an unknown writer.

#### Bon Appétit

While *Bon Appétit* doesn't outsource a great deal of material, there are some opportunities for freelancers as long as you are a walking and writing food encyclopedia—and can prove it. "Starters," in the front of the book, is about 50 percent freelanced. With items ranging from "very short" to 300 words in length, it's a great place for rookies to debut. Another freelancer-accessible department is "At the Market," which focuses on seasonal produce and ingredients. *Bon Appétit* also prints first-person essays, and submissions on just about anything are encouraged. Feature stories are a freelancer's fair game, but know that the odds aren't exactly stacked in your favor. If it's food or travel you hope to chime in on, you'd better have impeccable credentials, or in the very least, writerly excellence.

#### Cargo

While shopping magazines aren't known for being heavy on editorial, *Cargo* does welcome freelancers in most of its sections. In fact, some, like "Tech," "Grooming," and the monthly "What a Girl Wants" column are almost entirely freelanced. Also, some of the mag's front-of-the-book news items are assigned out. Everything fashion and entertainment related, on the other hand, is written in-house.

### Child

*Child* can be one of the tougher magazines to pitch. The front of the book, which includes columns on child development, health and safety, nutrition, entertainment, and pregnancy and babies, is written in-house or by contracted contributors. If you send in a great idea for one of these columns, and the editors want to do it, chances are you won't be asked to write it but instead will be paid a finder's fee for the idea. Regular freelancers usually take care of the feature well (the meaty section of the book where longer articles appear), too. But that doesn't mean it's impossible to break in. The back of the book offers two freelancer-friendly columns, the "How They Do It" profiles on parents with unusual jobs or lifestyles and the "What I Wish Every Parent Knew" personal essay. In rare instances, essays sometimes make it into the feature well.

### Elle Decor

Most ideas at the designers and decorators magazine *Elle Decor* are generated by the staff and then sent out to regular contributors. But that doesn't mean you're without a shot: if the editors are impressed with your clips, they may well assign you one of their in-house ideas. Freelancers often write for the following columns: "What's Hot! Shops," which focuses on a new retail shop; "What's Hot! People," which profiles product designers "Art," which introduces readers to new artists and their work; and "*Elle Decor* Goes To," which is a virtual tour of a city, including its top restaurants, hotels, museums, and shops.

*Glamour*

Freelancers produce about 70 percent of *Glamour* magazine. Most write service pieces, as about two-thirds of the magazine's content has a service slant. The front of the book is a good place for freelancers to start, with short service items that are fun, quick reads.

Sections like "Couple Time," "All About You," and "Your Work and Money" are also possible spots for freelancers to break in. The magazine is always on the lookout for compelling health articles. The "Health & Body Book" section is another especially freelancer-friendly area, with many pages to fill each month.

*Good Housekeeping*

Eighty percent of the time-tested magazine *Good Housekeeping* is written by freelancers. While the magazine's tried and true writers almost always write the features, there's still opportunity for newbies. "My Story" is a first-person (or as-told-to) article in which a woman shares her tale of overcoming an especially difficult impasse in her life. Also open is the section "Real Lives," which includes short features about inspiring, heroic, or fascinating people—including women entrepreneurs, celebrities, authors, or human-interest subjects. As at most magazines, fashion and beauty pages are done in-house, as are celebrity profiles. The columns in *Good Housekeeping* are written by the big shots—among them, Liz Smith, Heloise, Peggy Post, and Joy Behar—so save your printer ink regarding those. High-profile or name-brand writers usually write even the essays in this magazine.

*Mad*

*Mad* magazine has always been very kind to freelancers; in fact, in the old days regular contributors were taken on all-expenses-paid trips every year. Things are no longer quite that good, but if you've got some humorous ideas, this may be one of the last places to exhibit them in print. Freelancers often even create comic strips for the magazine. There are no departments or discrete sections of the magazine, and only a few regular features—among them "Spy vs. Spy" and the back page "Fold-In"—which you shouldn't pitch. Spoofs on movies are often done in-house since they have to be done far in advance to meet release dates. Otherwise, all your ideas are welcome.

### National Geographic Adventure

*National Geographic Adventure* has no staff writers, so it can be a great venue for writers looking to offer up their adventure expertise. The magazine welcomes pitches in almost every section of the book. The front of the book, called "Journal," is broken into several sections, most of which are pitchable. The opener, "Frontiers," describes a specific excursion. Writers can also pitch a one-page "City Escape," highlighting outdoor activities just outside major metropolises. Freelancers can also pitch the "Books" section, which rounds up typical *Into Thin Air* or Shackleton-type media fare, and "Essentials," a recurring primer on how to outfit yourself for a particular activity. Three travel service sections in the front of the book are written in-house: "Next Weekend," "Wild Roads," and "Where Next;" another front-of-book page, "First Person," is also mostly off-limits. The magazine accepts photography submissions for its back page, called "There & Back." If you're a photographer with a great shot from your last trip, pitch it to the photo editor—it could pave the way for future assignments.

### Oxford American

This publication appears only quarterly, but it is set up much like a monthly. While the writing in this magazine is diverse, the content all shines a lamp south of the Mason-Dixon Line. The magazine has shut down and relaunched a few times in recent years and the editors may ask writers to submit things on spec.

New writers can break into the only truly defined sections of the magazine, found in the front: "Site Seeing" is an essay highlighting little-known or aesthetically significant architecture of the South; first-person accounts appear in "Odd Jobs"; and "Just Cause" is a section on the region's charities. Sometimes articles that are pitched for the front end up publishing as longer pieces in the departments or the well. For example, in one issue, a "front" piece featuring short interviews with southern celebrity chefs—such as Emeril—became a feature.

The FOB (or front-of-book) columns "For Sale," "Calendar," and "Now Showing" are mostly written in-house, and the magazine doesn't run much celebrity coverage. Also, there is not much of an emphasis on travel or regional service. The magazine isn't a southern guidebook, it's about a way of life, and it's got a broad readership: if a piece about a place or a restaurant isn't worth reading for someone who will probably never go there, it probably isn't right for the magazine.

### Prevention

The big front-of-book section in *Prevention*, "News and Trends," usually contains about twenty bite-sized nuggets for freelancers to sink their teeth into. Features are typically assigned only to writers with lots of experience writing for national health magazines. But if you're not in that niche, there's a chance you could land a longer piece if you have access to subjects with riveting narrative stories. The food section is open to writers with fresh ideas, too.

### Real Simple

While the title may seem easy, *Real Simple* is a tricky book to pitch. You may flip through the magazine and naturally assume the editors are looking for product-based pitches. Unfortunately, the magazine has its beat editors developing and writing those kinds of stories all the time. Instead, your best bet to break in is with a clever conceptual conceit. The "Know How" section is one place you might want to

---

"The general misconception is that *Rolling Stone* is basically a magazine of essays and reviews of musicians and people, and we're much more than that. In the past few years, *Rolling Stone* has altered itself to be newsier and more competitive; stories are shorter and the magazine now takes a decidedly visual approach. And investigative reporting and music is always at the center of it all."

—Rolling Stone *assistant managing editor Eric Bates*

---

attempt to make inroads, as it is usually made up of ten or so items. The editors are also on the lookout for stories for "The Guide." The section is broken into six beats—style, body, beauty, life, home, and The Organizer. Don't bother pitching an essay to *Real Simple*, as those published in the "Life Lessons" section are almost always contributed by name writers, like Jonathan Safran Foer on vegetarianism, say, or Jane Smiley on beauty.

### Runner's World

*Runner's World* is a prime example of a magazine where the large front of book offers many opportunities for freelancers. Entitled "Warmups," the section is broken up further into a number of subsections, including "Human Race," "Training," "Mind + Body," and "Fuel," and is the freelancer's starting line. Each of these sections opens with a lead piece (accessible to freelancers) followed by advice-type columns produced in-house.

A little further into the magazine is the column "Personal Record," which is also open to freelancers. So are the "Gear" and "Racing Report" columns.

The feature well (the meaty section of the book where longer articles appear) is harder for freelancers to crack, except for "True Obsession," a two-page spread. It's not a classic-length feature story, but an easier, entry-level way to break in, especially for not-yet-established freelancers low on clips.

### Ski

Even a targeted magazine like *Ski* opens with a front-of-book section packed with short items. Titled "Fall Line," the front-of-book section opens with a trend story and then segues into several pages that contain pithy product reviews and the like. The section is pitchable but probably not worth the time, as most is written in-house. Essays, on the other hand, are better bets. The "On Skiing" column provides first-person reflections on the sport and is almost entirely freelancer penned. Next is a page called "Off the Map," which provides another great opportunity for freelancers. Generally a single page, "Off the Map" takes a look at a "strange, unusual, exotic, bizarre place" in the ski world. "Mountain Life," a lifestyle/shelter section, is accessible to freelancers who are knowledgeable about a terrific ski house, for instance, and who have experience writing home and design/décor content. And if you have a feature idea, the competition is tough, but pitch the magazine around mid-October, when the editors plan features for the entire year.

### Teen Vogue

Packed with features, the fashion bible's fashionable kid sister is open to writers of all ages. Young writers may get their start with the first-person "My World" features, but these features are also written by more seasoned writers in the "As Told To" format. Also assigned out are the health-related features that run in the front and center of the book. The fashion and beauty content is written almost entirely in-house, and the magazine has a stable of writers who cover the entertainment beat, so you'll have to come armed with an amazing idea—and amazing access—to get the editors' attention in those departments.

### Travel + Leisure

The front of the book is where aspiring *Travel + Leisure* freelancers should head first. The pieces in "T+L Reports" are very short and incorporate the latest news on everything from hotels and restaurants to the arts, fashion, trends, technology, and shopping. "Insider," a column in the magazine's "Next" section, is also open to pitches. It's informative and service based, almost always headlining a particular city, domestic or international. A hard, but possible, pitch is the "Update" section, which focuses on travel industry and destination news, strategies, technological innovations, and the intersection where political, economic, cultural, and environmental issues meet travel and tourism. Features are almost always reserved for well-established writers.

### Yoga Journal

Freelancers contribute about half of the content that appears in *Yoga Journal.* The front-of-book "Om" section and departments in the "Life" and "Wellness" sections are probably the best places for freelancers to break in. The "Om" pages contain short items covering a broad range of categories—health, nutrition, wellness, fitness, home, and travel—but they all must have a yoga connection. The media section in the back of the book is a tricky pitch, but welcomes freelancers who are tuned in to alternative media. Typical coverage includes reports on chanting CDs for instructor use, popular music with a spiritual component, and traveling art exhibits dealing with Hinduism, Buddhism, or the plight of Tibet, for example.

The magazine runs three or four 2,000- to 3,000-word features per issue, and freelance writers contribute most of these. There's a fairly strong travel component in the feature well, along with health features and stories on national yoga trends. Yoga experts—usually instructors—write the three Asana departments. The Anatomy department is off-limits, unless you happen to fall into that small category of writers who are also anatomists.

Detailed how-to-pitch guides for these and many other titles are available at mediabistro.com.

# 6

# What Kind of Article Should You Write?

## From Feature to Review to Q&A—What's the Difference and Which Should You Be Pitching

You've got your idea and you've got a good idea of the market for freelance articles. What's next? Figure out how to frame your article for the right publication. What does that mean? Let's say you want to write about your family's yearly ritual of stomping on grapes and making wine together. Perhaps it could make a heartwarming article for *Ladies' Home Journal,* which has a column dedicated to family connections. Or maybe it would work well on the Web site of a gourmet food magazine. Or, you wonder, might *Wine Connoisseur* be interested in this fun, offbeat piece? Or maybe you think of how proud your grandmother would be if you got the entire family featured in the weekend section of your city paper. Where do you start?

Devote a little time to thinking about what kind of piece you want to write. There are countless different types of magazine, newspaper, and online articles—features, columns, op-eds, profiles, essays, Q&As, and on and on. While not easily defined, because many of them overlap—a feature could be a profile, and a Q&A might be a column—they all have a place somewhere out there in the print world. Here are some of the most common:

## How-to

How-to pieces often appear in the front of a magazine and in the feature section of a newspaper. Rather than one long article, how-to items are usually short and grouped together with other bite-size pieces or other how-tos. While how-to pieces are "service pieces" (see page 93), they are usually shorter, quicker bits of information than what you'll find in a longer service article. Some magazines and some Web sites have a few pages that are actually labeled how-to pages and have a how-to editor who works only on this section. That's the person to pitch when you have a great short (often with a newsy hook) idea.

Many how-to pieces begin by discussing a particular subject, describe any tools that might be needed to do the particular task, and then take the reader through step-by-step instructions on how to do it. Examples of how-tos are projects like "How to Make Table Setting Cards," which you might see in *Martha Stewart Living,* or "How to Design a Wreath for Your Front Door" in *Family Circle,* or even "How to Teach Your Child to Whistle" in *Child.* In *Real Simple* you find how-tos like how to "Be Prepared," which focuses on what to know before embarking on various outings: to the butcher, the consignment shop, a road trip, a job interview, a parent-teacher conference, a red-eye flight. One month, *Real Simple* ran "How Good Is Your . . . ," which took to task everything from your immune system to your credit ranking. The magazine has also tackled concepts like "What's the best time to . . ." (ask for a raise or take your vitamins, for example) and "How to read . . ." (a wine list, a credit-card agreement, a real-estate ad). Business magazines publish stories on how to control costs, save energy, and increase efficiency. And men's magazines run the evergreen story "How to Get Six-Pack Abs" on a very regular basis. (An evergreen topic is one that can run any time, and that editors keep on hand to plug in when they need a story.) Perhaps your grapes piece could run as a fun "How to Make Your Own Wine" in an upscale men's magazine.

## FOB Piece

While how-to pieces are often found "in the front of the book," you may find other short newsy items in the first few pages of a magazine. These are usually simply referred to as FOB pieces or FOB items. Sometimes they consist of straight news; other times, often in news weeklies, they are funny or gossipy items.

## Q&A

Q&As appear regularly in publications and are often popular with readers, as they're usually quick and easy to take in. Most involve just one individual answering some questions, but sometimes they include two people with different viewpoints or a forum of three or more people. Q&As generally fall into two categories—either service or personality. Service Q&As are similar to how-to columns and conducted with an authority in a particular field of expertise. The more common personality Q&As are done with a celebrity or public figure (politicians, actors, filmmakers, artists, musicians, media professionals, royalty, scientists, criminals, everyday heroes, and so on). But playing off your winemaking piece, you might pitch an in-flight magazine a Q&A with a winemaker at an independently owned vineyard.

Make very sure that you have access to an interviewee before pitching a Q&A to an editor. And make sure the person is amenable to working with you on such a piece—and that he or she is a charismatic, outspoken, quirky, and insightful individual. Because a Q&A is just an edited transcription of your questions and the subject's answers, there's no way to hide a dull personality—it'll just be a dull Q&A.

Don't think that a Q&A is quick and easy to write. While the questions may be quick and easy to ask, it takes time and research to come up with good questions that will yield interesting answers. Also, some talented editing is necessary to work that content into a focused and intriguing piece suitable for publication.

A Q&A can run as a regular column in a magazine or as part of another section of the book. For instance, *Bon Appétit* sometimes includes Q&As in its front-of-book section "Starters." Obviously the magazine's Q&As are always food related, as in a recent one with Linda Ellerbee, the author behind *Take Big Bites: Adventures Around the World and Across the Table*. *Yoga Journal*, on the other hand, has a page called "The YJ Interview," which is always a Q&A with a well-known yoga teacher.

## Feature

Features are the backbone of most online and print magazines, and while news stories are usually the meat of newspapers, feature stories are commonly found in papers, too. Often promoted on the cover of the magazine, feature articles draw in the reader. Lengthy and in-depth, they address trends, issues, real-life traumas or successes, and

---

### THE ART OF THE FEATURE

"Successful feature stories often have a strong personality at their
core—and, of course, feature stories demand narrative prowess from
the writer."

—Business 2.0 *former executive editor Amy Bernstein*

---

more. Health articles, food stories, fashion and beauty spreads, and
relationship, lifestyle, and parenting pieces also often run in the feature well of a magazine. An editor may call anything longer than a
page (and sometimes even one-pagers) a feature. Just be aware that a
feature may mean one thing at one publication and something totally
different at the magazine down the street. You may be able to sell a feature idea to a newspaper—your grape-stomping piece could certainly
run as a big piece in the family or home section of a local newspaper.

## Profile

Profiles are often written about people or companies. For the most
part, those about an individual are written after an interview, or extensive interviews, with the person. Entertainment magazines also
sometimes publish "write-around" profiles, where the person, usually
a celebrity, is not actually interviewed. Instead the article is made up
of information and quotes grabbed from other articles or from interviews with "people close to the celeb." Presented as real profiles, these
pieces happen when the magazine is unable to land an actual interview with the celebrity. Just to make the terms a little more confusing, profiles often, but not always, run as features.

Back to your grape stomping: your own family saga might not fit,
but perhaps, using your wine knowledge for a magazine like *AARP*,

you could profile a retiree who launched his own winemaking business after leaving the corporate world.

## Service

Magazines (both print and online) are filled with service pieces—articles containing practical information, resources, and advice on a particular subject. These articles are the bread and butter of most women's magazines—they're dedicated to providing their readers with practical information to use in their own lives. Service pieces can address parenting, cooking, decorating, traveling, stress, shopping, health, career, happiness, money, science, sports, and business issues, and on and on. Services pieces are also sometimes call informative articles, which basically means they can be about any topic under the sun. They can run long, as a feature, or short, as a how-to. A big article on how another family could emulate your winemaking tradition, or simply an explanation on how to make wine, would be a service piece.

In fact, some magazines are nothing but "service books." *The Knot Weddings* puts out both a national edition and regional publications, and while they don't share much content (the national edition is more style focused—it's about the stuff you need—while the regional mags focus more on the people you should hire and where you can find them locally), the goal of both is always the same: service, service, service. *Real Simple* is another good example of a book very heavy on service. The magazine would never run a first-person essay about the trials and tribulations of moving. If they were ever to do a story on moving, it would be a story on *how* to move, which would be solely service oriented.

---

**AT YOUR SERVICE**

"Service pieces are typically intelligent self-help staples familiar to women's-mag readers: How do I cope with a difficult boss? When should I end a relationship? But rather than simply doling out advice, *Psychology Today* analyzes and explains the underlying situation."

—Psychology Today *editor-in-chief Kaja Perina*

---

## Exposé/Investigative

Exposés are found mainly in newspapers and magazines, but also occasionally online. They involve investigative reporting and usually reveal something new to the reader. They require thorough research and excellent writing skills, as well as extreme accuracy. Investigative pieces in a newspaper are most commonly penned by staff writers. And while investigative pieces have a home in newsy publications, they have also become more common in more service-oriented books. For instance, *Prevention* published a shocking exposé about tanning, titled "Killer Tan." While researching that piece on winemaking, you might discover that a top-selling winemaker still has employees' feet playing a role in the production process. That could make for a great exposé!

## In Their Own Words/As Told to

An "in their own words" piece—also called an "as told to"—is the tale of a personal experience, told in the first person. But they're not written by the person telling the story; they're written by a professional writer who has worked with the subject of the story to develop the first-person essay. These pieces are usually emotional, dramatic, intimate, and insightful. The byline often reads "by [the person who had the experience], as told to [the writer]."

The *Good Housekeeping* "My Story" column is often an as-told-to tale of a woman overcoming an especially difficult impasse in her life. One recent example, "I Couldn't Afford to Teach," was by a teacher who could hardly survive on her salary. *Teen Vogue's* "My World" column, about a teen's personal experience, is often done in an as-told-to format. Recent "My World"s include one about a teen animal-rights activist; one in which *8 Simple Rules* actress Kaley Cuoco describes her feelings about the death of her costar, John Ritter; another about two girls who fled from polygamy; and one about a girl falsely accused of writing bomb threats on her middle-school walls.

## Essay/Rant/Op-ed

A personal essay is the story of a private epiphany. A rant, on the other hand, is a piece about something that angers or annoys you—something you would like to change in the world. An op-ed is usually an opinion piece in a newspaper. In order to write an essay, a rant, or an op-ed, writers often interview themselves, by making a list of questions that will help reveal the details about an experience or a way of thinking. Essays, rants, and op-eds are more authoritative when backed up by reliable statistics and real facts. For these pieces to be interesting to the readers, they must address issues that touch them as well as you.

Web sites often feature these types of articles, such as the essay pitched to *Nerve,* featured on page 132 of this book.

Along similar lines, *Ski* magazine runs a column called "On Skiing," which is a first-person reflection on the sport. One recent column was developed from an e-mail sent by a writing instructor in Montana whose student had crafted a piece about a recent ski trip in Iraq. He wondered if the magazine might be interested in using it, and sure enough, *Ski* snatched it up. Even the health magazine *Prevention* sometimes prints essays. One writer pitched, and was assigned, a personal essay about her relationship with the scale, detailing the little things, like how she takes off her boots, hat, clothes, earrings, and watch before stepping on the scale at the doctor's office.

The op-ed page of a newspaper is a good place for a freelancer to demonstrate his tone and creativity.

## Roundup

In order to include many shorter topics or items in one piece, an editor may assign a so-called roundup. You'll find roundups like "Best-Selling Authors' Favorite Summertime Reading Picks" in the feature section of a newspaper, or "The Most Technical Off-Road Rides in the U.S." in a mountain biking magazine, or "Thirty Execs to Watch in Pharmaceuticals" in a business journal. *USA Today* recently ran a roundup of the latest ways in which colleges and universities are using technology to help build relationships with prospective students. Roundups do not have to be written as running text; instead, they might be detailed lists.

> When pitching a roundup—say, "The Weight Loss Secrets of Top Chefs" to *Prevention*—be sure you share some of the "secrets" in your query, to show that you have the ability to put a truly fresh spin on an evergreen topic.

## Travel

Who wouldn't want to be a travel writer? See the wonders of the world, taste exotic cuisines, experience adventures of a lifetime, and more, and get paid for it! While travel writing is considered one of the most competitive markets, the publications that print travel pieces have gone far beyond just *Travel + Leisure* and the *New York Times* Travel section. Many Web sites run travel pieces, and today, you'll even find a travel column in *Yoga Journal*. The publication's travel pieces are typically first-person essays accompanied by sidebars that address the practicalities of the trip—the when, where, and how to get there. Recent, unusual topics include a writer who went on a juice fast in Portugal, one who went on a vision quest in Arizona, and another who attended a yoga retreat at the Feather Pipe Ranch in Montana.

The most important thing to remember when pitching a travel piece is that not all travel articles are alike—some publications want a first-person description of a destination, others may want the writer to be invisible. So be sure to tailor your pitch to the specific publication you are querying. If you are writing that piece about your families' tradition of grape stomping, *Ladies' Home Journal* may be interested in a sidebar on kid-friendly wineries—*Maxim,* on the other hand, would most likely have no interest in a sidebar on kid-friendly anything. And if you're pitching a winery tour piece to an upscale travel publication, suggest a sidebar on "no kids allowed" venues and you'll probably have better luck. When pitching a travel piece to a newspaper, you might want to send along some JPEGs as well. While magazines usually take care of their own art, local newspapers are more apt to use decent photos that the freelancer provides.

Established travel writers are often offered "press junkets," which is a slang term for a "free trip" paid for by a resort, a city, or any other location or facility looking to get some positive press coverage. Be aware that some reputable newspapers, magazines, and online sites won't hire writers who take junkets.

## CONFESSIONS OF A PRESS JUNKET JUNKIE

"The first six years of my career I worked as a writer on staff at *Vogue, Mademoiselle, Seventeen,* and *YM.* Then I called up all my former editors and said, 'Spread the word, I'm going freelance.'

"One of the first bits of advice I got was to call *Bridal Guide* because I was told they needed travel writers. I took a test to rewrite an article, and they called me back a week later, saying 'We love it. Can you go to Barbados?'

"I made nearly twenty-five press trips a year for five years, traveling to Europe, the Caribbean, Micronesia, Hawaii, and South America.

"I am not afraid of the term press junket. I'm all for them! I'm just a writer trying to pay my bills in New York City. I've traveled all over the world and mostly on press trips. How do I manage to keep my objectivity? Look, if the service at a hotel is bad, you can't lie and say you had a great time. I'll write an article saying I had fun, but don't do this and this. For example, I went to Arizona recently. The first hotel was fantastic, but two other hotels were convention hotels, which didn't really excite me, so I'll write about the first one and about a spa treatment at one of the other two.

"To get on the inside scoop on trips and conventions, I suggest writers call tourist boards for different countries or islands and ask for their publicists, and get on their mailing list. Another insider secret: www.travel writers.com, a Web site that, for an annual fee of $89, allows writers to register to receive weekly updates of press trips around the world. One of this week's choices: New Year's Eve in Thailand. Doesn't sound too shabby, eh?"

*—Freelance writer Karen Bressler has written travel pieces for* Condé Nast Traveler, Ocean Drive, Fitness, Self, Elements, *and several other magazines. She's worked on several Caribbean books for Fodor's and traveled to Costa Rica and Tel Aviv for bridal magazines.*

## Reviews

Writing reviews is also a dreamy task, especially if you are a bookworm reviewing bestsellers, a foodie rating four-star restaurants, a music lover grading chart toppers, a movie buff comparing block-busters, or an artist evaluating lauded exhibits. Unfortunately, most reviews in magazines are written by staff members or regular contributors. But keep your eyes open for opportunities, a chance to propose a front-of-book item on a newly released book to a magazine that doesn't normally publish book reviews or to pitch reviews of restaurants to in-flight magazines. Newspapers may be more open to freelancers writing reviews, especially if you can write up local cultural events that the paper hasn't had time to send their own reporters to cover. Look for places that papers may be missing—new galleries, local theater productions—and offer to write a review. Web sites are also good places to pitch reviews, as they can be very timely—such as a review of an artsy film that will be playing for just one week at a local theater, or a review of the fall menu at a local restaurant.

## Quiz

Quizzes make for fun editorial in almost any publication. They require the reader to get involved and do a little thinking or analyzing. They work well on Web sites where they can be interactive. Quizzes often come in one of two forms—those that test one's knowledge and those that focus more on personality issues.

Personality quizzes often appear in teen's and women's magazines, with titles such as "Are You a Team Player?" "Are You Needy?" "Are You a Control Freak?" and "Do You Really Know Your Husband?" While the scenarios in personality quizzes may be fabricated, the results and analysis section is usually based on factual information acquired from experts or established research.

Know-how quizzes can be found in a variety of publications, and cover any topic: "Test Your Nutrition Smarts," "How's Your Geography?" and "Who Wore What to the Oscars?" Factual information is the basis of any knowledge-based quiz. *Shape* used a quiz to tackle the evergreen topic of sleep. The piece entitled "A Wake-Up Quiz" ran with a dek (the summary part of a headline) that read, "How much sleep do you need to be healthy? If you don't get enough, will you age faster? Gain weight? Here are a few facts that will surprise you."

## Now What?

Once you've zeroed in on the kind of article your idea is best suited for, where do you go? To the library, the bookstore, or the magazine stand. Start reading all the publications where you think your article might fit (and by now you know which pubs are freelancer-friendly). Think about the style and the tone of each publication.

While you might dream of writing that grapes-into-wine article for a certain upscale food magazine, perhaps you'll realize that your idea is a bit too out of the ordinary for that type of title. On the other hand, you might be surprised to find one foodie magazine that has an offbeat column in every other issue on creative ways to prepare food with a group. Perfect. Time to perfect your pitch.

PART III

# Pitch

# 7

# Getting Your First Assignment

**Getting Work Before You've Made a Name for Yourself**

The first freelance writing assignment is most definitely the hardest to get—you have no reputation in the field, you have few if any clips to present, and you're unlikely to have useful connections to assigning editors. So how do you do it? It all starts with the query letter (also called a pitch letter). Most all freelance pieces begin with a query letter, but when you don't have other credentials to your name, the letter takes on added importance.

A query letter is like a movie trailer. It lures an editor into the story, giving a taste of what's to come. And it should be an alluring taste. The editor has to want to read more and know more. The goal is to describe the article that your editor will receive if he buys your idea. The query letter also gives the editor a quick look at your writing ability, and, just as important, your ability to tackle that particular topic. It also makes it clear why that story idea is timely and pertinent.

Here's how to build a great query letter.

## First, Learn the Voice of the Publication Inside and Out

Once you've decided on a topic and a publication, keep reading . . . and reading. Get your hands on back issues. Your pitch will need to show that you have a good grasp of the publication's voice. The voice is largely determined by the demographics of the reader—basically who the publication is written for. Most pubs think of themselves as having a certain type of relationship with the reader and thus communicate to the reader in that way. For instance, some women's magazines see themselves as the reader's best friend and impart information in a casual, friendly, and kind way. Others describe themselves more as an older sister of the reader, providing advice in a gentle but somewhat authoritative manner. In the past, money and finance magazines used to present content in a somewhat bland, straightforward, corporate tone. But today there are magazines that thrive on providing their readers with serious content in a fun and accessible manner.

A great way to find out the inside scoop on a publication—who they consider their audience and other demographic information—is to call the advertising department and request a press kit or a media kit. These promotional materials are geared toward selling advertisements but can be very helpful to freelance writers gathering intelligence for a pitch.

Also, keep in mind that certain parts of the same magazine may have different voices. For instance, the front of the book might contain a news section in which the information is very matter-of-fact, opening with phrases like "Recent findings indicate . . . ," or "A new study reveals . . ." But, in that same publication, feature stories, appearing farther back in the magazine, might be more lighthearted, opinionated, or sarcastic.

Check out below how four different publications launch into stories about the same topic—how to shape up your abdominals.

### SELF, "PLAY YOUR WAY TO FLAT ABS"

*You want a flat, firm, I'm-so-sexy midriff—but you can't face another crunch. We at SELF can relate, which is why we came up with an ingenious way to get major tummy-toning results with minimum time and zero drudgery. We collected 11 favorite ab moves from five top fitness pros.*

### NEW YORK TIMES, "AMERICA IS STILL WORKING ON ITS ABS"

By Alex Williams

*By some measures the heyday of abdominal fitness was a decade ago.* Men's Health *magazine rode to publishing glory in the 1990s with a monthly cover model showing off his washboard stomach. The term six-pack entered the language of vanity. Driven by late-night television advertising, some 368,000 AbRollers, ABSculptors and . . .*

### GOOD HOUSEKEEPING, "LOSE YOUR BELLY FLAB—FAST!"

By Jim Karas

*Devote 20 minutes a day to these exercises, and you'll be ab-fab in no time. It's an unfortunate female fact of life: As women age, they get thicker in the middle. That's partly because weight distribution changes, but it's also due to a certain kind of fat (called visceral fat) that collects around your organs. This fat predisposes you to heart disease, high . . .*

*MEN'S HEALTH,* "UNLEASH YOUR ABS:
7 STEPS TO A 6-PACK THAT WILL GET
YOU NOTICED"

*By Scott Quill*

*Forget for a moment that the shape of your midsection largely determines how good you'll look on the beach this summer—and how well you'll play volleyball. We'll get back to that in a minute.*

*The pursuit of abs goes deeper. You strive for a six-pack as if your life . . .*

As you can see, each publication has a distinctly different approach to crafting the same type of story.

## Tailor Your Query

Knowing the magazine inside and out means nothing if you can't show off your knowledge in your query letter. For instance, you should not send the same query to three magazines and just change the addressee. You need to show extreme precision in terms of who your query is targeting. Every query letter should be different—even if it's for essentially the same article. You're going to want to make sure that your query letter matches the voice and tone of the magazine. This illustrates to the editor who receives the pitch that you "get" the magazine. Read at least three issues of the publication before you start writing the pitch. Then you'll have "the mood" of the pub in your head.

Having a great idea is wonderful, but if the editor gets the sense from your letter that you wouldn't be able to pull off writing in their style—or that you're using a generic template letter and haven't taken the time to tailor your query—chances are you're not going to get the assignment.

### HOW SHOULD A FREELANCER TAILOR THE QUERY TO A PARTICULAR PUBLICATION?

"Read it. I tell students that I meet (like the interns at my magazine, for example) to read at least three months worth of any magazine they hope to freelance for. Cover to cover. It sounds so obvious, but I swear half the freelancers who pitch me have no idea what kinds of stories we do."

—*Jennifer Tanaka, a senior editor at* Chicago *magazine and former technology writer for* Newsweek

"READ THE PUBLICATION! Know what it wants and doesn't want. If it's a regional publication, make sure you're pitching regional stories. Use an example in the pitch, comparing your story to an earlier one that appeared in the magazine. It shows you read the magazine, and saw a story that worked."

—*Doug Most, editor,* Boston Globe Sunday Magazine

## Address Your Query

The salutation of a query letter may not *make* the pitch letter, but it can certainly *break* it. Some writers send their query letters right to the top. That's a big mistake. Unless it's a magazine with a staff of only one or two, chances are zilch that the editor-in-chief reads unsolicited query letters. Find out which editor works on the section or column of the magazine you think your piece is right for, and pitch directly to that person. Not only does this help keep your pitch from being lost forever and never responded to, but it also allows you to follow up with one person, rather than being bounced around from editor to editor, each of whom says he passed your query along to someone else when you call to check in.

While some mastheads may indicate who edits what—and in fact some sections say "edited by so and so" right on them—remember that magazines are often sent off to be printed as much as a few months before you as a reader ever lay eyes on them. So even the issue that just yesterday arrived in your mailbox can be somewhat outdated in terms of staff. You can check out mediabistro.com's Revolving Door Newsletter (available to AvantGuild members) to find out which editor has gone where each week.

Don't be afraid to call the magazine's general number and ask for the editorial department. Hopefully you'll get an assistant on the line.

> Be kind and courteous and introduce yourself by saying, "Hello, it's Fredrick Jones," rather than, "Hi, my name is . . ." You'll sound more authoritative—and the person on the other end of the line might even think you are someone he should know.

Ask specifically who edits the part of the magazine you want to write for, and you can ask if that editor prefers submissions by e-mail or snail mail. If the assistant doesn't know, you might ask who that editor's specific assistant is and be put through to him.

Your diligence gives you a much better chance of getting to the right person. If all else fails, send health ideas, for example, to any editor with the word *health* in her title, send feature ideas to any editor with the word *feature* in her title, and if you have no idea, send it off to an associate or senior editor on the masthead, and hopefully it will be passed to the correct person. Never simply send a letter to "editor/name of publication." This is basically just asking for your letter to be thrown into a pile of mail that may sit unread for months.

Don't ever forget, before sending out any letter, to make sure you check and double-check the spelling of the editor's name, either with

## SUBMISSION GUIDELINES

Many magazines have submission guidelines that can be found on their Web sites or can be acquired by calling and asking further "submission" or "writer's" or "editorial" guidelines.

Here is a sample set of guidelines from *Sierra* magazine.

EDITORIAL GUIDELINES

*Sierra* is a bimonthly national magazine publishing writing, photography, and art about the natural world. Our readers are environmentally concerned and politically diverse; most are active in the outdoors. We are looking for fine writing that will provoke, entertain, and enlighten this readership.

Though open to new writers, we find ourselves most often working with authors we have sought out or who have worked with us for some time. We ask writers who would like to publish in *Sierra* to submit written queries; no e-mail queries please. Phone calls are strongly discouraged. If you would like a reply to your query or need your manuscript returned to you, please include a self-addressed stamped envelope. Prospective *Sierra* writers should familiarize themselves with recent issues of the magazine; for a sample copy, send a self-addressed envelope and a check for $3 payable to *Sierra; back issues* are included on the Sierra Club's Web site, www.sierraclub.org/sierra/.

Please be patient: Though the editors meet weekly to discuss recently received queries, a response time of from six to eight weeks is usual.

Please do not send slides, prints, or other artwork. If photos or illustrations are required for your submission, we will request them when your work is accepted for publication.

FEATURES

*Sierra* is looking for strong, well-researched, literate writing on significant environmental and conservation issues. Features often focus on aspects of the Sierra Club's work. For more information about issues the Club is currently working on, visit our Web site at www.sierraclub.org. Writers should look for ways to cast new light on well-established issues. We look for stories of national or international significance; local issues, while sometimes useful as examples of broader trends, are seldom of interest in themselves. We are always looking for adventure travel pieces

(continued)

that weave events, discoveries, and environmental insights into the narrative. We are more interested in showcasing environmental solutions than adding to the list of environmental problems. We publish dramatic investigative stories that have the potential to reach a broad audience. Nonfiction essays on the natural world are welcome, too.

We do not want descriptive wildlife articles, unless larger conservation issues figure strongly in the story. We are not interested in editorials, general essays about environmentalism, or in highly technical writing. We do not publish unsolicited cartoons, poetry, or fiction; please do not submit works in these genres.

Recent feature articles that display the special qualities we look for are "Beneath Wyoming Stars" by Geoffrey O'Gara (March/April 2004), "Lessons in Granite" by Daniel Duane (March/April 2005), "Dangerous Liaisons" by Marilyn Berlin Snell (May/June 2005), "Earth's Innovators" by Dashka Slater (July/August 2005).

Feature length ranges from 1,000 to 3,000 words; payment is from $800 to $3,000, plus negotiated reimbursement for expenses.


DEPARTMENTS
Much of the material in Sierra's departments is written by staff editors and contributing writers. The following sections of the magazine, however, are open to freelancers. Articles are 100-1500 words in length; payment is $100 to $1500 unless otherwise noted. Expenses up to $50 may be paid in some cases.

**"Lifestyle"** is a new section, debuting in our November/December 2005 issue, that provides a colorful, upbeat take on green living. At turns practical and whimsical, this lavishly illustrated section informs readers about the latest (and best) trends, products, and tips in food, fashion, housing, transportation, and other areas of their everyday lives. The section also includes brief Q&As with green innovators in the lifestyle field, and short takes about the books, music, movies, art, and other media that should be on any well-rounded environmentalist's radar. Writers are encouraged to submit queries on light, positive, inspiring topics that will help readers add more value to their lives, not more work—or more guilt. We especially welcome ideas that incorporate lists, factoids, photos, how-tos, recipes, quotes, statistics, tips, and other quick-hit presentations. Items should generally be 50 to 200 words in length; payment will vary depending on length and complexity.

**"Good Going"** succinctly describes a superlative place, including fascinating natural and cultural facts, in about 300 words.

**"Lay of the Land"** focuses on environmental issues of national or international concern. Regional issues are considered when they have national implications. At 500 to 700 words, "Lay of the Land" articles are not sweeping surveys, but tightly focused, provocative, well-researched investigations of environmental issues. Payment varies according to length.

**"Profile"** is a 3,000-word biographical sketch of a person doing important work to protect the environment. We try to broaden our readers' understanding of the environmental movement with subjects they haven't read about elsewhere: for instance, a pig farmer in Mississippi or an outfitter in Wyoming.

**"One Small Step"** features the first-person accounts of ordinary folks doing extraordinary things. We publish a 100-150 word quotation from an interview that explains the person's actions, motivations, and impact. Payment for all articles is on acceptance, which is contingent on a favorable review of the manuscript by our editorial staff, and by knowledgeable outside reviewers, where appropriate. Kill fees are negotiated when a story is assigned.

Address all queries to:
Managing Editor, *Sierra* magazine
85 Second St., 2nd Floor
San Francisco, CA 94105

*Reprinted with permission of* Sierra *magazine.*

the assistant or against the masthead. Misspelling an editor's name on a query letter is among the worst things you can do—not only does it offend the editor, but, on practical terms, he has to wonder, if you're that careless when pitching, what kind of mistakes will you let slip by when you're reporting and writing?

## Who's Who

Some publications seem to get by on shoestring staffs while others have numerous editors, including those with the most bizarre and random titles. Here's a rundown of some typical job titles and responsibilities of folks you may encounter when deciding who to pitch.

### Editorial assistant

Freelancers should befriend every editorial assistant they possibly can. As assistants to senior-level editors, EAs open the mail (your queries!), answer the phones (your calls!), get writers paid (your rent and food money!), and more. They may do some writing and editing of front-of-book and back-of-book short items.

### Assistant editor

Usually a step or two above an entry-level position, assistant editors may do some paperwork, such as reading queries and processing payments. Most write and edit (and may assign) some of the short front- or back-of-book items or departments. May write or edit some larger features.

### Associate editor

A step above assistant editors, associate editors often write, assign, and edit front- and back-of-book items and departments. More likely than assistant editors to write and edit columns and features, associate editors are often good folks to query, as they probably have some say in getting pitches moved along to more senior editors. In addition, editors at this level are often expected to come up with a certain number of ideas for the magazine. They are typically eager to present great ideas (and great new writers) to the higher-ups because, as young editors, they have something to prove. They want to illustrate that they are able to bring in good freelancers and fresh new ideas. Doing so helps their careers—so hook up with a good associate editor, and it's a win-win for both of you!

### Assigning editor

You seldom see this title on a masthead; it's really just a term applied to any editor who assigns stories to freelance writers. In most cases you can assume that senior-level editors are assigning editors; it is more often a question to ask of those lower down on the masthead— "Do you assign out stories to freelancers?"

### Senior editor

Senior editors spend much of their time assigning and editing stories for one particular area of the publication, and often work directly with freelance writers. Senior editors may report to the executive editor or the editor-in-chief, and probably have an editorial assistant, assistant editor, or associate editor working below them. Senior editors usually work on the feature well of the publication, but may also assign and edit front-of-book and back-of-book columns and departments.

### Features editor/Articles editor

If you have a terrific idea for a feature story, pitch the features editor, right? Well, maybe, although many publications now get even more specific with health editors, nutrition editors, sports editors, travel editors, news editors, entertainment editors, fashion editors, beauty editors, business editors, home editors, and so on, who work on the features for their particular area of expertise.

## AIM LOWER (ON THE MASTHEAD)

One mistake many freelancers make is ignoring the little guy. A writer might send an expertly crafted article idea to the editor-in-chief or another top editor. Then when that writer receives a rejection form letter or e-mail from an editorial assistant or assistant editor, he'll feel totally dejected and assume that the editor never even looked at the pitch—which may very well be true. Assistants, often assumed to be (and all too often treated as) simply secretaries, have more power than you think. Chances are, any query letter you send to a magazine will cross the desk of an editorial assistant first. If she dislikes your idea, that may be the end of the line.

On the other hand, if you receive a rejection letter from an assistant and decide to follow up, sending a kind response and further article ideas, chances are a lot better that she'll take time to consider your next idea. The assistant might even send you an e-mail telling you why you are not on the right track in how you're pitching that magazine. Remember, editors are always looking to find stellar freelancers to add to their Rolodexes. It makes them look good (and helps their career) if they can present their top editors with ideas from new promising writers. So if you get an assistant on your side, she might write a little note on the top of your pitch letter saying what a great idea it is, and pass it along to the editor above her with assigning power. Or—even better—the assistant might have some assigning power of her own, and be just waiting to find a great new writer to help her move out of the assistant ranks.

## Essential Query Elements

In most cases, a query should not run longer than a page. But you have to pack in quite a bit. Here's what.

### The grab

You need to get the attention of the editor reading your query right away. You cannot give her any opportunity to think, "This is just another ho-hum pitch," which would destine it for the recycling bin.

Many writers open with an anecdote or an intriguing quote. You

---

### ANATOMY OF A QUERY

"A great *How* query establishes a connection and a familiarity with the design field and includes a possible lede, a well-researched outline, clips, and, preferably, a list of design sources with whom you plan to speak."

—How *editor Bryn Mooth*

---

may want to write what you think will be the first few paragraphs of the actual article and use that to launch your query letter. If the editor reads that first paragraph and is left wanting to know more, then you very well may get the assignment.

Throughout your entire letter be sure you are *showing* the reader what a grabbing article this will be, and not just *telling* them. For instance, you should not have to say, "This is going to be a fabulous, well-thought-out, and well-written piece." Your query letter should make that perfectly clear on its own, by illustrating a fab idea, by being well thought out, and most important, by being well written.

For example, in a query letter sent to a Canadian newspaper, one freelancer was pitching a story about crazy new ideas for thirtieth birthday parties. Rather than saying something straightforward and dull, such as "I'd like to write a story about 30th birthdays," she grabbed the potential editor with "On Saturday, August 27th, my law school chum kicks off his thirtieth birthday with a Track and Field Party. In the tradition of grade school competition there will be competitions in the long jump, triple jump, shot put, 100 metre dash, 4 x 100 m relay, high jump and hurdles."

### The what

So you've gotten the editor's attention. Now you need to give him more detail. What is this article going to be about? Describe, in beautiful prose, your idea. Lure in the editor by including the most in-teresting details, the most telling quotes, the vital stats, and the valu-able tips on your topic. Don't leave out anything juicy, thinking you'll surprise the editor when you hand in the article. If you've got some-thing good, reveal it in the query letter. You can't worry about your great idea getting swiped. Despite popular belief, that seldom happens.

For instance, in the thirtieth-birthday pitch, the writer said, "If you'd like to pursue the idea of 'Youth-Affirming 30th Birthday Parties' in general, I also know of a roller-skating party that took place recently, as well as a Vegas trip for a group of girlfriends and an upcoming South Beach trip for another group of girls (the 30th birthday girl-bonding trip: another new trend). I'm sure further research would turn up other novel party ideas for grown-ups who still play like kids."

### PUT IT ALL OUT THERE

"I want to see an idea that makes sense for this magazine, one that has not appeared in this magazine. I'd like to see a certain amount—not too much, not too little—of reporting so that any questions I might have in the course of reading the query are either answered or it's clear that the answer is gettable."

—Texas Monthly *editor Evan Smith*

Be aware that most writers prereport their pitches—so you should, too. You need to do some digging to be sure the article will pan out, to find some possible experts to interview, and to get a few attention-grabbing details to plug into the query letter. (See Chapter 11 for some reporting tips.) You don't need to call and interview experts before you pitch a story, but it's good to have some compelling information to pre-sent. For instance, if you want to write a piece about the dangers of rock climbing, you better find out some stats on how many people

## STOLEN STORIES

"Here's the scenario: Multiple freelancers and maybe a staff writer or two pitch the same story. The story gets assigned to one of them or was assigned separately by another editor or perhaps was already assigned but hasn't run. The story appears and the pitcher's immediate reaction is to call the editor and complain that the story has been stolen from him. Editors have almost no incentive to steal a story under the worst of conditions and no incentive whatsoever under the best. I think editors stealing stories happens at about the same rate that people get struck by lightning. It's risky and unnecessary. As a result, nothing is more infuriating than to be wrongly accused of stealing a story and having to defend yourself as an editor—especially if the story in question is completely unoriginal and has been pitched multiple times.

"The freelancer, of course, has no way of knowing what has been pitched, what hasn't, or when and how stories are being assigned internally. And the natural corollary is that the freelancer has no actual evidence that supposedly stolen stories are, in fact, stolen. Accusations are backed only by the freelancer's suspicions and resulting similarities between the published story and whatever the freelancer had in mind, which is never self-evident proof of plagiarism. In the rare instances where stories are stolen and hard evidence is available, it's worth prosecuting, but if all you have is a suspicion and two topically similar stories, keep in mind that any spurious accusations will permanently destroy your relationship with that editor and, likely, that publication (and if the editor feels particularly insulted at having his or her professional integrity questioned, all of the editor's editor friends and their respective publications as well). Make the claim when necessary, but don't do it lightly."

—*Elizabeth Spiers, former editor-in-chief of mediabistro.com*

have been injured or killed doing so in the last year, five years, and so on. An editor reading a query letter about the dangers is going to want to know how dangerous it is. The thirtieth-birthday-party pitcher would be wise to include numbers on what percentage of thirty-year-olds have birthday parties (if that stat exists), or a fact such as "From ages 21 to 29, only 2 percent of the population holds birthday parties, but when it comes to hitting the big 3-0, 70 percent of people go all out, in some way." Or maybe a stat about a change in the times: "In 1972 only 8 percent of 30-year-olds had birthday parties. Today 76 percent of 30-years-olds have some sort of celebration."

> Sell an idea, not just yourself. You might have a slight ad-
> vantage if you've got great credentials, but every editor is
> looking for a brilliant, new, fresh idea.

### The how and where

If you have an idea that you think is absolutely perfect for a certain section of a publication, say so. Just not in so many words. (And, of course, you're already announcing your thoughts for the article by the very person you decided to send it to.) Basically, where an article fits into a magazine or newspaper is the editor's call. And chances are they probably won't appreciate your "telling them" that your idea should appear in a particular spot. Your thoughts should be more of a sugges-tion: "This piece may work in your front-of-book short items." Or "I can see this article running in your Q&A column, along with a short intro." It's okay to mention the structure you think the piece might take, be it that Q&A, a piece with twenty to thirty tips following a short intro, or a feature story of running text. In the thirtieth-birthday pitch, the author said, "I think this would be a really fun feature for the Arts & Life Section or the *Saturday Post*."

And of course, if you have any ideas for sidebars, include those, too. It can only help your case. (And you never know, they might like one of your sidebar ideas better than what you're pitching as the main text.)

If relevant, you should also consider mentioning in the query let-ter who your experts will be. Certainly you should do so if your idea is very controversial or involves some very surprising new information.

---

### ON TARGET

"I think the most frustrating thing for editors anywhere is getting letters from people who obviously aren't reading the magazine. Not only is the pitch way off target, but they belie a misunderstanding of the magazine they're trying to write for."

—Smithsonian Magazine *editor Carey Winfrey*

---

For example, if you state that diet sodas make people fat, you better mention the researcher or study that revealed this fact. And if you are promising an interview with someone famous and not easily accessible, you should make it clear in the letter how and, if applicable, when you'll get access to this person. If a friend of a friend got the author of the thirtieth-birthday piece invited to Britney Spears's thirtieth-birthday party, she would be a fool not to mention that in her pitch letter.

### The audience

Include in your pitch at least a sentence or two about why your story idea will appeal to that magazine's reader. This is another place where you need to show, not tell. Don't say, "Your readers will just eat up this story. It is perfect for the demographic." Instead, if you are pitching a piece on a strange new food allergy to *More* magazine, which targets women over forty, tie your pitch to their reader by saying something like "This unidentifiable allergen seems to cause extremely large hives in two out of every three women over forty." In that one sentence you have made it clear that you know their audience—and that this topic is of utmost importance to that audience. In the case of the thirtieth-birthday-party pitch, you better hope that the writer is pitching a publication that has twenty-seven, twenty-eight, and twenty-nine-year-old readers, or else the writer is off the mark.

### The timing

Whenever you can, make it clear that your article is timely. Editors—and their readers—are not interested in old news. So hook your idea to a new study, new findings, current events, recently released movies or books, an upcoming holiday, or the season of the year. Read newspapers, and get on the mailing lists of PR agencies and the press offices of universities, corporations, government agencies, nonprofits, and more. And don't forget that print publications work far in advance. Unless you are pitching to a daily newspaper or a Web site, you have to get your time-specific ideas out to editors months ahead. If your article idea is pegged to a particular event or date, make that very clear. For instance, if you are pitching an idea to *Martha Stewart Living* about the Christmas Stroll on Nantucket, make it clear early on in your pitch (which should be sent by June, at the latest) that the event you want to write about happens in December. No magazine is going to run that holiday story in any other month.

Go to the library and look at what the publications you want to target wrote about six to eight months ago. Those are the kinds of stories they want to hear about now, and this will give you some ideas of what kinds of things you can peg your article to.

### Plug yourself

Why are you the person to write this story for that publication? You need to show the editor that you are talented enough to write this piece—and that should be evident from how you expertly crafted your entire letter. Don't be shy, but be creative. Brainstorm your five biggest strengths, and make these evident in a clear and concise manner in your query letters. Again, be sure that you show editors why they should hire you, rather than just *telling* them how great you are. Apart from that, let the editor know, without being pushy or too self-promoting, if you have background knowledge on that particular topic, or if you have some type of special expertise in the area, or if

## CLIPS: A ROUNDTABLE

"If you don't have something [a clip] that's similar [to what you're pitching], I'm going to respect you for breaking out of what your supposed genre is. If you've never written about film before and you only have eats and drinks clips, send them to me. But the first couple lines [of the pitch] should tell me that you have an interesting idea. It's more about the ideas; we can save any writing."

—New York Press *former editor-in-chief Jeff Koyen*

"If I can't see what you're capable of from your clips, you really need to put on a show in your pitch."

—Good Housekeeping *senior deputy editor Evelyn Renold*

"I would like to see some clips beyond 'mywebsite.com,' but the pitch speaks volumes. If someone can't put together a succinct pitch that really gets the point and format of the story across, that's a red flag. Good clips could mean good editors anyway."

—Health Magazine *former senior editor Abigail Walch*

"Potential writers should pitch areas in which they already have a good deal of expertise and should be able to prove those smarts through relevant clips. If you want to write about music or film, the clips you send should not be from a city council meeting."

—Time Out Chicago *managing editor Amy Carr*

you somehow have access to pertinent information or to an important person. This section should also be short, only a few sentences, and can be a combination of personal and professional details. Be sure to include only information that is relevant to writing about this particular topic. For instance, the thirtieth-birthday-party pitcher mentioned, "As I rapidly approach my 30th birthday (it's just under four months away) I have become accustomed to receiving birthday party

invitations from friends who have reached that particular milestone."
For any other story, the fact that she is about to turn thirty would
most likely be irrelevant.

   Of course, if you have written for, and have clips from, other publications, go ahead and mention that here. If you are sending your
pitch via e-mail, you probably want to avoid sending clips as attachments; even pasting them in the text might not be such a good idea.
They can make the file too large or the formatting may make them

---

### PITCH PERFECT

"If pitching by e-mail, the best way to include clips is with links; it's
easy for editors to get overwhelmed by attachments, particularly if
they're graphics heavy and weigh in at more than one megabyte
each. But including a link in your proposal doesn't mean that anyone's
ever going to click on it. To that end, I think nothing's so impressive
as 8.5×11-inch photocopied sheets of paper. And if your article has
been teased on the magazine's cover or you've been written up on
the contributor's page, include that as part of your clips, too. For sending that many pages, nothing beats the U.S. mail—and on the pitch
level, the truth is the difference between e-mail and domestic snail
mail is only about two days. As for selecting clips, more recent ones
are generally better than old ones, provided they're as good. But
clips aren't dairy products, so they don't spoil. When I send clips, I try
to make a selection that will match my target publication, prospective editor, and proposed article best. I rarely use my fax machine for
pitching or sending clips anymore, but I still use it enough to keep it
plugged in."

   —*James Sturz is the author of the novel* Sasso *and more than sixty articles in
   newspapers and magazines.*

## THE FIVE WORST MISTAKES A FREELANCER CAN MAKE IN A QUERY LETTER

When pitching any editor, if you spell his name wrong, forget about it. That doesn't even count as a mistake. Aside from that, Kendall Hamilton, editor-in-chief at *Ski* magazine, fills you in on other faux paus to avoid if you ever want to see your name in print:

1. Don't send something totally blind. In other words: I've never heard of you and you've never heard of me, other than by looking at the masthead. Do some research. Information is gatherable. Failure to research your target results in pitches that are sent to people who've long since moved on or no longer handle the sort of thing you're pitching, junior editors with no pull, senior editors with too much pull to worry about your pitch, receptionists with fancy titles, the editor's family pet, etc. And don't—under any circumstances—send the same pitch letter to everyone on the masthead. Spam doesn't sell.

2. Don't send one of these I-got-it-out-of-a-book [formlike] pitch letters. It's cheesy and amateurish beyond repair. The tricky part here is that when you do meet an editor and he or she gives you his or her e-mail address and says go ahead, pitch me, you will need to write something convincing. Something grabby, something that explains who you are, what you've got, and why you think it's a good idea—something, in short, that actually functions in the way that the clichéd template attempts to, yet somehow doesn't register as a clichéd template. If you're a good writer, you'll figure it out.

3. Don't be presumptuous. Reeling off word counts, angles of interest to readers, advertisers, etc. can annoy an editor. You probably don't know the magazine or its readers as well as he or she does (or imagines he or she does). And even if you do, an editor will never believe it. So don't waste the energy trying to impress an editor with your deep understanding of the magazine and its universe.

4. Don't include typos, the passive voice, mixed metaphors, brutal clichés, any sentence longer than your arm, or other blaring Klaxons of bad writing. If you can't write a pitch, you can't write a story. It's that simple.

(continued)

5. Don't pitch something inappropriate. Often the line between what's right for a magazine and what's "not for our readers" is an invisible, shifting, and forever inscrutable boundary—even to an editor. So you're going to strike out a lot, whatever you do. But, really, don't pitch a fashion piece to a nudist magazine. Unless it's about hats, I guess.

—*Kendall Hamilton spent eleven years at* Newsweek, *going from researcher to writer, and to editor. He moved on to* Details *and* MBA Jungle. *He is now editor-in-chief of* Ski.

difficult to read. The best idea is to include clips as links, so the editor can just click and see your samples on your Web site or wherever you have them posted.

If you've got a great idea but little background writing in that arena, make extra sure that your pitch letter is clear, concise, and fascinating to read, and that it shows that you will be able to pull off the assignment brilliantly if the editor takes a chance on you. Never draw to the editor's attention that you've never been published before. Instead, just try and stand on the strength of your incredible idea.

### The payoff

If this article provides the reader with a real service, make sure that is evident in the query letter. Editors will want pieces that will let their readers take away some new knowledge or insight, or even let them just be entertained.

### And don't forget

Keep your letter conversational but not too informal. Be careful about grammar and punctuation. And we can't say this enough: Spell the editor's name correctly!

## Your Pitch Package

When it comes time to actually send out your pitch, provide the editor with everything he might need. If sending it by U.S. mail, lead with the actual pitch letter. Behind the letter, attach your best clips—probably three, four at the most. If you have clips related to the topic you are pitching, lead with those. If not, lead with the clips you are most proud of and, if possible, show the diversity of your writing. You can follow that with your résumé if you think it will help. But if you have a superstrong query letter and idea, and little experience to help your case, go ahead and simply send the letter.

If sending your pitch via e-mail, end your letter by either offering to send clips and your résumé if they are interested or by providing links to your clips posted somewhere on the Web. Do not send attachments or paste your clips after your letter.

---

### WHAT THE EDITORS HAVE TO SAY

Here's what editors of national magazines and newspapers say about the pitching process.

- Make it apparent that you have read and really know the publication you are pitching to.
- Make it very clear that this is not a general letter that you could send to just any publication, by clearly targeting it to the specific publication that you are pitching.
- If you are pitching a typical, evergreen topic, always give it a spin.
- More than one idea in a letter is fine, but more than three is too many.
- Include your résumé and three or four of your best clips.
- Keep the letter concise.
- If your idea is well thought out and appropriate for the publication, but just not quite right, you very well might get a call to work on another assignment.
- Try to make your pitch match the magazine's tone as closely as you can.

(continued)

- Give your idea a headline and summary, called a hed and dek. The whole purpose of a hed and dek in a magazine article is to draw the reader in. So draw the editor into your pitch with a clever hed-and-dek combo.
- Give the editor a sense of your writing style. Give your pitch the same kind of attention you would give to an article you are writing.
- Watch for typos, of course.
- Keep your writing lively; the sentences should not all have the same rhythm.
- Your idea should be clear.
- Even if your idea is rejected, take heart if you hear from the editor directly. It probably means that there is something about you that felt right.
- The more you conceptualize and package your story, the easier it will be for the editor to get your story approved. If you haven't thought out your piece and you expect the editor to do it for you, chances are he is just going to get annoyed.
- Never pitch the same idea to two editors at the same publication.
- Don't hassle editors about your idea. One follow-up, one to two weeks after submission, is enough.
- Do research ahead of time. Nothing is worse—or more damaging to a writer's reputation—than having your editor assign you a story, only to find out that your pitch was based on a hunch that turned out to be false.
- Tell the editor what, if any, press coverage this topic has gotten. This is very effective if one of the magazine's competitors covered the topic two years ago. You might find that a major change in the topic occurred, and that no national publication has covered this stunning reversal, of course.
- When possible, send clips similar to the type of story you're pitching.
- When sending clips, try to send a range of pieces, so the editor can see that you are versatile.
- If targeting a national publication, do not send an idea about something strictly regional.

8

# What Worked

Successful Pitch Letters

What makes a successful pitch letter? Check out these samples. Each one is a real pitch letter that led to a real assignment— and in many cases numerous follow-up assignments from the same publication.

## Getting a Foot in the Door

*This pitch resulted in the author's very first-ever assignment, published in* Time Out New York. *The piece the editor assigned was 700 words for $150. The writer was so thrilled to be published that she didn't care about what she describes as "the small payment."*

Dear [First name of the television editor],

Now we've done it. Broadcast networks are fed up with our reckless television viewing antics and they've decided to put a stop to the madness. What did we do? Let's not play innocent— we've been brazenly using personal recording devices to skip right over the commercials airing during our favorite shows. And to the growing anxiety of media executives, we are not isolated offenders.

One network is taking action. Responding swiftly to the escalating TiVo epidemic, Warner Brothers is cracking down on "ad-abusers" with the launch of a new television series so hardy, so slippery, even die-hard electronic gadget fans won't be able to find a way around the commercials. That's because the marketing messages will be cleverly embedded within every facet of the broadcast.

Promoted as a hip Ed Sullivan–type variety show, the WB's yet untitled hour-long program may be devoid of advertisements but will deliberately showcase a full roster of sponsors by designing sets around their logos and building comedy routines around their products. Pepsi and Nokia have already signed on for six hours of airtime each to support the show, which is scheduled to air this summer.

The move reflects industry-wide tension over the rapidly decreasing effectiveness of the traditional 30-second commercial spot. Since most networks rely primarily on advertising sales for revenue, there has been great pressure to create alternative ways to broadcast marketing messages.

I would like to submit an article of 1,000 words (or the length of your choosing) on the recent moves taken by the television industry to regain viewing power from audiences with too much remote control. This humorous and informative article will explore the effectiveness of network defensive tactics and the possible future of broadcast television programming.

Thank you taking the time to look this over. You can reach me by e-mail (xxxxx@hotmail.com) or at (xxx) xxx-xxxx.

Amanda Pressner

## How-to

*This query—specifically for a how-to piece—resulted in an assignment for exactly what was pitched. After this story, the magazine bought several more of this writer's pitches and started assigning her stories that were developed in-house. Two years later, she was asked to become a contributing editor. This was sent by regular mail to* Complete Woman *magazine.*

Dear Ms. [Last name of the executive editor]:

Dating, especially for high-powered career women, often takes a backseat to workplace demands. For this reason, would you be interested in a story, "The Busy Woman's Guide to Dating," which would focus on how women can approach dating in much the same way they would a job hunt?

For this story, I would interview top relationship experts to come up with 25 tips the busy woman can follow in order to find time to enjoy dating. Each tip would have a job-hunting theme, such as:

A. **Write Your Relationship Résumé:** While this is purely for your eyes only, it will serve as your starting point. List your strong points and be aggressive in putting your best foot forward.

B. **Get Referrals:** Networking can really pay off in the dating world. Being set up with a friend of a friend can often allow you to enjoy a great night out with minimal planning work involved.

C. **Screen Potential Candidates:** Whether it's through an online dating service or a chance meeting in a bar, learn to be a good judge of character by asking a few key questions—without prying—to simply learn if this is a person with whom you'd like to spend some time.

A former newspaper columnist, I'm a contributing editor for *Bridal Guide Magazine,* former features editor for *Contemporary Bride Magazine,* and feature writer for the *Star-Ledger* newspaper. I've also written for various women's publications, including *All Woman, Ladies' Home Journal Online,* and *MAMM* magazines. Please let me know if you are interested in this story idea. Enclosed are my résumé and some clips. Thank you for your time and consideration.

Sincerely,<br>
Tracy Propora

## Service

*This writer first pitched a profile to NYCPlus (a lifestyle magazine for the fifty-something New Yorker), but was told that the magazine had a staff profile writer. The editor encouraged her to send another idea in a few weeks. Her second pitch, for a service piece, was based on a personal experience, and the editor bought it.*

### A REAL PAIN IN THE BACK

#### By Nell Stundell

Who wants to undergo back surgery? Obviously, no one.

For those who suffer from chronic back pain and have tried the many prescribed remedies, there is a noninvasive medical technology to significantly reduce or eliminate the pain of degenerative disc disease.

As an athlete and a woman with degenerative disc problems, I sought a noninvasive treatment to complement exercise and swimming to reduce the pain. I researched alternatives and found a breakthrough in technology—at the office of one of the few medical professionals in the country using this state-of-the-art system. The end result of the treatment—relief from the neurocompression of discs associated with lower back pain—has shown to enlarge disc space, strengthen outer ligaments, and move discs back into place.

The subject matter would be ideal for NYCPlus. I have testaments from patients who have undergone this 3-week treatment—how it changed their lives. What better way to make a difference than to hark this remarkable technology?

Let me know if you're interested.

Thanks,
Nell

## Essay/Rant

*This writer writes personal essays and narrative journalism, and she chose in this case to send a completed piece along with a contextualizing note. This e-mail pitch got an enthusiastic offer of publication from* Nerve, *the online magazine of highbrow erotica, almost immediately upon submission. When submitting a complete piece, the pitch letter matters much less, because the editor can already see what work you'll produce. But, even so, the straightforwardness of the letter increased the possibility of its being taken seriously. The writer gave her credentials, introduced the wry, self-deprecating tone that the editor would then find in the piece, and didn't oversell or synopsize.*

*Interesting to note: the writer sent the pitch from a unique e-mail address she had set up in order to use a pseudonym. That way, only a response from* Nerve *would show up as new mail, and, if they didn't like it, there was no way for anyone there to discover her real name. After it was accepted, she switched to her real name for contract correspondence. She also negotiated to retain some rights the publication normally takes, since she planned to perform the piece and wanted rights to the audio and video.*

Dear [First and last name of *Nerve* editor-in-chief],

Here is "Urban Legend," a 1,800-word essay about my ersatz sex toy accident.

I'm a solo performer and writer and have had a couple of pieces on Mr. Beller's Neighborhood, did an NPR commentary, and published two pieces of personal journalism about Sept. 11 in *The Villager.* I attended the Wesleyan Writers Conference two weeks ago and both readers recommended submitting this to *Nerve.*

I'd like to use a pseudonym for this. I'm comfortable performing extremely personal material, but this one could seriously haunt me in some mythic future where I run for public office.

The essay follows both in the body of this e-mail and as a word.doc attachment.

Thanks,
"L. Divona"

## Travel

*This e-mailed query led to a 1,200-word article in the* New York Sun's *Travel section, complete with two color photos taken by the writer's now-husband. She thought she was ahead of the game by querying before the trip, but she didn't get the assignment until nearly two weeks after she'd gotten back. Luckily, she took notes while she was there anyway.*

*The writer was asked to (and did) provide some clips before she was given the go-ahead to write the piece.*

Subject: Travel proposal: Puerto Rico, from Laura Siciliano

Dear Ms. [Last name of features editor]:

My name is Laura Siciliano, and I am a freelance travel writer based out of Brooklyn. [A reporter at same newspaper], a friend of mine, might have mentioned that I'd be contacting you with a proposal for the *New York Sun*'s Travel section.

In a nutshell, my story idea is what to do in Puerto Rico for a long weekend away. I'll be doing this myself in two weeks, over the 3-day Martin Luther King Jr. weekend, when I travel to Puerto Rico with some friends. Not everyone realizes that Puerto Rico is perfect for its proximity, wealth of beautiful natural resources, rich history and small size—it is very possible to see a good bit of the island over three or four days. Moreover, it offers perfect "escape weather" for this cold and wet time of year.

The completed article, written in first-person, will use my own itinerary as a sample for readers who, when presented with a few days off of work, want to get away to someplace exotic, yet not too far off. I have visited Puerto Rico before, but plan on exploring more this time around: On the advice of some native Puerto Rican friends, I'll be renting a car and hitting at least 3 or 4 locales, maximizing our 3-night stay to really get a taste of the island. Our planned itinerary is as follows:

1. One day/night in historic Old San Juan
2. The beautiful drive west to Arecibo and south on Route 10 through the central mountains (stopping for lunch along the way) to reach the charming Mary Lee's By The Sea guesthouse in Guanica, home to the biologically diverse Guanica Dry Forest Reserve
3. Morning on the Caribbean Sea in Guanica, where

we'll rent kayaks to visit nearby islands (one of them is called Guilligan's Island!)

4. Drive to the colonial city of Ponce for a quick exploration, possibly dinner
5. Camp the night on a beach near Arroyo
6. Continue driving along the south and east coasts, stopping for a swim or two, en route to airport

Naturally, this plan may alter a bit, but not too drastically.

As I'm not leaving for this trip until Fri., Jan. 14, I can easily focus this piece further according to your specifications if we speak beforehand. Regardless of the angle, all hotel, car rental, and restaurant information will definitely be included with the completed article.

Photography is covered: My boyfriend is a professional photographer and will be shooting high-quality digital images; I will be shooting as well on both 35mm and slide film. My recent writing credits include *Time Out NY, International Living,* and *Travel Savvy;* please let me know if you would prefer I e-mail clips.

Please let me know if you are interested, or have any questions. I look forward to your response. Thank you.

Best regards,
Laura Siciliano

## Review

*The music editor at* Soma *magazine did not bite at this pitch for a music review, but she did ask the writer to send along some other writing samples. The editor also asked for some ideas for reviews of albums with later release dates. The writer sent along a list of possible albums, the magazine picked one, he wrote it, and now he continues to write for the magazine.*

Hey there,

Just wanted to check in and see if you were planning to run a review of the new Peppermints' record, which is out June 28 on the Animal Collective's label, Paw Tracks. In case you haven't heard the record yet it's really rough, dark, garage rock that sounds like Nico fighting in the studio with Lou Reed. It's dirty, stormy, and really creative—though nothing like the BBC-coined "new weird American folk" that the Animal Collective plays. I've attached writing samples (from "Hit It Or Quit It," "The Stranger" and "The Portland Mercury") and my résumé. Just briefly, I've been writing about 10 years, held a few staff jobs, done work for publications like "BPM," Insound.com, and "Skyscraper," and now freelance full-time. I'd love to review the Peppermints' record, or anything else you might need. Please let me know if you're interested.

Thanks!
Adam Gnade

## Feature

*This feature pitch was e-mailed to the real estate editor at the* New York Times, *and it resulted in a cover story for the Sunday Real Estate section—and steady work since then, three or four real estate pieces every month.*

Dear [First name of the "Real Estate" section editor]:

**First Floor Apartments: Happy exile, starter pad, or bargain-hunter's dream?** On Halloween, I took my daughter trick-or-treating and met two total strangers: the young couple who've occupied a lobby-level apartment in my chummy 10-story UWS building for two whole years. Like other first-

floor dwellers, they rarely had occasion to stumble into the social incubator otherwise known as the elevator. Socially speaking, this affable pair was living off the grid.

[Agent's name], a residential real estate agent at Douglas
Elliman, disputed my hypothesis that misanthropes might favor first-floor abodes for their relative isolation. "The noise,"
she says. "You have to really not mind hearing the noise from
the lobby and from the street, if you're in front." Other disad-
vantages include lack of light (especially in rear apartments),
window bars and security concerns, and less square footage
than other apartments in the line, due to the encroachment of
the lobby.

But for a certain type of buyer—not merely those seeking
live-work or separate entrance accommodations—these low-
lying spaces fit just right, at least for a while. For one thing,
the units sell for an estimated 20 percent less than higher ones
of comparable size, which makes them the perfect starter
pad—or an affordable way into a pricey neighborhood or
building. They make great discount pied-a-terres too.

This article would look at the first-floor apartment
through these various lenses by interviewing real estate agents
and owners. It would also explore the special considerations
in buying or selling a ground-floor unit and whether, as the
tide turns against commercial ground-floor tenants, more of
these spaces are coming onto the market.

I'm a freelance writer specializing in lifestyle, business, and
legal reporting. I've written for *Parenting, Worth, The New
York Post, Shape, Health, Cosmo,* and *The American Lawyer,*
among others. I hold journalism and law degrees from New
York University. If you would like to review my clips, please
see my profile on mediabistro.com, http://www.mediabistro.
com/TeriRogers.

Many thanks for your consideration.

Sincerely,

Teri Karush Rogers

P.S. For what it's worth, I am a **huge** fan of the redesigned Real Estate section. Keep up the good work!!

## Pitching a Few Stories at the Same Time

*Many editors welcome multiple pitches—although not more than three—in one query letter. This is a good example of sending a bullet-point pitch and getting a few ideas across briefly. The writer has written for this editor before, hence the chatty tone. She was assigned the Colombian Hotel piece.*

Hi [First name of *Wallpaper* travel editor], it's Rachel Sklar writing—we were in touch a while back regarding my contributions to this month's wallpaper* (Night Out in Toronto, Flushing Meadows Pool). I write this missive from Sydney, Australia, where I'm cheering my roommate on at the Gay Games. I've come across three spots that I think are wallpaper-worthy that have not been covered yet by any international publication, and I thought I would see if you were interested, so here goes:

1. Savage—Restaurant & Bar, Taylor Square

Tucked away on a quiet tree-lined street around the corner from Taylor Square (in the heart of Boystown) is Savage, which is a well-kept local secret. The food is excellent (their slow-roasted tomatoes—a Sydney specialty—are particularly succulent) and the vibe casual and chic against a backdrop of exposed brick, high ceilings, and spare furnishings (the modern-style bathrooms use floor lighting to great effect).

Good-looking waitstaff heightens the aesthetic appeal, and the snazzy wetsuit-inspired staff shirts they wear are for sale for a pittance in Aussie dollars (our party bought two). Upstairs a retro-minimalist bar/listening lounge offers beats for sale or for sampling with unique twelve-inch singles lining the walls, and if you sweet-talk the counterman he'll even lay a few tracks on CD for you. An exceptionally cool spot, open for just about a year, and has only gotten press within Australia (and conspicuously absent from the latest Lonely Planet).

2. The Colombian Hotel—Oxford Street and Crown (at Hyde Park)

This 1940s South American–inspired hotel has been open for under a week and has become an immediate hot spot (due in no small part to the discerning masses of gay men out and about at the Gay Games). The bar fronts onto Oxford Street, sans windowpane, and has an upstairs cocktail bar with a 180-degree outlook over Oxford with views of the Harbour Bridge and Opera House. The old-world Latin aesthetic is evoked through tiled walls, stone floor, and woody, earthy tones, plus a mirrored wall that's printed with an Amazonian jungle scene. The music is spun by local deejays with an official policy of "anything goes," which makes for an eclectic evening. I also think that the chandelier above the downstairs bar is Arn Jacobson (if you're interested in a write-up I'll obviously confirm that).

3. Wildfire, Circular Key/The Rocks, Sydney Harbour

This restaurant/bar has been open for about six months thus far but as far as I know it hasn't been written up outside Australia. It's a great space, on two levels with high ceilings and great light fixtures all done in shades of a crimson palette. A bar to the side serves up smashing cocktails with quirky ingredients and the food is excellent. A good-looking crowd accessorizes the sleek interior. Raspberry-lemon souffle is divine.

That's it—I'm here until Sunday (then to Melbourne) and can get shots for you digitally and e-mail them, if you're interested. I'm most bullish on the top two—they're my favorites—but wanted to throw Wildfire in there for your consideration as well. Hope you are doing well and hope you find these to be of interest.

Best,
Rachel

## Follow-ups

*As good as your pitch might be, it can always end up falling through the cracks once an editor receives it—a letter gets put aside and then buried under other paperwork; an e-mail gets buried among spam in the in-box. Following up on queries—without becoming a pest—is always a good idea. This writer sent her initial pitch by regular mail, and, after a few weeks passed with no reply, she re-sent it by e-mail. That time, the editor e-mailed her back immediately and assigned the piece.*

Subject: Follow-up: bad kid lit pitch

Hello [First name of the editor of the *Boston Globe Sunday Magazine*],

I'm following up on a hard-copy pitch I sent you several weeks ago about the phenomenon of bad children's books written by celebrities. I was wondering if you'd had a chance to look it over?

I'm thinking this piece could have a great public-service angle for the holidays: we're fast approaching the season when well-meaning but clueless aunts and uncles might stumble into the stores and actually buy one of these books, unaware of how awful they are!

The original pitch is pasted in below. I look forward to hearing from you.

Best regards,
Tracy Mayor

Dear [First name of the editor of the *Boston Globe Sunday Magazine*],

Now that Madonna's announced she's writing a children's book, I think it's time to take a closer look at the phenomenon of celebrity picture books for kids. Mrs. Ritchie's book isn't due till next year, but other B-list celebs like Spike Lee, John Lithgow and Marlee Matlin are all coming out with tomes for tykes this fall. They'll join the ranks of actors/anchors/etcs like Jamie Lee Curtis, Maria Shriver, Katie Couric, Julie Andrews and Lynne Cheney—all of whom have kids, but no other writing experience.

With built-in name recognition and ready-made marketing strategies, these books are a gold mine for their publishers and a nice feel-good credential for their authors. The only problem? Most of them are unreadable. I speak here not as a casual observer but as the unproud owner of "Budgie the Little Helicopter" by the Duchess of York. Bad as it is, it's a veritable "Goodnight Moon" next to Dr. Laura Schlessinger's "But I Waaaaaant It!"

I'd love to report a story for the *Globe* magazine that balances these admittedly cranky opinions with exploration of more serious underlying questions: are Bad Books by Famous Authors about Important Subjects ultimately good or bad for children's book publishing? Do they crowd out books of real merit? Or do they bring in buyers, stimulate sales, and raise ticklish issues (adoption, handicaps, bullying, etc.) that otherwise wouldn't get covered?

Sources would include owners of some of the top children's bookstores in and around Boston (Curious George, Banbury Cross, etc.), organizations like the Children's Book Council and the ALSC (the Newbery Award people); and non-celebrity New England–based children's authors like David McPhail or Susan Meddaugh.

I've published book-related essays on Salon.com and in *Brain, Child* magazine (winner of the 2002 alternative press award), and I report frequently on technology, management, and parenting for national publications. I've enclosed a few clips. Please let me know your thoughts!

Best Regards,
Tracy Mayor

## 9

# You Pitched. Now What?

......................................................................

### What You're Likely to Hear Back, and How to React to Different Replies

All freelance writers have experienced it—the frustration of spending days slaving over a pitch letter, perfecting every comma and dotting every i, sending it out on your finest résumé paper, and then hearing nothing. Did it get lost in the mail? Did it ever make it to the editor's desk? Did he hate it? Did he pass it along to someone else? Did he file it away for another day? Did it go straight into the recycling bin? It's a horrible feeling—but don't worry, we have all been there.

Editors are busy people—some busier than others. Some read their own mail; others have their assistants or interns read it. Some read pitches as they arrive. Some pile them all up in a box in the corner of the office and then spend one day a month filtering through all the queries at once. But however they do it, here's the truth: you spent hours and hours perfecting your pitch, but the decision of whether it goes into the "yes," "no," or "maybe" pile happens in just a few seconds. If those opening sentences of the pitch don't grab the editor's (or assistant's, or intern's) attention, your letter very likely ends up in the "no" pile. This reject pile then goes to one of two places: either right to the trash, or, if you're lucky, to the editorial assistant instructed to send out "no, thank-you letters."

Let's say your pitch makes it to the "maybe" pile. If that "maybe" pile resides on the editorial assistant's desk, eventually it will get passed along to a more senior editor who makes another judgment call. Rejects there will again receive a letter or hit the trash bin.

If you haven't gotten a reject yet, great! But there are still a few more flaming hoops for your idea to jump through before you get your assignment.

## Idea Meetings

Most publications have idea meetings on a regular basis, at which editors gather to talk about article possibilities. Sometimes the editors present their own ideas, but they also toss around ideas from freelancer pitches for discussion. So even if the editor to whom you addressed your query letter loved it, unless the other editors and the editor-in-chief agree your idea is fantastic, it could still be rejected at this stage. For this reason, it's in your best interest to always do whatever you can to be on an editor's good side. You want him to go to bat for you and fight for your pitches in these idea meetings. Also, keep these meetings in mind when you're crafting your pitch letters—you need to convince the colleagues of the editor you're pitching just as much as that editor. So remember that it's a good idea to provide your editor with ammunition (great stats and quotes) to help support your story at idea meetings.

It's important to note that the frequency of these meetings varies from publication to publication. Obviously, the more often a publication comes out, the more often the editors need to have idea meetings. But even among monthly magazines, the variation may be great. At one magazine, the editors might gather twice a month to go over new ideas. Another monthly might map out six issues at a time, and thus those editors have idea meetings only twice per year. It could very well take weeks or months before you hear a definitive "yes" or "no."

## WHAT GOES ON IN THOSE IDEA MEETINGS?

"As a weekly magazine, we get dozens of pitches every week. We sift through looking for potential cover stories, or middle features, or simply one-page profiles. We look at the writers, sometimes look up their work online, and we make sure the idea has not been well covered locally, especially in our own newspaper. The editors usually have different opinions on stories, as they appeal to different people. Our give and take is strong and useful, and it usually weeds out the weak pitches."

—*Doug Most, editor*, Boston Globe Sunday Magazine

"Basically everyone sits around a conference table and brings up ideas— their own, other people's—and the group discusses them. These meetings vary a lot in their tone. Some places have very lively, fun, and productive idea meetings. At other magazines, the meetings can be brutal, as if the editors are serfs, with each called upon in turn to offer up tribute to the feudal lord (or, as we know him, the editor-in-chief). You want to write for the first kind of place."

—*Kendall Hamilton, editor-in-chief*, Ski

"Response time varies tremendously depending on where editors are in the magazine's production cycle when they get your note. Bad pitches are probably rejected quickly, so don't despair if you don't get an immediate response. It's okay to follow up with a brief e-mail or voice mail reminder if you haven't heard anything after a couple of weeks."

—*Liz Mazurski, editor-in-chief*, Spa *magazine*

Let's look at some possible scenarios after you pop your finely crafted query in your local mailbox, and consider how best to proceed in each.

### You get no response

Don't panic. As we've seen, there are a variety of reasons why you might not hear back from an editor right away. If it's been only a week, wait

---

### MONOGAMOUS PITCHING

"You should never multiply submit proposals. If an editor doesn't respond to your follow-ups, then you absolutely should send your proposal somewhere else. When that happens, I never formally retract the first proposal, I just assume that it has died on the vine. Then if I suddenly hear back from the first publication with a surprise yes, I consider my situation: Is my proposal now awaiting a response at Publication 2? If so, I stall. Then if Publication 2 says yes, I accept its assignment and tell the first publication I hope we can work together on something else soon and then I do my best to come up with some great ideas. But, of course, if Publication 2 turns me down I clamber onto Publication 1's bandwagon like we've always been the best of friends."

—*Freelance writer James Sturz*

---

a few more days. After two weeks, it's time to plan your follow-up. In most cases, e-mail is probably the best route to go. Keep the message short and to the point—something along the lines of "Dear Mr. Lawrence, I am following up on a pitch I sent you on the fifth of April. In case you did not receive it, I am pasting it below. Please let me know if I can provide you with any further information. Sincerely, XXX."

If you don't have an e-mail address for the editor you queried, make a few phone calls to the publication or do a bit of searching on the Web and see if you can get the e-mail address. If it's a magazine you're pitching, check the masthead page. Some list editors' e-mail addresses, or at least the e-mails of a few people on staff (sometimes on the advertising side). If you can get one address, you may be able to figure out the company's system: for example, namename_lastname@condenast.com.

---

#### @ WORK

"Contact editors via e-mail. Pitches should be a couple of paragraphs long and should demonstrate that you've already done some reporting and mastered your material to some degree. You can follow up again by e-mail if you haven't heard anything after a week."

—Popular Mechanics *deputy editor Jerry Beilinson*

---

If you can't figure out an e-mail address, draft another quick letter, again stating that you are following up on a pitch you sent. Be sure to include the original pitch letter, just in case the post office really did lose the first one you sent, although chances are better that it got lost on the editor's desk.

Three days after sending a follow-up e-mail and a week after sending a follow-up letter, you may want to make one phone call to the editor. If you get voice mail, leave a quick message mentioning your story idea and any related experience you have (publications you have written for in the past, etc.) and, of course, your contact information (both phone and e-mail so they can contact you in the manner they prefer). If you, in fact, get to speak to an editor, remember that he or she is sure to be busy, and might even seem put off by your call. Make your pitch quick and snappy. Don't assume that the editor has read your letter. Introduce yourself, mention that you sent an idea, and then quickly summarize the main points—fast:

"Hi, *Rolling Stone* editor. This is Freddy, the freelancer. I sent you a pitch letter via snail mail and e-mail within the last week. I thought your readers might be interested in hearing about a groundbreaking new singer-songwriter music festival that will take place in the hip little town of Shepherdstown, West Virginia. The event takes place in August, so I'd love to get working on a piece about it for you as soon as possible."

---

## HOW LONG TO WAIT?

Queries are usually responded to within a month. A follow-up e-mail is acceptable after a few weeks. Do not call. Please. Really.

—*According to* Jane *former senior editor Karen Catchpole*

It normally takes the editors about a month to respond to a pitch, but the time varies. If you haven't heard after a month, feel free to follow up via e-mail.

—*According to* Travel Savvy *former editor-in-chief Gina Masullo*

Queries are typically responded to in six to eight weeks, and a follow-up phone call is acceptable at that point if you haven't heard back from the magazine.

—*According to former* Marie Claire *senior features editor Julia Savacool*

---

It's then in the editor's court.

If you do all of the above but never hear back from (or never make an actual connection with) an editor, it's time to move on and pitch another publication. Don't wait more than a month if you've gotten no response—wait even less time if your idea is timely. Head back to the drawing board, revamp the letter, and send your brilliant idea elsewhere.

### You get a reply: "Not for us"

Get used to rejection. If you want to be a freelancer, you need to be able to handle rejection—often. All writers, even the most talented, have received rejection letters. Garrison Keillor, whose radio show *A Prairie Home Companion* reaches more than four million listeners each week, still tells the story about when he was first starting his career: He went to his mailbox daily and looked for envelopes from *The New Yorker*. He knew his fate before even opening the letter, because back then *The New Yorker* sent rejection letters in envelopes of one color and acceptance letters in envelopes of another color. Despite this fact, Keillor hoped and prayed for an acceptance as he walked back up his long driveway with the envelope in his hand— hoping that any reject-colored envelope would miraculously turn into an acceptance before he got up to the house.

---

### THE WAITING GAME

"Regarding response rate, you'll either hear back immediately, within several weeks, or somewhere in between. You may get a boiler- plate rejection note if we're swamped."

—Elle *executive editor Alexandra Postman*

---

Despite the dreaded rejection letters, successful writers forge on. So, whether you retool your pitch for another publication, totally revamp the idea, or simply trash the idea for something new and fresh, be sure to keep your head up. View a rejection as a learning experience and move on.

But don't just toss out your letter or e-mail of rejection. Take a closer look at it. Is it directly from an editor, or is it just a form letter? If it's a basic form letter, go back to the drawing board. But if it's a real letter, from a real editor, this is your little in. Jump on it fast. Within the next week or so—the sooner the better—get back to this editor with three more terrific story ideas. Address them to that same editor, beginning with something like "Thank you for responding so quickly to my last pitch; enclosed are two other ideas that I think might work for you." You don't want to wait two months, or even a few weeks, to get

## DEALING WITH REJECTION

"I mention in my book about crying after receiving rejections from both *Esquire* and *Playboy* on the same day. I used to save all my rejections, always thinking, 'I'll show them.' I always talk about how hard it is, but I also think it's glorious. If you have talent, persevere. Some give in. Writers are writers because they can't help but be writers; they have to get it out there. I feel more whole and reassured when I've written something. I try to discourage my students from a writing career most of the time. The ones who get beyond it are really meant to do it."

> —*Lawrence Grobel, freelance journalist, author, and biographer, writes for* Playboy, Esquire, *and* GQ, *and he's a go-to guy for* E! *'s* True Hollywood Story *series. His book,* The Art of the Interview, *is both a primer on the subject, which he teaches at UCLA, and a humorous in-depth look inside the exasperating and exciting world of celebrity journalism.*

"I had clips from *Premiere, People,* and *Parenting*, but I was dying to write for *Details* magazine. For as long as I can remember, in every incarnation, whoever's been editing it, I always wanted to write for it. I would take my clips every six months or so and color copy them and send them off to the magazine and I was very accustomed to never hearing anything. I even knew people who said oh you should send this to so-and-so, and I would always do it. And I didn't take it personally for whatever reason, I just totally grew accustomed to sending it and then never thinking about it again. And I was utterly shocked when one time I got an e-mail saying 'Hi, I'm the articles editor of *Details,* I'd love to meet you.' And so persistence definitely paid off there, and now I write for *Details*. And what I always tell people is that I never took it personally when they didn't respond. I'm a completely oversensitive person, I take everything personally, but for whatever reason magazines not getting back to me I don't take personally, and it really serves me well. I now understand that there are editors who are just too busy to ever get back to people; I know editors who have promised assignments who I've never heard from again. It's totally a numbers game."

> —*Anna David, formerly a staffer at* Premiere *and* Parenting, *now writes a monthly column for* Razor *and also writes for* Details, Playboy, Cosmopolitan, Maxim, Redbook, *and* Teen Vogue, *among others.*

---

### TRY, TRY AGAIN

"Being rejected doesn't mean you shouldn't pitch again; you should be able to tell from the tenor of the rejection whether a future pitch would be welcomed."

—Travel + Leisure *features editor Nathan Lump*

---

back to an editor. Editors receive more queries than you can imagine, so you've got to jump on a contact while you're still fresh in their mind.

#### You get a reply: "We just did a similar piece"

Congrats. You obviously know the types of pieces that this publication goes for, so you're on the right track. This note must have come right from an editor, so be sure to follow up with more ideas as soon as possible. Do not wait more than a month. Your name is fresh in this editor's mind, so take advantage of that.

But here's something to check on: When did the publication do that similar piece the editor mentioned? If it's so recent that it has not yet appeared on the newsstands, or that it's appeared since you sent your pitch, good for you. But if it was in one of the last few issues, not so good for you. The editor may not think so highly of you if it's clear you did not read the most recent issue before sending your pitch. Always try to read at least the last three issues of a magazine before drafting your pitch. Hunt around on Web sites to see if they've tackled a similar idea recently; and check search engines, such as LexisNexis, to see what a newspaper has recently covered.

#### You get a reply: "No, thank you, but send more ideas"

You've been given a great opportunity. This editor either liked your idea but couldn't use it for some reason, or else she simply really liked your writing style or clips. She's interested in working with you. This is an invitation to an assignment. Act quickly, and get some more ideas off to this editor right away. Even if the editor didn't tell you *why* she rejected your first idea, resist your urge to ask why. Just get working on some new ones!

**You get a reply: "Can you develop this idea further?"**
Okay, so the editor is interested, which is great. But just what is he looking for? Before going forward, make a phone call or send an e-mail. Maybe the idea is on target but the editors want an expanded proposal or a more detailed outline before signing off. Or maybe the editor liked your general concept but not your angle and wants you to massage it into something slightly different. Make sure you know what your editor is looking for before you devote more time (without pay) to polishing the pitch.

**You get a reply: "We're thinking of doing a big package on this topic; we're going to hold on to your idea"**
This is a positive response, but it could mean that your idea will float off into the ether, never to be heard from again. Follow up. Call or e-mail the editor. Find out if the big package is scheduled for an issue in the near future—within the next six months or so. Even better, ask if you can set up a time to discuss this "package" with the editor.

---

### GETTING TO KNOW YOU

"Since we're always trying to establish new writer relationships, we'll hold on to your work if we like it. Even if you don't fit our immediate needs, we might call you down the road for assignments."

—*Former Time Inc. Custom Publishing managing editor Bill Shapiro*

Offer to help develop the entire package. If you've never worked for this publication before, they might not take you up on the offer, but they will certainly be impressed by your initiative.

### You get a reply: "We're interested, but at 150 words, not the 1,500 you proposed"

Now the ball's in your court. Obviously this offering isn't what you hoped for. But if this is your first opportunity to work with this publication, you might not want to pass up the chance. This is your foot in the front door. If you do a great job with the 150-word piece, you'll stand a better chance of getting the big feature assignments down the road.

But if you really believe that you can sell this idea as a big feature to another venue—and if you're *very* sure of it—it's always okay to say thanks but no thanks. Be sure not to burn any bridges, though; the editors obviously liked some small part of your idea, so you should be sure to pitch this publication again as soon as you can.

### You get a reply: "We love your idea, but we want someone else to write it. Can we send you a fee for your idea?"

Receiving this response is no fun at all. It means you were on target with your idea, but, even so, the editors don't want you to write it. The thing to remember is that it's a lot better than a reject letter. Sure, you could just take the offered money (don't expect it to be much) and run, but try to make this work to your advantage.

Take a look at your original pitch letter. Was it a bit sloppy? Were there any typos or grammatical errors? Are you sure you got the editor's name right? Did you really give it your best effort? Your idea sold, but your writing somehow fell short. Do you think you fully grasped the voice of the magazine in your pitch? This is a case where you should probably have someone else look over your query letter and give her feedback. If you feel comfortable doing so, pop the edi-

tor a quick e-mail inquiring as to why you were not given the assignment. Hopefully you will get some feedback that will improve your
pitching technique.

### You get a reply: "We love your idea. Will you write it on spec?"

Usually, a writer signs a contract to write a piece, delivers a draft, and
then works with an editor to finalize a version both the writer and the
magazine like. If the piece doesn't work out, the writer gets a pre-
arranged "kill fee," some portion of the contracted fee. If you write
on spec, however, the magazine is basically just agreeing to take a
look at your completed draft. They might like it and buy it, but if
they don't, you'll get nothing.

An established writer wouldn't bother with a spec piece—it's not
worth the time and effort if there's no guarantee of a payday. But if
you're new to freelancing, and you respect the publication offering
the spec deal, then go for it. Hopefully, you will do a stellar job, get
paid in the end, acquire a nice clip, and line up some more work for
that publication in the future.

One middle ground is to see if the editor would be willing to consider a standard, rather than spec, contract, after you develop the idea
further and present a more detailed outline. That could be a way of
showing the publication that it's worth taking a chance on you, without devoting all the effort required to write a complete piece without
any guarantee of payment.

### You get a reply: "We love your idea"

An actual acceptance, however phrased, often comes by phone,
sometimes via e-mail, but rarely via snail mail. (FYI, publications
rarely ask for or expect self-addressed stamped envelopes with pitch
letters these days. Don't expect to get the clips you send back,
whether you get an assignment or not.)

Even when an editor calls you to assign a piece, don't expect it to be assigned exactly as you pitched it. Chances are the editor will want you to alter the concept in some small or big way. Good editors explain, in great detail, exactly what they expect from you, even if they just reiterate what you proposed in your query letter. Listen carefully and take notes to ensure you write the article to their specifications. Remember, you want another assignment from these folks, so you want to do the first one right.

When editors call, make sure you nail down the contractual specifics—due date, word count, and payment. Then get down to the details of the assignment: how they want the piece set up, if they want any sidebars, how many experts they want quoted, and so on. The editor should feed you this information. If not, ask questions. And before you hang up, find out when they'll be sending the contract.

**You get a reply: "We love your idea. Can you have it to us in a week?"**

Get used to it. Editors often need assignments yesterday. They often ask for revisions overnight, too. Be as flexible as you can be, but don't make any promises you can't deliver. If you do that, you will be putting your editor in a difficult situation with her superior, and you're almost guaranteeing that you'll not work with that editor again.

But if you really can turn around a piece in a week, then do it. You might get offered a slightly higher than usual pay rate for the quick turnaround. If it's not offered, it can't hurt to ask. Say something simple, such as "Wow, that's a quick turnaround you need. Can you compensate me a bit more since I'll have to put this assignment on the top of my priority list?" If the editor agrees, great. If not, still move ahead with the assignment; perhaps you'll be offered more in the future. Plus, you'll go down in that editor's Rolodex as someone who can be counted on to help out in troubled times—which may be often!

## Building the Relationship

Once you have a connection with an editor, milk it for all you can— again, without being a pest. Check in with him regularly, keeping in mind that most editors generally prefer to be contacted via e-mail. It's less intrusive than calling too often, but less formal—and more likely to be seen by its intended recipient—than regular mail.

When you check in, don't simply ask for an assignment. That might be one of the most annoying e-mails an editor can get— someone asking for work without providing any ideas. Perhaps Sebastian Junger can simply mention he's looking for some work and get something. But you can't. Most desirable to your new friend the editor: send a few terrific story ideas. Another option, less desirable but still acceptable, is to send a message letting the editor know about stories you have in current issues of other magazines—even in a rival publication—or telling her about articles you'll have coming out soon. Along with your quick update, ask if there are any types of stories the magazine needs. Beware, though, of sending these e-mails too often— especially if you don't receive a response from the editor. You want to be on the editor's radar screen, not on her "desperate for work" list.

> Also, don't forget the importance of befriending your editor's assistant, who may control everything that makes it (or doesn't make it) to your editor's desk—or voice mail.

All editors are always looking for amazing story ideas to present to their top editors and then to the public. It is in their best interest to develop great stories with you. So, after writing two or three stories for the same editor, set up a meeting with him, either in person or over the phone. Tell him exactly why you want to meet with him: to talk about story ideas. There is no better way to get immediate feedback, and to get the inside scoop on what types of stories his publication is looking for.

Inevitably, when you are talking with an editor, she'll like some of your ideas, hate others, and see some sort of possibility in many of the rest. Listen to and take notes on any of the tips the editor might have. For instance, perhaps you have an amazing story idea about a man who overcame terrible odds to reach some sort of success. The editor may think the tale is indeed inspirational but not enough to stand entirely on its own. She may feel the piece needs to address a broader topic than just one man's story, or perhaps it would work well as one story in a grouping of four or five inspiring stories.

By working with an editor, the ideas you originally propose will most likely change, develop further, and flourish into something bigger. Of course, an editor could also suggest that your fabulous feature idea is only worth running as a short sidebar alongside another article already in the works. Then the ball is back in your court; you need to decide whether you are willing to write the abridged version of your idea or whether you'd rather try to sell your piece elsewhere.

Remember, especially when starting out, to be flexible. There are many writers out there, and if you are too married to your ideas and only want to do them your way, chances are you'll miss out on some great writing opportunities—and some money.

# 10

# All About Contracts

Before writing and delivering any assignment, be sure you have a
signed contract in hand. Even if you've gone over all the details
of your assignment with an editor—even an editor you've worked
with in the past—and been promised a certain payment, it's best to
hold off on sending in a piece until you have a contract that verifies
all of the particulars. Most editors will send you a contract immediately after you've discussed the piece via phone. If you don't receive
one in a week or so, pop your editor an e-mail asking when you
should expect to receive it.

## Read It

Haven't you always been told to read documents thoroughly before
signing on the dotted line? Contracts for writing assignments are no
different. Read each one from beginning to end to be sure you are
getting the deal you discussed. You certainly don't want to sell all
rights to a short story for a thousand bucks, and then watch the
magazine take your tale to Hollywood and make millions. You need
to protect your interests. And in addition to keeping control of your
creations, you want to be sure that legally you are not taking on some

unnecessary risks. Don't be afraid to speak up and ask questions if you think something doesn't sound quite right.

Most editors are happy to explain their publications' policies. If you do ask for further explanation on a contract, be sure to keep copies of all correspondence concerning your rights, whether it is by letter or by e-mail. If you chat on the phone, keep detailed notes. If something sounds controversial or problematic, get it in writing. In the future, if a disagreement occurs, your correspondence can take the place of a legal contract, as long as it clearly illustrates what was agreed to.

In most cases your own judgment should be enough, but if you are negotiating a big deal, such as a book or a long-term project, then you might want to have an agent or an attorney help review your contract.

The key is to remember that as soon as you write anything, it's yours. You own the copyright until you sign a contract selling the work (that is, the story, article, poem, book, whatever) to someone else. Knowing your rights can only help you—both legally and financially. Here are some of the basics.

### First North American (FNA) rights

First North American contracts are probably the most common contracts freelance writers in the United States receive from publications, and such a contract is probably the kind you'll want to sign. Basically the publication is borrowing, or licensing, your work. Also called FNASR (first North American serial rights), these contracts allow the publication to use your original material one time, in publications distributed in the United States and Canada, and then basically return all the rights to you. Under such a contract, you cannot allow anyone else to publish the work before the publication with whom you've signed this agreement does.

The contract will probably ask you to verify that the material you submit has not been published before, that you are the sole author, and that you have not sold rights to the piece to anyone else in the past.

The contract will also most likely state that you can't sell the article to any other publication for a certain amount of time after it is first published. This amount of time varies, but for monthly magazines it's usually around ninety days or so. After the designated time frame, you are free to do what you want with the piece. You may be able to sell it to another publication that does not require "first" rights. (See Reprint or second serial rights below.) Or you could sell it to a publication in another country, for first British rights or the like.

If the first publication bought only the print rights to your work, you may be able to sell it to an online publication that buys electronic rights.

### First serial rights or worldwide first publication rights

Basically these rights are the same as those found in an FNA contract, but in this case they are not limited by geography. The publication can be distributed worldwide. Some online publications use these contracts, as anything on the Internet is available everywhere.

### Simultaneous or onetime rights

Although rare, onetime rights allow the publication to print the work just once, but other publications may be printing the same information at the same time. This might happen with an article that is very time sensitive—let's say the review of a soon-to-be-released movie. Usually the work is sold to a variety of publications, each with a different audience, or in different areas geographically. In addition, in some cases onetime rights may also be sold when the piece has already appeared in another publication.

### Reprint or second serial rights

When periodicals publish excerpts from books, they often purchase first or second serial rights (first are those published before the book is on sale). Some publications—*Reader's Digest* is a popular example—buy reprint rights to articles previously published in other magazines and newspapers. While the author of the reprinted material is seldom paid as much as he was for the first rights, chances are he didn't have to do any further work on the piece, either. So it's a win-win situation. Also, since second serial rights are usually nonexclusive (also called nonexclusive reprint rights), they can be sold to more than one publication at the same time. Just be sure that the publication purchasing the piece is fully aware that the piece has appeared somewhere else already—even if you just had it on your own personal Web site.

### All rights

Writers are often warned to stay away from all-rights contracts, since they mean you are selling all of your ownership of your work. You can never reuse or resell that piece. You will most likely get a byline saying you wrote the material, but the publisher can basically do what it wants with it. The article can be reprinted as many times as the publisher likes, in whatever format, and there's no obligation to pay you another nickel—even if, say, there's a lucrative Hollywood deal for your piece.

Increasingly, publications request all-rights contracts because they want to be able to include your work on Web sites or in digital databases that will exist in perpetuity.

If offered an all-rights contract, kindly ask for an FNA instead. Some editors are just waiting for the request and will simply send you a different contract. In other cases, the editor may stand firm, stating that the publication offers only all-rights contracts. If this occurs, you have to decide whether the assignment is worth giving up your rights. If you do sign an all-rights contract, and you want to reuse your work sometime later on, you will have to ask for—or, even worse, purchase back—the right to do so.

> ## YOUR WORK WHILE ON STAFF
>
> It's important to note that when you are on the staff of a publication, the work that you do for that publication belongs to that employer, not to you. So if you are an editor at a magazine and write an article that is published in that magazine, you do not have the rights to take that piece and sell it elsewhere, no matter how much time has passed. The employer owns the copyright to that work. If you print the same article, or something very similar, in the future, you'll be infringing on the company's copyright.

### Work for hire

Freelancers are sometimes asked to sign "work for hire" contracts. This is often the case when working on a big project for a publication or perhaps when developing a series of articles from conception through publication. Work for hire contracts are also common in ghostwriting situations. In all of these cases, the work produced belongs to the hiring company. The company owns all rights and it owns them forever. Usually the author is given credit for the work, even though he doesn't own the rights, but in some cases contracts may ask the writer never to reveal his identity.

### Electronic rights

Electronic rights can mean a lot of things. In the recent past, it meant just exhibiting the work on the publication's Web site around the same time it appeared in a print version. Today it can include everything from putting the work on the Web and into permanent archives accessible by the public, putting it on CD-ROM, distributing it through an online database (such as LexisNexis) or other electronic information storage and retrieval systems, or producing the material on any other electronic, digital, or optical system—some of which may not even exist yet.

Currently it seems that for every different publication out there,

## IS IT LEGAL TO REPRINT YOUR OWN CLIPS ON YOUR OWN WEB SITE?

Welcome to the gray area of copyright law. The general rule is that the copyright owner owns all rights to the protected work. There is, however, an exception known as the "fair use" doctrine. This doctrine permits the use of copyrighted material under certain circumstances. According to the U.S. Copyright Office's Web page concerning fair use (www.copyright.gov/fls/fl102.html), "reproduction of a particular work may be considered 'fair' if it fits within the realm of the following four statutory factors: (1) the purpose and character of the use, including whether such use is of commercial nature or is for nonprofit educational purposes; (2) the nature of the copyrighted work; (3) the amount and substantiality of the portion used in relation to the copyrighted work as a whole; and (4) the effect of the use upon the potential market for or value of the copyrighted work."

That being said, try and get written permission from the copyright owner (the publisher) to use the protected work on your Web site at the time you sell the work. Unfortunately, obtaining written permission is not always easy. While I can't endorse or otherwise give an across-the-board approval or opinion, I strongly suggest that if you use a protected work without the copyright owner's permission, make sure that you (1) give proper credit to the copyright owner; (2) stay within the statutory factors stated above (you can find them codified under 17 United States Code, Section 107); and (3) follow the guidelines set forth on the U.S. Copyright Office's Web page.

Remember—you *must* be careful when using a copyrighted work or you could expose yourself to a lawsuit.

—*Ken Jewell is a New York–based attorney who practices employment and commercial law.*

there is a different way of stating electronic rights. So if you don't understand how it is written in the contract, ask your editor to explain.

Some Web sites may want to buy first electronic rights or first world electronic rights, which will allow them to be the first to exhibit the work on the Internet or via e-mail. Other publications refer to electronic rights only when publishing material on CD-ROMs or other electronic devices. They use the terms *Internet* or *Online* to reference material on a Web site or delivered by e-mail. If this distinction is of importance to you, be sure you are well informed about what you are selling.

All of these issues hold true when writing for Web sites of any sort—online magazines like *Slate,* companion Web sites like *New York* magazine's NYMetro.com, or even blogs. Before you write for these publications, figure out whether you're signing an all-rights or work-for-hire contract, or maybe something more limited. If you're signing only an electronic-rights contract, for example, to write something for a Web site, you still have the rights to sell your piece in a traditional print venue.

### Anthology rights

Some contracts, especially with magazines that publish collections of their articles, will request anthology rights. Often you will be paid a small percentage of your original assignment fee if your article is used in any anthologies compiled by your publisher. This should be noted in a clause in your original contract.

### Archival rights

Back in the old days (that is, a decade or two ago), archiving a piece meant keeping it in a library of past issues, or copying an article onto microfiche. Today, due to the Internet, archived material is much more accessible to the general public. If you want to reprint an article in the future, be sure you have not sold your piece into archives forever.

## Independent Contractor

You may receive a contract that refers to you as an independent contractor. This is making it clear that the publication is not legally responsible for you—basically meaning that they are not deducting taxes from your pay, and most likely that they are not providing you with benefits such as health insurance.

## COPYRIGHT INFRINGEMENT

Everything you write should originate with you. If you use, or reference, another writer's work, you must either gain permission to use that information or, in some cases, credit that writer or the publication in which the work first appeared.

What happens if you find that something you wrote has appeared elsewhere, without your permission, or without you being credited or compensated? First, be sure that you own the rights to the work you think has been swiped. For instance, if you sold all rights for an article to a publisher, that company may have allowed someone else to reprint or reuse your work. In that case, you have no recourse. You might want to check with the publisher to see whether it allowed the third party to use your work. If no such permission was granted, the publisher is the one whose rights were infringed, not you.

If you indeed own the rights to the plagiarized material, make sure that you can prove that you first printed the material (a dated clip is best). If your material appears on a Web site, you might simply want to request that it be taken down, or you can ask for compensation for the use of your material, or request that you be given credit for the work. Of course, you can take the matter to a lawyer, but unfortunately, in many cases doing so is more costly than it's worth.

## Negotiating Contracts

If you are uncomfortable with something in your contract, don't sign it. Let's say a magazine is asking for all rights to a piece that you think could be developed into an even larger article for another publication in the future. Call your editor and talk about the contract. In some cases, editors are just hoping that you will sign the all-rights contract without argument and then they don't have to worry about paying

**JESSAMINE COUNTY PUBLIC LIBRARY**

(859) 885-3523

**Customer ID: \*\*\*7407**

**Items that you checked out**

Title:
  Get a freelance life : mediabistro.com's
  insider guide to freelance writing
ID: 32530606049987
**Due: Wednesday, August 08, 2018**


Total items: 1
Account balance: $9.30
7/18/2018 3:59 PM
Checked out: 5
Ready for pickup: 0

you anything more in the future. But if you ask for a less-binding contract, the editor might just have an alternative contract at the ready that she'll send right over to you.

Another thing to look out for is indemnity or warranty clauses. These are items in a contract that say something along the lines of "You will hold the publication harmless from any and all loss, damage, and/or expense (including attorneys' fees) that we may suffer or incur by reason of any claim arising from the breach or alleged breach of any representations or warranties made by you." Basically you are agreeing to take the financial blame if anything in your article is plagiarized, defamatory, libelous, or in any way against the law anywhere. This is a heavy burden for a freelancer to endure. Ask if this clause can be deleted altogether or talk to a lawyer about how it might be altered slightly so less of the responsibility falls on your shoulders.

If there is just one clause in a contract that you are not happy with, an editor may give you the go-ahead to cross out or change that statement, initial it, and send it back to the publication for the editor's initials.

If your editor, or the publication, refuses to give you a new contract or to make a change, then you have to decide whether to agree to the terms or walk away. That is a decision only you can make. You may be able to sell your article elsewhere under better circumstances, but there is no guarantee. Keep in mind that publications often are required by their parent company's legal department to obtain certain kinds of rights, and your editor may not have any flexibility in the contract you're offered. Especially when you're starting out, it may well be worth giving up more rights than you should, just so you can get a clip and build a relationship.

### Getting more money

If you are unhappy with the dollars offered in a contract, you can always ask for more. The worst your editor can say is no. After working for a publication on a few articles and establishing a relationship with an editor, asking for more money is fair game (for more on money, see Chapter 19).

In cases where you think the magazine will reprint your article on a Web site or in an anthology, ask if you will be given more compensation. If you think the publication will be profiting from your article in the future, you should benefit as well.

### When will you get the money?

Contracts often state that you will be paid for your work either upon acceptance or on publication. Being paid on acceptance (which is more common) means the publisher will pay the writer when the assigned article is completed, revised if necessary, and accepted by the editor. Being paid on publication means the publisher pays the writer when (or soon after) the article appears in print.

Many writers argue for being paid upon acceptance, since technically this is when your work is done. But when it comes down to it, pinpointing when an article is actually accepted is difficult and in many cases does not differ so much from when it is published.

### Word count

Most magazines pay by the word (whereas newspapers generally pay a flat fee). For example, an editor will call and ask you to write a 1,000-word piece. "We can pay you a dollar a word," he says. He is offering to pay you $1,000 for the piece. Many folks not in the industry laugh when they hear this. "Oh, I bet you put a lot of 'ands' and 'buts' in your work," they'll say with a chuckle.

Word count is not something that editors or writers look at with a fine-toothed comb. Rather, word count is giving the writer a general guideline as to the length of a piece. If an editor told you to write a two-page piece, what would that mean? Two pages double spaced? Two pages single spaced? What size font? You get the point. Word

## MEETING DEADLINES

"It's very important for writers to meet their deadlines. But if the writer needs more time, they shouldn't be afraid to ask. Sometimes the piece might not be so time-sensitive (perhaps it's not yet scheduled to run in an upcoming issue) and the editor won't mind giving a few extra days. If the deadline is looming, however, she'll let you know."

—*Jillian Lewis, a freelance writer in New York City who held staff positions at magazines in Sydney, Australia, and New York before launching into a life of flexible hours, writes primarily about health, fitness, sex, and relationships.*

count is the easiest way to describe the length of a piece without having to go into nitty-gritty details.

That being said, if you get assigned that 1,000-word piece for a dollar a word, don't expect to be paid $1,244 if you hand in a 1,244-word piece. Just as if you hand in a 900-word piece, the editor is not going to knock $100 off your check.

So remember, word counts are general guidelines. If assigned that 1,000-word piece, try to hand in a piece somewhere around 950 to 1,300 words. You don't want to give your editor too little (they might not be able to fill their space) and you don't want to give them way too much, either (you don't want to make their editing process extra difficult).

### Due dates

Before signing a contract, be sure you can meet the deadline stated. If you don't think you will be able to meet the deadline, say so up front, before signing. Your editor will appreciate your honesty and can probably adjust the due date.

Writers who do not hand in articles on time often put their editors in tight spots, and may make their job more difficult. Editors seldom continue to assign articles to writers who don't meet their deadlines.

### Kill fees

Contracts usually discuss the kill fee, which is the amount of money you will be paid if your article is completed as assigned but never appears in the publication. A kill fee is most often a percentage of your originally agreed on payment for the article, usually 20 to 30 percent, but sometime it's a flat rate. A kill fee is paid only if you hand in your piece and the publication declines to run it. This might be decided right when you hand it in or the publication may hold on to it for months and then finally decide to kill it; when you get paid a kill fee totally varies.

If you do all the research and interviews for a piece but never actually write and submit it, it's very unlikely you'll receive a kill fee. The kill fee comes only when you have done all the work that was expected of you, not if you don't finish the job.

### Expenses

Contracts should give some mention to the expenses you may incur while reporting and writing the piece. Some contracts will simply state that you need to get prior approval from your editor for any expenses for which you expect to be reimbursed. Some publications will reimburse you up to a certain dollar amount, and anything over that needs prior approval. Others may refuse to cover any expenses, including phone calls related to the piece. Be sure you know what you can and cannot expense before beginning work on your article.

If you feel overwhelmed by all of the things you need to consider before signing a contract, think about talking with a lawyer or an accountant who works with freelance writers. You may be able to hire someone who will look over contracts before you commit.

PART IV

Write

# 11

# Rules of Reporting

Tips and Tricks for Learning Information

Some people are great reporters and others are great writers. Most editors can easily identify writers who underreport their stories—and these are, usually, the same people who tend to overwrite. These writers try to extend what little information they have to make it look big. The guy who goes out and asks all the questions, on the other hand, can find the real meat of the story and is then able to zero right in on it. That reporter has no need to fill in extra space with dispensable words.

If you ask some of the most talented reporters working today how much of what they learn while researching a story ends up in the actual piece, you'll find that it is often only a very small proportion. But they've got to report every last detail to make sure they find the right ones for their story.

Some of what makes a great reporter is innate—a sense of curiosity, an ability to make sources feel at ease, an understanding of the right questions to ask, and a willingness to risk embarrassment by asking tough questions. Some of what makes a great reporter comes only with time and experience—a network of reliable sources, an ability to tell when people are being truthful and when they aren't, a deep and comprehensive understanding of the subject you're covering. But most of what makes a good reporter comes in between—techniques, tricks, and systems that can be studied and learned.

## Where to Start

Before picking up the phone to track down a source, begin with a bit of research. Spend half an hour—or all morning, or three days, if that's what you need—educating yourself. You should know the basics of whatever topic you're writing about before you begin reporting. In the past, reporters went to the library or the courthouse for background information, but now almost everyone begins their research on the Internet.

While you can find a great deal of background information by conducting simple Internet searches, you need to be careful, too—much of that information is best used as a jumping-off point for deeper reporting. You have to be very cautious about what sources you're relying upon—there's no guarantee that just because a piece of information is on the Internet it's true. Further, even when things are true, you're not going to want to write a piece with citations like " according to a Google search" or "according to the Internet." That is amateur and nonspecific. Dig deeper and go directly to the subject and make sure the information is still accurate. It's a good idea to always double-check and confirm any information that is questionable or from a questionable source.

Where you go to verify information depends on the subject matter. Sites like www.infoplease.com contain a vast compendium of statistics, facts, and figures, atlases with information on hundreds of countries, a dictionary guide, and a comprehensive encyclopedia. The U.S. government also has many sites overflowing with information, such as census information at www.census.gov and information on countries around the world from the *CIA World Factbook,* at www.cia.gov.

Often you can confirm facts by checking public records. A student in a mediabistro.com writing class was interviewing a source who refused to tell her how much he paid for his house. This was a detail that she really needed for her story. At first she thought she was stuck. Not so. She didn't have to prod her source to give her this information. Real estate transactions are a matter of public record, and she was able to grab the information she needed from the *Washington Post*'s real estate Web site. She could have also headed to the local courthouse to confirm the amount.

Information such as people's ages, current and former addresses, and any legal matters in which they've been involved is all part of the public record. Hard-core reporters purchase access to databases, such as LexisNexis, which, in addition to its famous news archives, contains more legal data than you can imagine. LexisNexis's SmartLinx allows reporters to access billions of pieces of public-record information, such as real estate information, identity information, business and personal asset information, criminal records, and more.

### Q&A: GO LOOK IT UP! WITH DON MACLEOD

Don MacLeod is a law librarian and author of two editions of *The Internet Guide for the Legal Researcher*. He also is the editor of the monthly newsletters *Internet Law Researcher* and *Internet Connection*. He teaches seminars on research techniques for mediabistro.com and is currently working on a guidebook on the techniques.

**Q. What do you think are the ten most helpful Web sites to freelance writers when it comes to researching an article?**

A. Ah, the ever-popular Top 10 list! When it comes to research, every article is unique. What might qualify for inclusion in a greatest hits list for one article might not be the same for another. That said, there are some reference sites that every writer should know about to make

(continued)

tracking down facts much easier, no matter what subject he's searching. These sites, taken together, make up a vast reference library. They will give the writer a grand universe of factual information to tap, whenever and wherever.

Because each of these sites is far ranging in content, freelancers should acquaint themselves with the contents of these pages. There is a ton of information available and it's easy to overlook some of the gems if you don't spend some time idly clicking and browsing. Best part of these sites? At a total net cost of $0 to use, these sites don't cut into the writer's bank account.

## 1. REFDESK: HTTP://WWW.REFDESK.COM
At the top of any list of sites freelancers can't live without is RefDesk. RefDesk is the handiwork of Bob Drudge, father of parajournalist Matt Drudge and collector of the finest reference sites that the Web can offer. This immense Web site won't win any beauty prizes, but for sheer functionality and the richness of information it contains, it can't be beat. It's like having a million dollars' worth of reference books for free at your fingertips. Tracking down simple facts—Was Lincoln the fifteenth or the sixteenth president? What's the population of Topeka? Is aspirin toxic to cats?—can be a frustrating exercise. RefDesk does a lot of the legwork for you, delivering thousands of links to fact sites. Get to know what's on here and use the site regularly.

## 2. LIBRARIANS' INDEX TO THE INTERNET: HTTP://WWW.LII.ORG
The reference selection from LII is more modest than RefDesk's, but this site comes with the added benefit of having been compiled by information professionals, trained in the craft of information research. The sites LII selects are uniformly excellent.

## 3. YOURDICTIONARY.COM: HTTP://WWW.YOURDICTIONARY.COM
Words! Words! Words! The site features not just definitions and spellings, but the built-in thesaurus, antonym links, glossaries, and links to specialized dictionaries for jargon and foreign languages make this a must-not-miss for any wordsmith.

## 4. FIRSTGOV.GOV: HTTP://WWW.FIRSTGOV.GOV
Who's the biggest publisher on the planet? The United States government. The federal government has gone ga-ga for the Web and now publishes

uncountable numbers of studies, statistics, white papers, and news on just about anything.

The government also writes laws and regulations, which are here, too, as well as the underlying legislative documents that lead up to the adopted laws. Like RefDesk, FirstGov.gov is a portal that pulls together a huge amount of disparate info into one place. It's also a site that requires some getting-to-know-you time before you can take full advantage of the cornucopia of facts, figures, and data that Uncle Sam puts on the Web.

5. JOURNALIST'S TOOLBOX:
HTTP://WWW.AMERICANPRESSINSTITUTE.ORG/TOOLBOX/
The American Press Institute puts together the Journalist's Toolbox, a mar-velous collection of well-vetted sites of interest to the editorial set. This one Web page links out to thousands of other sites, from ones that pro-vide reporting tools to editing and fact-checking resources. Every free-lancer should know this site inside and out.

6. NEWSPAPERS.COM: HTTP://WWW.NEWSPAPERS.COM
This site deserves mention for its role as a double-dipping resource. It's a listing of Web sites from newspapers in the United States and around the globe. Use it as a research guide to locate local media that covers people, companies, or topics of mostly regional interest. But that's not the only reason to use Newspapers.com. It's also a good way to locate newspaper outlets for your articles: a New York–based freelancer might want to find a Texas newspaper travel editor to pitch an article about where to find bar-becue in Brooklyn for homesick Texans.

7. ADVANCED GOOGLE:
HTTP://WWW.GOOGLE.COM/HELP/REFINESEARCH.HTML
Think you know how to use Google? Guess again. If you're not using the tools and techniques outlined by the experts from Google, you're cheating yourself out of some great ways to find information faster and more accu-rately. Professional researchers swear by the + and – system, as well as the ability to restrict searches by specific domains and the often overlooked "cached" feature can be a lifesaver. Take fifteen minutes to become a Google expert by reading these tips and the Web will be your oyster.

(continued)

## 8. WAYBACK MACHINE: HTTP://WWW.ARCHIVE.ORG

The Web is an ever-changing, ephemeral place, as we all know. But the Internet Archive is keeping a record of Web pages past. The WayBack Machine makes for a superb site for looking up out-of-date information and otherwise inaccessible data. This site is great for tracking down that which once was.

## 9. STATISTICAL RESOURCES ON THE WEB: HTTP://WWW.LIB.UMICH.EDU/GOVDOCS/STATS.HTML

I know, "Lies, damn lies and statistics," but when it comes to making abstract concepts clear, statistics sometimes tell the story succinctly. For the most monstrous collection of statistical resources from across the Web, try this site from the University of Michigan.

## 10. PEOPLE FINDERS

I'm going to cheat here and include a number of sites under the single heading of "people finder" sites. Some will help you nail down addresses, phone numbers, and sometimes even e-mail addresses for individuals. The reverse lookups are great if you know a phone number and want to locate the address associated with the number. AnyWho provides links to international phone directories: AnyWho.com: http://www.anywho.com; WhoWhere.com: http://www.whowhere.com; BigFoot.com: http://www.bigfoot.com.

## 10½. BONUS SITE: PUBLIC RECORDS RESEARCH

Public records are such a great source of information that freelancers need to really have a handle on what's available and how to go about getting public record info. For that, I recommend the Web site (and the publications) of BRB Publications, Inc. (http://www.brbpub.com). The company publishes first-rate guides on mining the public record. The free *BRB's Public Record Resource Center* at http://www.brbpub.com/pubrecsites.asp is a great place to learn about public records and to find sites for retrieving them conveniently.

**Q. If a writer needs to find a great expert for an article, where do you suggest they begin?**

A. The cliché we use in English to indicate that someone is an expert on a subject is to say, "He wrote the book on it." Indeed, an author of a book, or a series of books, on a particular topic, is by definition an expert. To find an author, turn to that lowest-tech and cheapest experts database that I can think of, the online library catalog. Start with the big ones, such as the Library of Congress (http://www.loc.gov) or the New York Public Library (http://www.nypl.org). Once you've got the name of an author or authors, Google or use one of the people finder Web sites to locate a phone number, address, or e-mail by which you can contact the author directly, or to find a publisher through whom you can contact the author. Don't forget the special libraries that have collections built around a single topic: the librarians there can usually help you find experts. To locate library Web sites from around the world, refer to LibDex (http://www.libdex.com/).

Where else can you look? Find associations that are interested in your subject. For instance, an article about speedboats might begin with a visit to the Web site of the American Power Boat Association. The site could probably provide the names of spokespeople whom you might interview directly or recommend experts in the field who might make good subjects for an article.

It's worth the time to search FindArticles.com (http://www.findarticles.com) to see who already has been interviewed as an authority on your topic. Use Google and the online directories to track down the talking head for your own article.

Other sources for finding experts are ProfNet, a service of PRNews (http://profnet3.prnewswire.com/enter/index.jsp), which will hook you up with more than 12,000 industry spokespeople and government agencies, which usually have a PR person willing to speak ex officio. Take a look, too, through the links on experts from the Journalist's Toolbox. It lists some great resources for finding authoritative interviewees.

**Q. Do you suggest freelancers subscribe to LexisNexis or other such research aids?**

A. Nexis, and its legal information counterpart Lexis, is unquestionably one of the great information systems. Subscribing to Nexis would be great for a freelancer, assuming that the freelancer rakes in half a mil-

(continued)

lion dollars a year. And the great cost of Nexis is really the only knock against it, since it is otherwise what most info professionals would consider the best editorial database in the world.

**Q. Can information on InfoPlease be trusted? Are there other sites like that which you recommend to writers?**

A. InfoPlease can be trusted precisely as much as any other site, which is to say, inaccurate until proven otherwise. Writers and researchers need always to be skeptical. Mistrust any source, unless you can verify that the information is accurate. The best way to do that is to double-check all purported facts with different sources. An encyclopedia site like InfoPlease is certainly convenient, but do double-check everything. For similar sites, check out the links to encyclopedias available from the Librarians' Index to the Internet at http://lii.org/search/file/reference.

How do you know if a site is any good? They are published by reputable people or organizations such as universities or well-known media outlets. (I would trust something from the *New York Times* more than something from a Web site written by ChipHead213.) Information on reliable sites is updated regularly; there is a contact address listed on the site and what's written there passes the "smell test": the content sounds and looks reasonable and restrained. Common sense and a skeptical eye will be your best guides to figuring out which sites are good and which are not. Use government sites for official information, which you can always attribute.

**Q. Do you think message boards are a good place for researching particular topics?**

A. A message board can be a useful source of information. It's like having dozens of people you can tap on the shoulder for advice on a subject ready 24/7. Message boards are where people with shared interests hang out. Since there are so many message boards or bulletin boards (or "groups" as Google calls them) on such a great variety of topics, these places offer an untapped resource of expertise. It's like being able to crash a party where everybody there cares about the same subject: antique quilts, alternative medicine, the New York Mets, you name it. Need to know what the latest trend in surfing is? Try a surf message board and ask the dudes.

These "bulletin boards" are as close as the nearest Google.

Google Groups, in fact, is one of the best to both find topical message boards and to participate in them. All the details that you'll need can be found at http://groups.google.com. Yahoo!, like Google, also hosts groups. See how to find groups, read messages, and post to specific groups at http://groups.yahoo.com/.

The people who participate in these sites can sometimes deliver an answer when your own Googling or research can't. Just keep in mind that the rule to be skeptical goes double for message boards.

Never believe that anyone is who she says she is and verify any bit of information you get with a trusted resource.

## Going to the Source

When you are ready to start interviewing sources, who should you speak to first? It's a good idea to start at the very beginning, with the subject most connected to the topic. For example, when reporters at the *St. Petersburg Times* in Florida reported a series of articles on teens, they began by interviewing countless teenagers all around their city. Only after all this general research did they then decide to focus their series on one small group of teens at one school. They started big, and then narrowed down their subjects as the piece really began to take form. This is often necessary when reporting. Talk to the generalists first, then get nitpicky when you see where your article is going.

How do you find these sources? It depends on the topic of your piece. If you are writing an investigative article on teenagers, perhaps you'll begin by interviewing teenagers you know, or by pasting up flyers in places teenagers frequent asking for volunteers willing to be interviewed, or by posting a request on online chat boards that cater to teens. In most cases, you should identify yourself as a reporter and provide your e-mail address. If you are writing a piece about a topic that has already gotten some coverage, perhaps you'll come across the name of a person already quoted on the subject who seems informed and in-the-know. In your research you may come across university studies on the topic you're looking into. The experts who conducted these studies will probably make good sources. There are also databases, such as ProfNet (www.profnet.com), which help reporters connect with thousands of expert sources. Of course, any time you talk to a source, you should ask for recommendations of other people knowledgeable on the topic. (See page 173 for more info on finding sources).

> As you begin researching a story, and throughout the reporting process, you should save all of your notes, any background articles or information you use, tapes (if you recorded interviews) and notes of all interviews you conduct, and any other background information you collect. Most reputable publications will ask you to hand all this information over to their fact-checking department when you submit your story. Even if they don't, it is best for you to keep your backup materials saved and organized, in case any sort of question about your piece or your reporting comes up sometime in the future.

### Setting up an interview

The easiest way to set up an interview is to simply get on the phone. Sound confident and diplomatic when making an initial call. Introduce yourself as a writer. If you are calling about a piece that you have an assignment for from a publication, then you can introduce yourself as a writer for that publication. If you do not yet have an assignment and you are doing some background research for your pitch letter, you can say that—quickly. "Hello, my name is Margit Ragland. I am a writer doing some background research for a piece on teen pregnancy. I'm hoping I can set up a time to ask you a few questions." (Don't try to ask questions in the initial call, unless the source suggests that it is a good time to do so. Let the subject set a date when she'll be able to spend some time talking to you, and when she'll be ready for questions on your topic.)

If you're simply gathering material for a pitch and don't yet have an assignment, don't lie if the subject wants to know who you're writing the article for. You might mention a magazine you plan to pitch, but it's probably better to keep it a little more open-ended. "I'm planning to pitch the story idea to a major city newspaper and would like to get some background information from you to support my pitch. I won't take much of your time." You can also say, "After my assignment is finalized, then I would like to get back in touch and set up a more formal and in-depth interview with you."

The most important thing to keep in mind when calling an interviewee is that you are asking him to do you a favor. So be very accommodating to his schedule. Let him pick the time and place for the interview.

You usually get the best material when you meet with your interviewee face-to-face, but if time and location prohibit meeting with your subject, phone interviews will work. (Get yourself a headset for your phone so your hands are free to type or write.) If your subject is very busy, you can always offer to just send your questions via e-mail for him to answer when he has a free moment. But this form of interviewing should be avoided, if possible. You can't ask follow-up questions via e-mail, information can be misinterpreted, and the answers you receive are often dull and short (and too neatly composed) compared to speaking directly to someone.

If a source is unwilling to be interviewed, don't give up too quickly. Here are some tactics that can help you.

**Make it quick:** The source may just be busy and doesn't feel she has the time for an interview. Tell her it will take only about 10 minutes and that you have just a few quick questions to ask.

**Make it easy:** If the piece is rather straightforward and you are not asking any controversial questions, offer to send the questions ahead of time via e-mail, so she'll be prepared for what you will be asking about.

**Make it in the source's best interest:** If she doesn't want to talk with you because you are writing about something controversial, let her know that you want to talk directly to her to be sure you've got her side of the story straight. Explain that you'll be writing the story regardless, and you wouldn't want to get some information about the source wrong because she wouldn't talk to you.

**Divert the attention:** Get your source talking about the easy stuff first. Once she feels comfortable, she'll be more willing to reveal her own secrets.

**Ask for the why:** If you've done your background research, you probably already know many of the facts of your story. Tell your source so: "I know what happened; I am just trying to nail down *why* it happened. I want to be sure I get it right."

**Keep trying:** People do change their minds. Perhaps you caught them at a bad time, or called them at home when they prefer to be contacted at work (or vice versa). Try contacting them again by using a different approach.

## WHAT'S RIGHT

CODE OF ETHICS
Many freelancers, and writers of all types, abide by the Society of Professional Journalists' Code of Ethics. Here the codes are briefly described. For a more detailed description visit http://www.spj.org/ethics_code.asp

**Seek Truth and Report It**
Journalists should be honest, fair and courageous in gathering, reporting and interpreting information.
• Test the accuracy of information from all sources and exercise care to avoid inadvertent error.
• Diligently seek out subjects of news stories to give them the opportunity to respond to allegations of wrongdoing.

- Identify sources whenever feasible.
- Always question sources' motives before promising anonymity.
- Avoid undercover or other surreptitious methods of gathering information except when traditional open methods will not yield information vital to the public.
- Never plagiarize.
- Avoid stereotyping by race, gender, age, religion, ethnicity, geography, sexual orientation, disability, physical appearance or social status.
- Support the open exchange of views, even views they find repugnant.
- Give voice to the voiceless.
- Distinguish between advocacy and news reporting.
- Distinguish news from advertising and shun hybrids that blur the lines between the two.

**Minimize Harm**
Ethical journalists treat sources, subjects and colleagues as human beings deserving of respect.
- Show compassion for those who may be affected adversely by news coverage.
- Be sensitive when seeking or using interviews or photographs of those affected by tragedy or grief.
- Recognize that gathering and reporting information may cause harm or discomfort.
- Recognize that private people have a greater right to control information about themselves than do public officials and others who seek power, influence or attention.
- Show good taste.
- Be cautious about identifying juvenile suspects or victims of sex crimes.
- Be judicious about naming criminal suspects before the formal filing of charges.
- Balance a criminal suspect's fair trial rights with the public's right to be informed.

**Act Independently**
Journalists should be free of obligation to any interest other than the public's right to know.

(continued)

- Avoid conflicts of interest, real or perceived.
- Remain free of associations and activities that may compromise integrity or damage credibility.
- Refuse gifts, favors, fees, free travel and special treatment, and shun secondary employment, political involvement, public office and service in community organizations if they compromise journalistic integrity.
- Disclose unavoidable conflicts.
- Be vigilant and courageous about holding those with power accountable.
- Deny favored treatment to advertisers and special interests and resist their pressure to influence news coverage.
- Be wary of sources offering information for favors or money.

**Be Accountable**
Journalists are accountable to their readers, listeners, viewers and each other.
- Admit mistakes and correct them promptly.
- Expose unethical practices of journalists and the news media.
- Abide by the same high standards to which they hold others.

### Conducting an interview

It's best to prepare a list of questions before heading into an interview—and even before you make an initial phone call, in case your source is willing to chat right then and there. Being ready with what you want to talk about will help you look and sound more professional. As mentioned, some sources will ask to see the interview questions ahead of time. If you feel comfortable doing so, go ahead and share the questions. It may save you some time during the interview process.

At the beginning of the interview try to break the ice by talking about something casual rather than what you've come to them to discuss—unless you sense that they are in a hurry, then get right to the point. It's okay to ask the subject how much time he has, so you know when to start wrapping things up.

Start with some broad, general, and easy questions. You might want to ask your source to quickly review her career history, or something along those lines. If you have some sensitive or difficult questions to ask, leave them for later in the interview when you both feel more comfortable—just be sure you don't run out of time with your source before asking the important questions.

If you're interviewing your source in person, it's best to take notes with a pen and paper. Jot down the main ideas and important direct quotes. Immediately after the interview transcribe your notes onto your computer, filling in the blanks with the information you did not get down word for word. Many writers have their own form of shorthand. So experiment and see what works best for you.

Some subjects are uncomfortable being tape-recorded, while others don't mind. Always ask your interviewee if it is okay if you tape the interview if you want to do so—especially if you are interviewing

### CONFLICTS OF INTEREST

Whenever possible, don't write about people or institutions with which you have personal connections. If you're forced to cite a source with whom you have a personal relationship, you should probably reveal this in your article. At the very least, discuss the issue with your editor—before the piece is assigned to you. For instance, if you pitch a story to the *New York Times* about the fact that George Bush has been hitting on his chef in the White House, then you better let the editor know ahead of time if that chef happens to be your wife.

### PLAY FAIR

Always be objective when reporting. Any time you have one source who accuses someone or something else publicly, it is your job as the reporter to get the opposition view and include it in the story. If a doctor tells you that McDonald's French fries will clog your arteries and cause people to have a heart attack, call McDonald's and see what the company's response is. If McDonald's refuses to talk with you, state that in your story and move on.

her over the phone. Depending on what state you work in, taping a call without consent may be illegal.

## What Did They Say?

You'd think that only investigative reporters would have to worry about what's "on or off the record." But surprisingly, many times when interviewing a subject, even about a mundane topic, an interviewee will stop short and say, "You won't print that, will you?" Here are some basic rules on what's what when it comes to quoting sources and using revealed information.

### "On the record"

Once you call a source and identify yourself as a reporter, the interview is assumed to be on the record. You can quote whatever the source says to you, and you can attribute the material to him. You do not have to explicitly say, "This is on the record." If a source wants to tell you something off the record—in other words, material that you cannot use without corroboration from another source—he must go off the record *before* he says anything. Sources may not place information off the record after the fact.

The key, however, is that you must have identified yourself as a reporter. Undercover reporting is generally frowned upon, and if you're undertaking an undercover investigation, be sure to discuss with your editor the standards you should be following.

But, at the same time, reporters still have the same rights as normal citizens. If the mayor of your town walks into the restaurant where you're eating and starts telling racist jokes in a voice loud enough for all the other customers to hear, you don't need to explicitly identify yourself as a reporter before reporting that information. Things you observe going on around you as a normal citizen are acceptable to be reported upon.

### "Confidential sources" or "not for attribution"

If a source agrees to be interviewed but does not want to be identified, this information is called not for attribution. For example, a former high-ranking tobacco-company executive might agree to talk to you about what went on in the company, but without his name attached. You should agree upon the attribution *before the interview begins,* not during the interview or later. Try to get your subject to agree to the most specific attribution possible without giving away the source's identity. For example, if the tobacco company had nine vice presidents, maybe your source will agree to be called "a past vice president." This will help your credibility. Everything the source says may then be directly quoted, but attributed to "a past vice president," not to John Smith. If possible, try to encourage "not for attribution" sources to go on the record after the interview. Sometimes letting them know that other sources are being named, or that other sources will talk if they reveal their identity, will make them more willing to reveal their identity.

Many publications have firm rules against using "not for attribution" facts or information because they are easy to fabricate and give less credibility to a story. Talk to your editor if this issue arises with your article.

### "Off the record"

When your source tells you something he says is "off the record" and you agree to this, then the information you learn from this source can inform your story but you cannot use it in print. It can, however, be used, without revealing the source, to coax information from another source. In general practice, information cannot be placed off the record retroactively.

## REPORTING IS PARAMOUNT

"People often underestimate the amount of reporting that goes into one of our features. They require thorough research and a great deal of resourcefulness. (For example, in a feature on safe-haven laws, a free-lance writer was responsible for quickly finding a teen who had thrown away her baby and was willing to talk about it; and, as any experienced writer of real-life stories will tell you, that's damn-near impossible.) We need writers who will knock on doors, call up everyone they know, and not give up until they find what we're looking for."

—Teen People *former articles editor Sandy Fernandez*

"You don't live or die on the strength of your idea; you live or die on your reporting skills."

—Shop Etc. *deputy editor Karen Catchpole*

# 12

# Writing

Journalism professors used to begin newswriting classes with the inverted pyramid, telling students to start their articles with the most important information first and then dwindle down to the unimportant details. The article's lede was to contain the who, what, where, when, and why. Some news stories on the front page of your local paper are still written this way, but there has been a move away from this type of writing. Writers want to grab their reader with an interesting anecdote and keep them reading right on through to the end to find out what happened. Especially in magazines, and in the feature pages of newspapers, narratives and service pieces are the norm, and you'll be hard-pressed to find a piece written in the inverted-pyramid style.

## Structure of an Article

First, let's talk about the terminology used in discussing a typical article these days.

**Hed:** A shortened version of the word *headline, hed* refers to the title of an article. It is intentionally misspelled, as many publishing-production terms are, so that editors, designers, and others involved

---

IN THE BEGINNING . . .

"I have worked with some good editors over the years, and they
have helped me be a better writer. I remember one editor rewrote my
lede, and I was blown away by how much better it made the whole
story. Since then, I pay a lot more attention to how I open an article."

—*Chicago freelancer Ann Logue, who is an organizer of the Chicago Magazine
Writers Conference and who has contributed to* Barron's, *the* San Francisco
Chronicle, *and the* New York Times

---

in the production process won't accidentally think it is real text that
should appear in the publication.

**Dek:** The *dek* is a sentence or few sentences below the headline of
an article, which quickly summarizes what's in the piece. This term,
like *hed,* is also intentionally misspelled.

**Lede:** When assigning an article, an editor will often say, "Please
open with a grabbing lede." The purposely misspelled term *lede* refers to
the first sentence, or first few sentences of an article. Some writers open
with an intriguing quote; a shocking statistic, fact, or figure; or an en-
gaging anecdote that illuminates the key issues and tension of the story.
The lede should pull readers in and leave them wanting to read more.

**Nut graf:** Following the catchy lede, many articles have a nut
graf, which is basically a paragraph or two that neatly summarizes the
points of the article and lets the reader in on what's to come. Also
called a trumpet or billboard graf, it's something like the thesis statement in a term paper. Also used as a transition paragraph, it takes the
reader from the lede into the body of the article. It's basically a road
map showing the reader exactly why the story is important, how to
interpret it, and what it's about. In an article about breast cancer, the
lede may describe a young woman in her doctor's office receiving

what sounds like a death sentence. The nut graf will go on to tell the reader that the article will follow the young woman through four months of grueling treatment. The nut graf can be thought of as the *telling* graph, which follows the *showing* graf, the lede. (And, as you've probably figured out, graf is a misspelled abbreviation for paragraph.)

**Narrative structure:** Depending on the type of article, the narrative structure will differ. For instance, in a profile, the structure might follow the chronology of someone's lifetime, from birth to death. In a travel story, the structure could be built around the journey toward a particular geographical goal.

**Body:** The meat of the story appears in the body of the article. Sometimes called running text, or the main bar, it is distinct from sidebars and charts and other elements of a piece. In a news story the body of the text will go into detail about the events of what occurred; in a feature story it will take the reader on a journey; and in a service piece it will provide the reader with important, usable advice. This is where good reporting is key.

**Kicker:** *Kicker* is another term for the final paragraph or sentence of an article, basically the ending. It's the place where everything should tie together. Perhaps you bring the reader back to the lede scene or answer a nagging question. As its name implies, you should try not to let your piece end on a dull note. Instead, it should conclude with a burst of energy, a striking quote, an interesting conclusion, a bit of knowledge, or something for the readers to take away with them.

**Sidebar or box:** Often used interchangeably, sidebars and boxes can be straight running text, a list, or a chart that is separated from the main body of the piece. These highlight additional information related to a story.

**Quotes:** Quotes can add a great deal of life and color to a piece, but they can also be overused, so place them cautiously. If a quote appears in quotation marks, the words should be exactly as the subject said them. (There is some controversy around this point, but some publications will allow you—and even encourage you—to "clean up" quotes by correcting grammar or slips of the tongue. Don't do this unless you know it's what the publication for which you're writing expects.) If a direct quotation is too unclear to be useful, feel free to paraphrase what a source said without quotation marks and with the attribution "according to [so-and-so]."

Ellipses in quotations represent words that have been removed. For example, "The squatter's camp near David's house is a tense and magical place," could be rendered as "The squatter's camp . . . is a tense and magical place." Words that are inserted for clarity must be offset by brackets. For example, "The squatter's camp near David's house [which the city is trying to tear down] is a tense and magical place."

## Sharing Your Draft

You should avoid agreeing to let a source read your story before it's been published. In most cases you'd be setting yourself up for a big headache. Sources frequently feel differently about things they said once they see their words in print. They may also want out of the piece altogether if they don't like the direction the article ended up taking.

## Rewriting Your Draft

You're done! Or are you? Take a step back from that draft and put yourself through a self-edit before you zip it to your editor. Giving your piece a closer look will undoubtedly result in some form of rewriting—and in a stronger story. Often you know the story has problems, and sometimes you even know what these problems are, but it's tough to figure out how to fix them. So how can you best do a strong revision?

- Start with an outline. Many first-draft problems are organizational ones. An outline can help. Instead of trying to rewrite the piece, pull out the main points and determine if they are being presented in the correct order. If they are not, shuffle things around in an outline form before you begin to rearrange entire paragraphs or sections.

- It may also be helpful to describe your entire article in two or three sentences. Brevity leads to clarity. Oftentimes writers have too many threads and need to simplify and focus on the basic tensions or themes of their stories.

- Try giving yourself distance. Attempt to finish an assignment a few days before it's due. Then go to a movie or out with friends and put your mind in a totally different place. Reread your work slowly aloud a few days later. You'll often see things you didn't in the triumphant moment of finishing the first draft of an assignment.

- If you are new to writing, you might want to show your work to a first reader before submitting it to your editor. Your first reader can be a friend, a spouse, or anyone whose opinion you trust and who will tell it to you straight. You don't want someone who will want to totally revamp your piece, but you do want someone who will point out glaring errors, typos, or sections that don't flow well or are not really clear.

- Because good reporting and accurate facts are the building blocks of a good story, a good revise often requires some rereporting. Don't be afraid to go back to your sources with follow-up questions. You'll be surprised at how many new questions reveal themselves in the process of writing and rewriting. You might not get to the juice of the story till you talk to the experts two or three times.

- Brainstorm. Think about what details, facts, or information could make the scene or the entire story richer. Then go back, find this information, and weave it into your piece.

## Fact-checking

Good writers strive to deliver error-free pieces. This means a draft free of grammatical, as well as factual, errors. The bigger the publication you are writing for, the greater the likelihood that it employs copy editors to catch grammatical errors and fact-checkers to catch factual mistakes. (Copy editors read over every word in a publication before it goes to print to ensure that it is error-free. They confirm that all the copy adheres to the publication's style guidelines, and they are the resident spelling, grammar, and style gurus. Copy editors at newspapers often do double duty as headline writers.) You can, and should, ask the publication if they have fact-checkers. Most magazines employ such people, whose job is to verify that every fact in your article is accurate. But even if there will be a fact-checker involved, you are still expected to deliver accurately reported articles. And if you don't, and a fact-checker discovers numerous errors, you probably won't be writing for that title again.

### Be your own fact-checker

Different publications have very different fact-checking standards, and different degrees of intensity in their fact-checking processes. Some magazines verify every fact in an article twice. Other publications check only numbers and dates. And still others go right to print, with no checking at all. You may be given a written set of "writer's guidelines," which tell you how that particular publication checks their articles, and what your editor expects you to deliver with

---

### BACKING UP . . .

"We usually don't receive annotated manuscripts from writers. The writers just usually provide backup by way of printed info, pertinent Web sites, and, of course, phone numbers of people quoted in the article (I prefer home, cell, and work)."

—*Ruth Manuel-Logan, research director*, Woman's Day *magazine*

---

your piece. For instance, some magazines require that you transcribe all of your interview notes and hand them in with your piece. Their fact-checker may just double-check your notes with your finished piece. In other cases, the fact-checker might not be interested in your

### WHAT CONSTITUTES GOOD BACKUP OR SUPPORTING MATERIAL?

- An annotated copy stating all sources used in reporting the story.
- Photocopies of all material referenced in the article, whether directly quoted or not.
- Photocopies of interview notes.
- The name, phone number, and e-mail address and a brief bio of every person interviewed.
- The all-important spellings of names. Always check and double-check the spellings of names. Sources are generally unforgiving if you misspell their names. And don't assume anything: Is it Jon or John? Ask. And confirm letters after names, too. She may be a doctor, but is she an MD or a PhD? Ask.
- Sources' birthdays. If you are including a subject's age in a piece, find out his exact birth date. Especially for a monthly magazine, it can take months for an article to appear in print, and if the subject's birthday falls in there, he will be a year older by the time the publication hits the newsstand.

(continued)

- Attributions. Make sure that all opinions appearing in your piece are attributed to someone. For example: "Blondes have more fun, according to John Smith, PhD, an expert on hair color's effect on personalities at Makeover University, in Beauty, West Virginia." Unless it's an editorial, make sure your opinion remains your own.

notes at all, and may call your sources to confirm all the information in the article attributed to that source, word for word.

Some publications will ask for an annotated copy of your article, although the practice may be fading. This means indicating on a draft where every bit of information in your piece comes from. They also may require that you submit your backup, which includes all your notes, interview tapes, copies of text from books, copies of material referenced on Web sites, and anything else that contributed to your piece.

Keeping good notes and records will not only help you if your editor has follow-up questions after you hand in your assignment, but will also cover you in case anyone takes issue with any of the facts published in your piece.

13

# The Path of a Story

As a freelancer, you may never see the inside of a magazine office. But what happens there certainly has an impact on the carefully crafted prose you submitted. Some of what goes on behind those closed doors makes perfect sense and is easily understood (as described below), but many times unexplained happenings leave you frustrated and confused: you hear nothing from your editor for a month or more and suddenly he calls needing revisions on your piece tomorrow! Or you hand in your great piece, and your editor flat-out rejects it, with no explanation. Below is the inside scoop on how your draft makes its way (or maybe doesn't) to the printed page of a magazine.

## Filing a Story

Find out ahead of time how your editor prefers to receive finished articles. Most now prefer you to simply send them in via e-mail (ask if it should be sent as an attachment or pasted into a document). Some editors want a hard copy sent via U.S. mail, along with all your backup materials. Plan accordingly. The editor should receive your finished piece on the due date in the form requested.

## Meeting the Deadline

This is a simple rule: meet your deadlines. Always meet your deadlines. If for some reason you can't make a due date, let your editor know as soon as possible. Editors value writers they can count on, so make sure you get your work done on time. If you can turn in your article early, that's great, but don't expect to hear back from your editor—or to be paid—any sooner.

---

### PLAYING NICE

"How to make yourself indispensable to cranky, moody editors: a lot of it is just being reliable. Don't blow your deadlines. Write the piece that you're assigned to write. Don't write your magnum opus, don't write your fiction piece—just do what you're asked to do. Keep open the lines of communication. There'll be times, especially if you're not going to make your deadline, when your editor will get cranky, but it's so much better for the editor to know [the piece is going to be late]. If you don't understand something, ask your editor. I know you might feel that you're being annoying, but it's really much better to get the terms of what she's looking for straight. If you don't understand what the editor is asking you to do, just ask very politely 'I'm sorry, it's not clear to me, could you explain it again?' And it's much easier to do that than to get sent the piece back for a rewrite, then for another rewrite, and another; you're both wasting time."

—*Former metropolismag.com editor Julie Taraska*

---

## Now What?

When you submit a story, ask your editor to confirm that she received your assignment. If you don't hear back, follow up. You don't want to be accused of missing a deadline if your opus got stuck in a spam filter or got inadvertently deleted or simply went wherever those pesky, never-seen-again e-mails sometimes go.

Assuming all goes well, you'll probably receive an e-mail like this soon after submitting your draft: "Got your piece. Thx. I probably won't be able to look it over for a few days. I'll get back to you."

Then the waiting game begins. In most cases, busy editors will not get back to you for a while. But stay on your toes, because when you do hear back, they might want a rewrite, or the answers to some follow-up questions, *right away.* Freelance writers complain about this all the time: they hear nothing for weeks (sometimes months) after handing in an article, and then suddenly the editor rises from the dead asking for the world—immediately! Expect this, and deal with it. Getting angry, or being uncooperative to an editor's demands (no matter how demanding they may seem), will do no good—and may very well prevent you from getting that next assignment.

## The Dreaded Rewrite

It's easy to view a request from an editor for a rewrite as rejection, or to take it personally. Don't. It's not. There's no use fretting. Every writer rewrites, even the best of the best. (In fact, the best of the best spend a lot of time rewriting before their editor even lays eyes on the first version, as we mentioned in Chapter 12.)

When asked to do a rewrite, don't expect it to be a quick fix. Sometimes articles need just minor tweaks, but some pieces need to be totally restructured, rereported in some sections, written with new nut grafs, or expanded or cut back. Editors look fondly on writers who have the courage and tenacity to truly overhaul a piece. If asked to do this, though, you will hopefully have some time. Follow the editor's instructions as closely as possible, whether she asks you to do more reporting,

## THE UNEXPLAINABLE "WOOING" THE EDITOR

You've been waiting to hear back from your editor about the piece that you really put your heart and soul into. You interviewed dozens and spent weeks fine-tuning every sentence so it flowed just right. Now you've heard nothing.

Finally you see the title of your piece pop up in your in-box. The message from your editor is short and not-so-sweet. "Your piece contained some interesting info, but we are unable to run it. We'll be sending you a kill fee. Thank you."

"That's it?" you want to scream. What are you going to tell all those experts to whom you promised copies of the article to frame? What are you going to tell your friends who have heard you going on and on about this story for months? What are you going to tell your landlord? You were counting on that BIG check to pay your rent.

Once you get over your initial shock, the question becomes, why? What was wrong with the piece that you were sure you hit out of the ballpark?

Kim Atkinson, former editor at *More* and *Boston* magazines, and now editor-in-chief at *Boston Common,* offers some insight into what might have happened.

**Q. A freelancer hands in what he assumes is a great piece, but the editors flat-out reject it, without an explanation. Can you give the freelancer some insight into what might have happened?**

A. While this seldom happens, it may occur if the story is just so plain bad it's unsalvageable. An editor might be so disgusted at the effort that she's not willing to even try to work with the writer. Lots of people think they're great writers, but not everyone is. A lot are really lazy reporters and might turn in something so thin it can't be used. Or maybe the editor-in-chief decides he no longer likes the story idea or wants the story to go with a different angle. In that case, it would be so much work to get the story going in the right direction that an editor might rather kill the story (and assign the newly positioned article to someone else) than put in the time and effort to get it right. So often these types of things happen during ship week or on the tightest of deadlines, and there simply isn't enough time to work with the writer to get the story to meet the needs of the magazine.

**Q. Why do editors sometimes take pieces and totally rewrite them without giving the freelancer the opportunity to rewrite?**

A. Again, time is always the issue. If a writer is slow and has completely missed the mark, a lot of times an editor may just decide it would be easier to take it into his own hands than send it back for revise. But tone is also important. It's up to a freelancer to not only write and report a good story, but to produce one that's right for the publication in which it's running. It's just plain lazy to write a piece without studying the publication and determining the voice and needs of the publication. As a freelancer, you're working for us, not the other way around. And you might think you're the best writer, with the best voice in the world, but at the end of the day, you're writing for our magazine, and we're paying you to do a job for us.

**Q. Have you ever had to lie to a writer?**

A. I've had editors-in-chief ban writers from the magazine for which I worked, for various reasons, but sometimes inexplicable ones. Sometimes they were writers I really liked and wanted to use, but was forbidden to. So I would have to tell the writer that we weren't using freelancers for a while, or our budgets were cut, to explain my inability to assign them work.

to change the structure, or to reconceptualize your piece. Remember that editors don't keep giving work to difficult writers. So be easy.

Also, be aware that some of the comments or questions your editor has for you may be coming from someone else. At many magazines, your assigning editor will do a first edit of your copy, make changes, ask questions, make marks where the writing is unclear or needs more work, and on and on. They may turn around and come back to you for a rewrite at that time. Or they may send along that marked-up copy to an editor above them in the magazine's hierarchy, such as the editor-in-chief. Editors-in-chief and executive editors (usually the second in command) seldom spend their time assigning stories to freelance writers, unless they work for a small publication.

## HOW NEWSPAPERS DIFFER FROM MAGS

The flow of your article at a newspaper is somewhat different from at a magazine. Below, David Hochman, who has been writing for more than a decade for newspapers and magazines, including the *New York Times, TV Guide, Forbes, Playboy, Esquire, Money, Entertainment Weekly,* and *Men's Journal,* comments on what it's like to freelance for a newspaper.

FEWER EDITORS
"With newspapers, I mainly work with an assigning editor until the last minute, when a copy editor and one or two of the higher-ups weigh in. Top editors only comment if they really, really like something or really, really hate something. It's usually better not hearing from them."

FEWER REVISIONS
"In most cases, newspapers edit far less than magazines. I rarely get pieces back for revision. Occasionally, I'll be asked to elaborate or go deeper on an aspect of the article but generally—and somewhat shockingly—the pieces publish as is."

LESS TURNAROUND TIME
"The turnover time in newspaperland is very fast. Often I write something on a Tuesday that ends up in Sunday's paper. If I'm writing for the week-day paper, I can turn a piece in on Monday and see it in Tuesday's edition."

RELATIVELY FASTER PAYMENT
"I usually get paid [for newspaper pieces] three or four weeks after a story runs."

BUT LOWER PAY
"Newspapers pay less than magazines."

For the most part these so-called top editors read over articles after the editor who assigned the piece has edited them. The other editors will add their comments and questions, which your editor would then bring back to you. (The editors' comments may even contradict one another. In most cases, editors will defer to the most senior editor's comments.) This can be a frustrating time for a writer, but take the high road and try to provide your editor with everything he needs. If there is a question that you simply can't track down the answer to, let your editor know. And if your editor seems to be taking your piece in a direction you don't like, voice your opinion gently. Perhaps your editor will see your point and agree. If not, decide whether you want to continue to work with this editor in the future.

When you do turn in your revised version, the process starts again, this time with the assigning editor most likely doing a more comprehensive edit to your piece. This top editing process can occur many times before an article makes it to its final form, and at any point in this process your editor may come back to you with questions.

## Art Meetings

Somewhere in this cycle, usually when editors are still fine-tuning the words in the article—and sometimes even before you turn in your draft—meetings will occur to discuss the design and layout of your piece. Prior to the meeting, the art director and/or designers of the publication get a copy of your manuscript. The art and editorial departments then get together and brainstorm. They discuss whether they need to set up a photo shoot for your piece, or whether stock art can be used, or if perhaps an illustrator should be hired to create some art to go along with your article. For the most part, a writer has little input into what art will run with her piece or how it will be laid out on a page. Of course, when you hand in your piece you can mention some ideas for art—if, for instance, you interviewed a prominent businessman who said he'd love to be photographed on his new ruby-red yacht, feel free to mention that to your editor. Some writers also like to send along pictures to go with the pieces they write. That's fine, but be aware, they very likely will not be used. However, you may be asked to provide the art department with contact information for the people in your article who will be photographed.

## Dummy Copy

When the art director, or a designer in the art department, designs the layout for your article, they usually do so with "dummy copy," which means the actual text of the article does not yet appear on the page. At this stage, the art department usually passes the layout by the assigning editor and the top editors to be sure everyone is relatively happy with how the pages look. Again, the writers are usually not included in this review.

## Headlines and Coverline Meetings

Somewhere in the mix, editors hold headline and coverline meetings. They are sometimes held at the same time, sometimes separately. In these meetings, editors brainstorm headlines for articles and ideas for teasers to appear on the cover of the magazine. Coverline meetings are vitally important to the magazine, as the coverlines need to be lively, creative, and intriguing in order to draw in the reader. While it varies from publication to publication, in most cases top editors are the main players at coverline meetings, midlevel editors are sometimes invited into these meetings when their stories are being discussed, and depending on the size of the staff, entry-level editors may or may not attend these meetings. Some magazines have freelance editors who come into the office just to help with writing headlines and coverlines. They are that important.

Once the headlines and coverlines are determined, this information is sent along to the art department so it can design the articles with the appropriate title in place, and so it can get working on designing the actual cover of an issue.

## Fact-checking

As we mentioned in Chapter 12, sometime during the editing process, the fact-checking department of a publication gets a copy of the article, along with all the backup material sent in by the writer. Some publications give this material to a research editor or fact-checker as soon as the writer turns it in, so fact-checking can start right away. Other publications wait till the article is fairly far along in the editing process, so that the fact-checker doesn't waste time checking any content that may be cut from the piece later on down the line.

As a writer, you should know you might get a call from a researcher working on your piece if he is unable to verify a quote or a fact or figure in your article. Fact-checkers usually work on tight deadlines, so if you get a call or an e-mail with a fact-checking question, get back to that person as soon as you can.

## Merging Copy

Once the layout of an article is completed, and the top editors have approved it, then someone on the magazine staff (often in the production department) will take your edited work and "flow" the text into the layout. This is called the merging of copy—basically the pictures and words are being merged together.

## Cut to Fit

After the text is merged into the layout, it goes back to the editor. Seldom do art departments design pages that fit exactly the number of words you wrote. So at this stage the editor must cut the copy to fit if it is running too long. Or she may have to fill content if the article is too short. Again, the editor usually does this work, but she may give you a call if she wants your input on what can be cut from the article, or if she needs further information to make the article longer.

Freelancers often complain that the beautiful 2,000-word piece they wrote was slaughtered down to, say, 800 words. Don't take your frustration out on your editor—chances are she didn't play a large role in determining the layout. And the editor is the one who had the tough job of cutting your piece in half. (And at least you got paid for 2,000 words!)

(If you feel strongly that your editor completely ignores your vision, changes your style, and destroys your work, the best strategy is to finish the story, get paid, and simply never work with her again.)

## Deks and Captions

After the copy is merged, the editors then write the deks, captions, and pull quotes (snappy quotes from the article highlighted in large type throughout the piece, to break up the text). Editors appreciate writers who suggest deks to go with their articles, but they're often changed to meet the needs of the publication. Writers seldom write the captions under pictures, since they are not usually privy to what pictures are actually appearing until the piece is printed.

## Copyediting

Far along in the process, an article will be handed over to a copy editor. This individual reads the entire piece very carefully, looking for errors of any kind, but especially for grammar, spelling, and style mistakes. Copy editors usually bring problems or mistakes to the attention of the assigning editor and do not contact writers directly.

## Galleys

Editors will sometimes say that a piece is "in galleys"—also called proofs. This means the text has been combined with the layout and the article is now looking like a sample page of the magazine or publication. This occurs sometimes before and sometimes after fact-checking and copyediting. At this point, a freelancer is sometimes allowed to take a look at her piece. If your editor offers, take the time to read your piece in this form. You can check for errors that others may have missed or mistakes that were introduced into the piece during the editing process. You may even find that your byline is misspelled. Just beware of suggesting any big changes when you see the piece in this form. It is probably pretty far along in the editing process, and major changes can be difficult.

## Last-Minute Changes

At any point before your article is shipped to the printing plant, last-minute changes can be made. Situations with advertising sometimes precipitate the altering of editorial copy. For instance, if an advertiser drops out, there may be a change in the size of the publication. Or a three-page article may suddenly need to become a four-page article to fill a void from a withdrawn ad, or vice versa if an ad comes in late.

In other cases, a fact-checker may find a glaring error in an article right before it is about to ship.

Sometimes top editors (some are notorious for doing this) will out-of-the-blue ask for a big change to a piece, right before it is set to be printed. If you get a panicked call from your editor, this could be what's happening.

## GETTING YOUR EDITOR TO COMMUNICATE BETTER

Editors are busy managing a stable of writers, multiple deadlines, and some-times multiple bosses with conflicting demands. They don't always focus long enough on one writer working on one assignment to give solid feed-back. Here are a few strategies for getting your editor to tell you what she really wants.

"Just try to engage him/her on the phone as much as possible and take notes. Sometimes I find that editors really just want you to write what they are saying so sometimes I just throw their words back at them. Another thing I might try, depending on the stage I'm in on the piece, is to do a de-tailed outline and let the editor take a look."

> —*Daryn Eller, who has written for many magazines including* Health, Natural Health, Parenting, Organic Style, Self, Fitness, O, Spafinder, *and* Prevention. *She has also authored, coauthored, and ghosted a total of eight books.*

"I keep asking questions until I'm sure I know what she wants. Sometimes I will offer to e-mail an outline of what I envision for the piece, so she has a chance to review it and make comments or changes. Also, as I write the piece I run ideas past her and ask for input and comments—I try to keep her in the loop as much as possible so that we're on the same page in the end."

> —*Jillian Lewis, a freelance writer in New York City who held staff positions at magazines in Sydney, Australia, and New York before launching into a life of flexible hours*

"I ask lots and lots of questions. If I still can't get a clear 'This is what I want,' I offer to flesh out a proposal. Sure, it takes time—but it'll be a lot less time (and a lot less aggravating) then overhauling the story in revise because you and the editor weren't on the same page while you were con-ceptualizing the piece."

> —*Nicci Micco, former staffer at* Self, More, *and* YM *and now a contributing edi-tor at* Self. *She also writes for* More, All You, Cooking Light, *and* Men's Health *from her home in Burlington, Vermont.*

## Final Read

Before going to press, all articles are given one last final read, by the assigning editor, and most likely by a few top editors, to be sure they are error-free. If any mistakes are found, the text is corrected, and the piece is sent around the office for another final read. This cycle continues until all editors sign off that the article is ready to be printed.

## Closing

On a certain date, the story will "close," which means that the galleys go to the printer and no further changes can be made. Several weeks after this date, the story will appear on newsstands. (The terms *close* and *ship* are often used interchangeably.)

## Shipping

Once the piece is entirely ready to go, it is shipped off to the printer. In the old days, this meant the page, looking exactly like it would appear in the publication, was put in an envelope and sent along to a printing facility. Of course, most of this is now done electronically.

In general, no changes to a piece can be made after it is shipped. If, for some reason, an error is discovered after this time, changes can sometimes be made, at a very high cost.

## Blues or Bluelines

Before the final print run of an issue happens, the printer sends the publication a full copy of the entire issue printed all in blue. It is folded to look almost exactly how the actual version of the magazine will look. The top editors and art director usually look it over for any

## GIVE ME MY MONEY!

"It's customary for publications to mail your check about thirty days after they receive your invoice, or in some cases, thirty days after publication of your article. If this doesn't happen, the very first step is to contact your assigning editor. Try sending a friendly reminder e-mail asking for a status update of the payment. Alternatively, you can call and ask her on the phone. Either way is appropriate. And, as always, be sure to communicate in a professional tone—without being combative or threatening.

"If for some reason your editor does not respond within a week, make a second attempt at contact. Sometimes a delay can be due to a vacation or illness, or perhaps she has been on deadline with other articles and didn't realize your payment was overdue.

"What do you do if you still get silence? Call the accounting department of the publication. Call the main switchboard of the publisher and ask to speak with the person in charge of processing payments to freelance writers. When you get this person on the phone, calmly explain your situation. Stay positive and proactive. The accounting person will be able to find out when the check is going to be issued. Or, you may even learn that your editor hasn't yet informed the accounting department to send your payment. Time to put in another call to your editor (or ask the accounting person to do it for you—or both). Usually, when an editor is made aware of the fact that a writer is making calls to accounts payable, the process gets kicked into high gear.

"That said, there may be situations when a tougher approach is necessary. If you happen to be hunting down a payment from a small publishing company that's in financial trouble, don't be surprised if even the accounting person puts you off. In this case, you might try saying something to your editor or the accounting person along the lines of 'I don't want to have to get my lawyer involved in this situation.' Chances are your check will appear in your mailbox soon after.

"The truth is, however, that more often than not, a delinquent payment is easily corrected. It usually takes one call to your editor to hear the words 'Your check's already in the mail!' "

—*Celeste Mitchell, former deputy editor of* Cosmopolitan *and senior features editor at* Family Circle, *writes for magazines and teaches magazine writing courses for mediabistro.com.*

mistakes or printing problems. This is the very last chance for changes (expensive ones) to be made.

## First Bound

A small batch of each issue is often printed before the real print run happens. These copies are sent to the staff of the publication. Your editor may send you one of those versions so you can see your piece before it appears on the newsstands or in subscribers' mailboxes.

## Payment

Depending on what your contract stated, freelancers are usually paid upon acceptance of an article or upon publication. As mentioned in an earlier chapter, these stated times can be hard to determine. *Upon acceptance* may be when a top editor signs off on your piece, or after the fact-checking department says your piece is good to go, or perhaps it's when the article is being shipped to the printer. *Upon publication* is just as iffy. Technically it should probably mean you get paid when the publication hits the newsstand or readers' mailboxes. But it is often sooner and sometimes later. The important thing is to keep track of your assignments, and follow up if you are not paid in a timely fashion.

## WHAT DO YOU DO WHEN . . .

### THE MAGAZINE IS GOING UNDER AND YOU HAVEN'T BEEN PAID

"This is always tricky. I have gotten left out in the cold before when this happens. Often, editors will try to hurry your payment so that you will get paid before it closes but that's only if they're still there. Sometimes you have to cut your losses and try to resell your piece."

> —*Daryn Eller, who has written for many magazines including* Health, Natural Health, Parenting, Organic Style, Self, Fitness, O, Spafinder, *and* Prevention. *She has also authored, coauthored, and ghosted a total of eight books.*

### YOUR EDITOR WANTS YOU TO ADD A SIDEBAR OR BOX TO YOUR PIECE BUT DOES NOT OFFER TO PAY YOU MORE

"If an editor wants more research or an extra sidebar, I just ask how much more they'll be able to pay for the added work. I like to start from the expectation that of course they'll pay more if they want more than the contract outlines. I learned this from an editor who volunteered to pay extra because he was asking me to do more research than originally expected. At the time, I hadn't even thought of asking for more. Most editors have been very cooperative about this. Now, if you just didn't get the assignment right or left holes in the story, that's a different situation."

> —*Sally Lehrman, who writes about health, medicine, and science policy for* Scientific American, Nature, Health, *the* Washington Post, *Salon.com, the DNA Files, and other publications and sites*

"I would first ask if the word count goes up and then see if I can get more money for the additional words. If I feel I'm on shaky ground (perhaps it's an editor I don't know very well, who's not very nice, or [I'm dealing with] a magazine I want to keep writing for), I may just cut my losses and write it. In addition, if it's a magazine that doesn't have a very big budget and I like the mag and the editor (and there's not a huge amount of work involved), I'll just keep quiet and do it."

> —*Daryn Eller*

"So many editor/writer questions are situation-specific. From an editor's point of view, the sidebar might involve nothing more than taking part of the story and putting a new lede on it. If the writer sees it as a new piece of work, he/she should say, 'I'd be glad to, what kind of payment are you offering.' Again, it depends [on the specific situation]."

> —*Steve Friedman has written for* GQ, Esquire, *the* New York Times, *and many other publications and is the author of two books. Some of his work is at Stevefriedman.net.*

"I do it happily. If it requires a lot of extra reporting, I might ask for a small extra fee. If it's compiling more of the research I've already gathered, I usually don't ask. I feel like these things always even out—and, as a former editor, I know that it's great to work with writers who are able to roll with story reinventions. If it happens repeatedly with the same editor, I'd probably ask. But often the editors acknowledge the 'pain in the butt' extra and repay you by assigning you more work."

> —*Nicci Micco, former staffer at* Self, More, *and* YM *and now a contributing editor at* Self. *She also writes for* More, All You, Cooking Light, *and* Men's Health *from her home in Burlington, Vermont.*

# 14

# How to Get Your Second, Third, and Three Hundredth Assignments

## Leverage Your Connections to Build a Career

- Build on connections. If you've worked with an editor once, keep in contact on a regular basis.
- After submitting an article, deliver more ideas soon after.
- Determine what an editor needs. Listen when editors talk about new columns or areas where they are always looking for more ideas.
- Take advantage when you're in good favor. If you've been assigned a few articles by the same editor or same publication, keep feeding him more ideas.
- Establish a beat. Write a few articles on the same subject and then begin billing yourself as an expert in that area.
- Be flexible. If asked to work on something new, take a stab at it. You never know.
- Network inside a publication. If you are working well with one editor, ask him to recommend you to editors in other departments at the same publication.

- Keep up with your editors regularly. Whether by phone or e-mail, remind editors that you're out there. Send them copies of recent clips.

- Brainstorm ideas with your editor. Set up lunch meetings, or even fifteen-minute phone meetings, with editors to discuss article ideas.

- Act before you're asked. If you hear about something new, approach your editor about tackling the topic.

- Fill voids. If an editor ever mentions needing help in any area, jump on the opportunity.

- Be in demand, or at least hint at it. Never simply ask an editor for some work. Busy writers get more work. When between assignments, pitch all you can.

PART V

# Mind Your Own
# Business

# 15

# Manage Your Finances

The great part of self-employment is the first half of the term: you report only to yourself. But perhaps the most important part is the second half: you're the employer, the boss, the one responsible for running the business. As we mentioned in Chapter 3, if you want to be successfully self-employed, you must be organized and keep good records. When you're embarking on a freelance career, you become your own bookkeeper, your own office manager, and your own secretary. Sure, you can hire other people to help you out with these tasks, but even they can't do much if you don't start them off with well-documented and properly arranged information. If you fail to make note of all your assignments and how much you are to be paid for them, your accountant will never know the difference if that check never comes. And you sure don't want to be working for free, do you?

Keeping good records on a very regular basis helps you to:

- Monitor your successes (and pinpoint those places where you are losing money).
- Be ahead of the game when tax time arrives.

* Save on taxes, especially when you keep track of all those deductible expenses.

## How to Stay Organized

Find a record-keeping system that works for you. Some freelancers jot down everything in a notebook; others have a few Excel spreadsheets that they constantly update, and some use computerized programs like FileMaker Pro, Access, Quicken, or Microsoft Money, which can do a lot of the work for you. It's important to tally your expenses and compare budgets from month to month or year to year. And remember, if you keep your budget information on a computer, back it up electronically (and print out a copy) regularly, just to be safe.

The most important things for freelancers to keep track of are due dates, expected payments, payments, and expenses.

A calendar hanging on your office wall or a datebook on your computer may be all you need to keep track of due dates. If you need reminders that you can't ignore, set up a calendar on your computer that dings every morning reminding you of upcoming deadlines.

Find a way to record when you hand in an article and when you expect payment. Even if this is a list in a notebook, refer to it often. If you haven't been paid by that expected date, it's time to call your assigning editor. Be just as on top of it when you do get a check in the mail. Make note of it right away, before you forget.

You also may want to keep track of your time, to help zero in on which assignments are actually earning you money. If you want to track exactly how much you are being paid for your time, work like a lawyer (there are even software programs that can help you do this!): keep track of every hour of every day. Then if you work on one article for two hours on a Wednesday, three hours on Thursday, eight hours on Friday, and so on, at the completion of a project you can add up all the hours you spent on that one article (include pitching time and time for revisions and sidebars and interviews). Divide the number of total hours spent on that piece by the total fee you were paid to come up with your hourly rate for that piece.

## Keep Track of Every Expense

Begin by dividing your expenses into two categories: one, those expenses that apply to your business generally and which you will deal with come tax time, and the other for expenses attached to a specific assignment. Some general expenses you'll want to remember in April are your mortgage or rent (some portion of which you can deduct as a home-office expense), your business phone, your office supplies, your computer, your Internet access, some travel expenses, magazine and newspaper subscriptions related to your work, and so on. (If you write on arts and culture topics, movie tickets, CD purchases, books, and maybe even your cable bill can be considered deductions.) Expenses associated with an assignment—for instance, long-distance phone calls made for an article, travel associated with the story, any postage expenses involved with the piece—will hopefully be reimbursed by the publication. If they're not, they're also deductible business expenses come tax time.

### General business expenses

Tallying your expenses is not something you should wait until tax time to do. Chances are, come April, you'll forget things. Better to be organized throughout the year, and input all of your expenses into a database at the end of each working day. At the very least, keep all receipts in a folder and at the end of each month take the time to log in every expense.

All sales slips, paid bills, invoices, pay stubs, receipts, deposit slips, and canceled checks should be kept in one central location. And even once they are entered into your database, keep these documents in order and in a safe place. You may still need to refer to them come tax time. They can be organized by month, or type of income, or kind of expense. Whatever system works for you is fine, as long as you can access what you need, when you need it.

### Expenses linked to a story

Keep track of all expenses while working on a story—even if it is 75 cents to park at a meter while interviewing a subject. And be sure you know the expense guidelines of any company that gives you an assignment. Most contracts with publications will state whether they cover writers' expenses and set a maximum amount the writer can spend without getting written approval for an expense ahead of time. For instance, the contract may say, "We cover all reasonable expenses up to $100. Any amount over $100 requires prior approval from your assigning editor."

Also, many publications require that you send them the original receipts—no photocopies or credit card statements allowed—when submitting your expenses. The exception to this rule is your phone bill. You can usually send in a photocopy of your home or cell phone bills, with the business calls highlighted.

Make sure you keep copies of all the receipts you do send in for reimbursement, just in case anything is lost in the mail, or in some black hole in a publications' accounting office, or in that other black hole on an editor's desk. Unfortunately, those black holes are very common.

Publications also often require that you submit expenses associated with a story within a certain number of days of handing in your story. Miss this deadline and you will be embarking on an uphill battle to get back the money you spent.

Also, be aware that some magazines have very fine, bordering on tedious, details when it comes to what you can and cannot expense.

---

### MONEY, MONEY, MONEY

"Submit your expenses. For mysterious reasons, many writers don't turn in any expenses. All the phone calls, photocopying, and other minor charges can add up to hundreds or even thousands of dollars a year."

—Backpacker *executive editor Peter Flax*

"When you're starting out, you're not going to find anyone who is going to want to give you $3,000 for a trip. But if you can find one story in Berlin about a bar, maybe you can get one magazine to pay for two nights at a hotel. Then from there, hopefully you can find a story in Berlin that you can sell to someone else, who will maybe pay extra because they're not paying for your expenses. You have to sort of strategically put together a whole trip. Ideally, you'll get one magazine who will pay for an entire trip where you write a 3,000-word story. But that probably won't happen; instead you just have to cobble it together and there may be trips where you end up spending more on expenses than you make back in writer's fees. If you go to these editors and say, 'Look, I'm going to bring this story from Berlin; can't you give me a few hundred dollars to cover meals?' there's some flexibility. Even if they can't cover your whole trip, they'll try to help you out."

—Condé Nast Traveler *contributing editor John Newton*

---

Some such rules might be:

- "You will not be reimbursed for gratuities above 20 percent."
- "When on overnight travel, breakfast and dinner expenses can be submitted for reimbursement. Lunch is not reimbursable unless it includes a meeting with a source."
- "The following items are not reimbursable: parking tickets,

dry-cleaning or pressing (except on fashion shoots), movie rentals, hairstyling, babysitting, personal expenses, office supplies."

But when putting together your expenses for a publication, don't go overboard. Remember, you want to write for this pub again (even if they don't pay for your scotch on the rocks at the end of a long day), especially if they continue to send you on trips!

### How long to keep records and receipts

This is always a tough question. According to the IRS, you must keep records that support any deductions you make for three years from the date you file the income tax return on which the deduction is claimed. A return filed early is considered filed on the due date. Also, always keep copies of your filed tax returns. You may need them in case of an audit, but they will also help you when preparing your returns in future years.

It's also a good idea to hang on to pay stubs, as well as other information that shows evidence of your work as a freelance writer, including copies of pitch letters and even rejection letters for three years. Then in case of an audit you can prove that you are indeed making your way as a working writer.

## Set Up a Business Account

Whether you're a full-time freelance writer or you just write on the side, you should open a business checking account, separate from your personal checking account. This way, all of your transactions related to writing will be in one place. This will help with recording your business expenses. Deposit all of your checks for freelance work into this account. Also, if possible, get a credit card or ATM card that is linked to this account. Then all business expenses can be paid for out of this account, rather than your personal account. Again, this

## FINDING AN ACCOUNTANT/LAWYER

"It is absolutely necessary for any business (even a sole proprietorship, which is a business owned and operated by one person) to have an attorney and an accountant. The best way to find an attorney or an accountant is through referrals. Find others who have started small businesses, call them up, and simply ask them. Many people have called or e-mailed me and offered to take me out to coffee to pick my brain. I've never turned them down.

"Most folks will be glad to share their experiences—we remember how hard it was to get going, so we're more than glad to help anyone coming up.

"You can also look online for CPAs or lawyers in your area (don't go with a law firm—their rates are way too high for any small business starting out). Call them up. Ask them if they specialize with companies in your situation. Meet them. And then go with your gut. Every accountant and lawyer is different. They will have intimate knowledge about your business and your personal finances, so you really have to feel comfortable with who you go with."

—*Duy Linh Tu, founder of Resolution Seven, LLC. Duy is a writer, videographer, motion graphics designer, and photographer and he teaches new media at the Columbia University Graduate School of Journalism.*

will make tax time go a whole lot more smoothly than if you have to spend all of March trying to remember which withdrawals from your personal account were related to your freelance work and which were not.

You might want to get your hands on a checkbook that gives you room to note the source of all deposits. You can then note which magazine paid you $1,200 and for what article.

Still keep track of all transactions in your log as well. When you receive your bank statement for your business account, you can double-check the information in your log—and you have a backup.

Use your business account for business-related purposes only. If you need cash from that account for other personal expenses, transfer it first to your personal account.

## Set Up a Budget

A surprising number of Americans keep no semblance of a budget. As a freelancer, you should have at least some way to keep track of what's coming in and what's going out—and how much you need to live on.

Start by figuring out what you currently spend. Compile all of your bills, bank statements, credit-card statements, and checks from the last year. Come up with an average of what you spend per month. Include rent/mortgage, phones, electricity, heat, television, food (including meals out), other necessities (such as toiletries and cleaning supplies), any loans, auto (or public transportation) expenses, insurance (health, homeowners, life), other medical expenses, accounting expenses, home-improvement expenses (include furniture and any sort of upkeep needs), clothing, travel expenses, entertainment and recreation, freelancing expenses (office supplies, memberships in organizations), gifts, and other miscellaneous expenses. And if you have children, don't forget all of the added expenses (child care, babysitting, lessons, classes, etc.) that go along with them. You should also include as an expense money you want to set aside for savings. You can also either include what you expect to pay in estimated taxes as an expense or deduct that out of your earnings when figuring your income.

Because some expenses—heating oil, for example—vary over the course of the year, tally how much you spend on that expense for the entire year, and then divide by twelve for a monthly estimate.

Then take a look at your income. This is where things get tricky for freelancers. Your income is not going to be consistent from month to month, and you always have to remember that Uncle Sam is going to take a large percentage of what you earn. (The percentage, of course, depends on your tax bracket and where you live.) If you've

---

### EBB AND FLOW

"There will be many, many, many slow times. The best advice is to save your money. One good month can be followed by six dry months. So, when you get that first big check, don't blow it all in one place. Also, don't give up in slow times. Use slow times to do things that you won't have a chance to do when you are busy, like writing marketing copy, getting your Web site going, setting up your office's file server. Every moment should be productive."

—*Duy Linh Tu*

---

been freelancing for a few years, you can probably make a rough estimate of what you'll be bringing in. If you're totally new to freelancing, make a modest guess about how much freelancing income you hope to make. Remember to include in your income any stock dividends, interest, trust funds, and the like.

Of course, you need to be sure that you can make enough money freelancing to cover your expenses; if not, make a plan to "bridge the gap" when times are tough.

## Easy Places to Save Money

As your mother always said, compare prices! For freelancers, this is hugely important when deciding on things like long-distance phone carriers and Internet service providers. Get the best deal you can. And stop paying for those extra cable channels you never watch. Consider package plans—maybe you can save money by getting your phone, Internet, and cable television all from one company. Also consider one of the new Internet telephone services, like Vonage (www.vonage), for your business calls.

## Q&A: FREELANCER FINANCE
## WITH HOWARD SAMUELS, CPA MST

*Howard Samuels, CPA MST, is the managing partner in S&C LLP, a NYC-based Certified Public Accounting firm specializing in tax for small businesses and individuals.*

**Q. How should a freelancer go about finding an accountant who specializes in working with freelancers?**

A. Generally, Internet portals (like mediabistro.com) provide some guidance and suggestions. Overall, the best way is really through referrals from other freelancers. You should also be sure the accountant is a CPA and has ample experience with other freelancers.

**Q. How often should a freelancer meet with her accountant? Just at tax time?**

A. You should have somewhat regular contact with your accountant during the year. If you are doing your own estimated taxes (or if your accountant has provided you with your quarterly estimates ahead of time), you should touch base a couple of times a year—even if it is just a quick e-mail.

Additionally, you should contact your accountant with any major changes in your life, such as marriage, children, buying or selling a residence, moving to a new state, and any other changes that you think might have some tax consequences. Better safe than sorry come tax time!

**Q. Is a freelancer a sole proprietor? What does that mean?**

A. A sole proprietor is an individual conducting a business without being incorporated and without operating as a separate legal entity. Basically, if you are a freelance writer and have not done anything fancy (like becoming incorporated or setting up a separate business entity), you are automatically a "sole proprietor." There is nothing to set up or do. Most freelance writers are sole proprietors.

The income and expenses of sole proprietors are reported on the individual's personal income tax return (Form 1040) and all taxes (income tax and Social Security tax) are paid with the individual's personal tax return. Generally, all expenses related to conducting this business are tax deductible, including home-office deductions for rent or mortgage and utilities assuming certain criteria for a "qualified home office" are met.

If an individual is conducting business on his own (meaning no taxes are taken out of the paychecks), and he is not set up as a separate legal entity, there is basically no choice but to be a sole proprietor.

**Q. Should a freelancer incorporate?**

A. This is a very confusing area. Basically, if your net profit (income less expenses) will be approximately $70,000 or more, you may be able to save some money by incorporating. Below this amount, it is generally not financially beneficial. However, instead of incorporating, you can become an LLC—actually you would be considered a "single member LLC" (*LLC* stands for limited liability company). There are *no* tax consequences to doing this other than a small annual filing fee (about $50 to $100). As a single-member LLC, there is some additional liability protection. Freelancers should consult an attorney, not an accountant, regarding this liability protection.

It generally is not worth the price difference to incorporate in a less-expensive state like Delaware or Nevada. The price difference is not that great financially. The simplest way to go is to incorporate in the state you do the majority of your business. If you incorporate in another state, there are still annual filing fees and reports that have to be filed in the state of incorporation as well as in the state you do business. This can become quite tedious.

See if you can save by paying some bills annually rather than monthly—this is often the case with health insurance, homeowner's insurance premiums, or dues to associations. Magazines have discounts on subscriptions if you sign on for two years or more—and subscriptions are always far cheaper than buying magazines off the newsstands.

Remember that you don't need to buy every new gadget meant to make your life easier, even in your work life. And take care of the things that you already have. Take precautions so you don't spill water or coffee on your laptop—and use surge protectors.

Also take advantage of the fact that you have a flexible schedule. It may just save you money. For instance, go on vacation off-season, when nobody else has time off. Rates will be lower and you'll avoid the crowds, too. Or take off for a spa for two days during the week, and make up for it by working some other weekend—rates are almost always lower on Mondays and Tuesdays than on Fridays and Saturdays. You can even join gyms and pay the discounted membership for going at odd hours. Hey, you're a freelancer; you can work from 6 till 10 in the morning and then go to the gym from 10:30 to 11:30.

## Plan for Retirement

Freelanceers aren't known for being the most financial-savvy bunch, but there are some things that it pays to prepare in advance for—such as retirement. Yes, it may seem like a way-off thing, but start saving now, and you'll be thankful you did in the future.

The best way to prepare is to think of retirement savings as any other expense, and put away a certain amount every week or every month, or perhaps a certain percentage of every check you get.

When you work for a big company and want to put aside some money for retirement, they do it all for you—setting up a 401k and taking dollars from your paycheck before you have time to miss them. While it may be a challenge, you need to do the same for yourself. For, as you know, the earlier you start saving and investing, the more time your money has to grow. Here's a quick rundown of some ways freelancers can save for the golden years.

* Individual retirement accounts (IRAs): Putting money into a tax-deferred savings program such as an IRA will help your savings

grow more quickly. While you are not taxed when you invest your money, you will be taxed when you make withdrawals.

- Simplified employee pension plans (SEPs or SEP-IRA): Popular with the self-employed, these are easy and relatively inexpensive to open and have fairly flexible contribution rules. So, basically, you can contribute a large chunk of cash one year (around 25 percent of your income), and, if your well is running dry, not as much the following year.
- Keogh plans: A bit more complicated, and perhaps more costly to set up than SEPs, Keogh plans permit contributions of about 25 percent of your income. And that's tax deductible. Upon retirement you get a set annual income from the plan.
- Roth IRAs: Yet another way to save for retirement, Roth IRAs allow you to put away $3,000 ($6,000 if you are married) per year toward retirement. These plans are after-tax dollars, so you do not get taxed when you take the money out after you retire.
- Stocks and bonds: If you are willing to take on some more risk, stocks and bonds may be the way to go. Although stocks are more volatile, the potential for making more money is greater. Lower growth bonds are more stable.

Indeed, you are a writer, and not an accountant, but if you don't take an active role in your finances, chances are your freelance career will be short-lived. You don't need to sign up for an Economy 101 class, but staying on top of where your money is and where your next check is coming from will allow you to succeed in the world of the independently employed.

# 16

# Affordable Health Insurance

Unfortunately for freelancers, affordable, independent health insurance simply does not exist—the only great option is to ride on the handlebars of your significant other's company plan. Indeed, because there are so few good options, and because health plans can be so expensive, many freelancers and other self-employed workers end up simply going without. But that's a very risky move—what happens when that cab you're riding in veers off the street and into a parking meter, or you find that strange lump, or your tooth begins to ache, or you become the cliché and actually do slip on a darn banana peel? Without coverage, one little accident or problem can mushroom into a major financial crisis.

So what are your options for getting insured?

## Join an Association

Because the price of insurance for just one person is usually sky high—if such an option is even offered by an insurance company in your area—you should consider joining an association that offers members the opportunity to buy into health insurance at a group rate. Mediabistro.com's AvantGuild program, for example, offers members access to a group plan. (See Resources for other writers organizations.) To purchase insurance through a professional association, you typically have to pay membership dues to the group—but remember that those dues are tax deductions (as are your insurance premiums). Some groups even require you to join before you can investigate the health insurance plans they offer. (At mediabistro.com, you must be an AvantGuild member to get insurance, but we're happy to tell you about plans and benefits before you join.) Of course, insurance through an association will be like any other health insurance—it may not be available in all parts of the country, it may not be as comprehensive as you'd like, and your existing doctors may not participate in the plans. These inconveniences, unfortunately, are realities for everyone in the current health-insurance climate.

Because freelancers foot the entire bill for their health insurance, some who are young and healthy may instead want to consider purchasing so-called catastrophic health insurance. Such plans are less expensive, but they typically have high deductibles. And, for the most part, they're only useful if you are hit by a truck or develop cancer. Payment for an exam when you have a sore throat will have to come out of your pocket.

## Company Ties

If you were recently laid off, or if you chose to leave your job to take up freelancing full-time, you're likely eligible to extend your coverage with your former employer's health-insurance carrier under COBRA. You'll have to stay on the exact same plan you had as an employee (no bumping down to the less-expensive plan that you didn't pick when you paid only a small portion of its cost), and you'll be charged the same amount your company paid for you (including any contribution you were required to make). You can remain on a COBRA plan for only eighteen months, and then you need to find your own coverage. Because you're keeping the same coverage you had as an employee, COBRA plans usually offer better coverage than what's available through associations, but they also usually have higher premiums.

## Help from Uncle Sam

Yes, there are government-subsidized insurance programs. But they're probably not right for you. You qualify only if you are making below a certain income (usually around $25,000), and you may not qualify unless you've been without insurance for a period of time. Visit www.govbenefits.gov for more information.

## Homeowner's Insurance

Hopefully you already have renter's or homeowner's insurance. Now that you're working from home—or if you have a part-time home office—you'll want to make sure you're covered, and covered adequately. Most basic homeowners policies cover only a few thousand dollars worth of home-office equipment. Ask an insurance agent what would be best for you, depending on your specific needs. There are deals that cover the loss of equipment both at home and on the road (say, if something happens to your laptop when you are traveling for a story), and some may provide protection help if the FedEx man—or a source, or a friend stopping by for a morning coffee break—slips on ice outside your front door.

# 17

# Taming Your Taxes

Tax Time Is Very Different for Freelancers
Than for Employees

Yes, yes, yes; the two things you can count on in life are death and taxes. But if you handle things right—even as a freelancer, whose tax returns are infinitely more involved than a regular old salaried employee's—tax time doesn't have to feel like a near-death experience. In fact, if you develop a plan, and follow that plan, and save and organize all your records during the course of the year, paying taxes can even be a life-affirming experience. Well, almost.

The reason tax time is so harrowing for most self-employed folks is that they've been receiving freelance fees all year, but, unlike regular biweekly paychecks, nothing has been withheld on these payments. At a salaried job, if withholdings are handled correctly, you've paid the government most—if not even a little more—of what you owe during the course of the year, leaving only a small payment, or perhaps a refund, in April. For a freelancer, however, at tax time suddenly everything's due. And as painful as it is to write a big check to Uncle Sam, it can be even worse if the money's already been spent.

Don't let that happen to you. Make sure you're ready for tax time, and ready to pay the government what you owe.

## Planning Ahead: Estimated Taxes

If you freelance full-time, or even if you're doing it only part-time but will owe more than $1,000 in tax from your freelance work, you have no choice but to plan ahead—and pay the government quarterly. Estimated taxes are due in April, June, September, and January. Failure to do so will result in penalty payments. It's a good idea to open a separate bank account strictly to set aside money for tax payments. Deposit a third of each freelance check you receive into that account. While that kind of financial discipline can be hard, it will make your life easier in the long run and will ensure that you won't be socked with your entire tax bill come April. Plus, you can look at it this way: that extra money really doesn't belong to you in the first place. If you were on staff someplace, that third would have been withheld by your employer; it never would have hit your checking account. It can help to fool yourself into believing the same about one-third of every freelancing check you get. (Setting aside a third of your pay for taxes is obviously just a rough estimate. The amount you'll actually owe depends on your state, your tax bracket, your deductions, and more. It is typically somewhere between 20 and 35 percent of your untaxed income.)

You should also continually keep track of how much you are paid by each different publishing company you work for. At the end of the year, you should have a running tally of checks from each company, and that total should match what the company reports to the IRS (and to you) on a 1099 form. (A 1099 is the freelancer's equivalent of the W2 forms employees receive. Companies are required to send a 1099 only if they pay you more than $600 in one year, although some companies will issue them for smaller amounts, too.) Double-check and make sure your 1099 is correct, because you don't want to be taxed for work you didn't do or paychecks you never received.

## Q&A: FREELANCER TAXES
## WITH HOWARD SAMUELS, CPA MST

*Howard Samuels, CPA MST, is the managing partner in S&C LLP, a NYC-based Certified Public Accounting firm specializing in tax for small businesses and individuals.*

**Q. Who must pay estimated taxes?**
A. Generally, anyone who receives income with no taxes taken out. The tax law says you have to pay tax on income as you earn it. The government has set up four quarterly dates to do this during the year. If you make below a certain amount of money (generally around $2,000), you may not need to pay them. However, everyone has other financial matters in their lives and you should be sure to consult with an accountant to determine if you need to pay estimated taxes or not.

**Q. In general terms, how much must a freelancer pay in estimated taxes?**
A. Generally, anywhere from 20 percent to 35 percent of the money earned is going to go to taxes. This is just a safe guideline. Again, everyone is different depending on other financial matters in their lives.

**Q. Do freelancers need to put more into Social Security than they would if they're employed—because when you're employed your employer puts in some for you?**
A. Yes. That is correct. As a self-employed person, you pay all the Social Security tax. When you are an employee, the employer pays half of it on your behalf.

## Choose the Right Accountant

Even if you are a numbers person, and are smart enough to file your taxes on your own, it's a good idea to talk with an accountant if you are now filing as a freelancer. Accountants who specialize in working with self-employed clients, and those who work specifically with writers, know the ropes. Most can even guarantee they will find places where you can make changes—a new way to write off something here, or depreciate something there—to keep more of those hard-earned dollars. Ask other writers in your area if they know a good accountant who specializes in freelancers. Failing that, check the yellow pages, looking for an accountant who has expertise in working with the self-employed.

## What You Can and Can't Write Off

Always check with your accountant for a final verdict on what can and can't be taken as deductions—tax laws are always changing, and tax professionals are the best sources on current regulations. But here are some general guidelines on the sorts of things that can be taken as deductions.

**Home office:** If you work "regularly and exclusively," as defined by the IRS, in your home, apartment, condominium, mobile home, boat, garage, studio, barn, or greenhouse in your backyard, you can write off a portion of your living expenses. You may be able to deduct part of your mortgage payment and real estate tax. If you rent your residence, you can deduct a portion of your monthly rent.

How much you deduct for your home office depends on the percentage of your home that you use for business. To figure that out, compare the portion of your home that you use for your writing to your entire residence. So, let's say your office is 12 feet by 20 feet, or 240 square feet. If your home or apartment is 1,200 square feet in total, then your office is 20 percent of the total area of your home. When it comes time to pay taxes, you can write off that 20 percent from your deductible mortgage interest and real estate taxes if you own your own home. (Anyone who itemizes deductions can make this deduction, which helps save on income tax as well as on Social Security tax if you deduct these costs against your freelance income.) You can also deduct that same percentage from any bills you paid that year for repairs, maintenance, or insurance on your residence. Let's say your furnace needed replacement. Purchasing that new furnace benefited the entire home, including your office space. So if you use 20 percent of your home for your work, you can deduct 20 percent of the cost of the new furnace at tax time. A percentage of a security system can also be deducted.

Expenses for utilities and services, such as electricity, gas, trash removal, and cleaning services, usually are considered personal expenses, but you can again deduct that 20 percent as a business percentage. (Be careful, though. A cleaning service, for example, could be questionable if you never have clients in your home.) Do you pay gratuities to your doorman? You might be able to deduct a portion of that, too.

It is important to be sure that your gross income (from the business you run out of your home) equals or exceeds your total business expenses. If not, your deduction for certain expenses for that business use of your home is limited.

**Phone:** The basic local telephone service charge, including taxes, for the first telephone line into your home is considered personal and therefore is not deductible. However, charges for business long-distance phone calls on that line, as well as the cost of a second line into your home used exclusively for business, are deductible business expenses. You can also deduct a percentage of your cell phone costs—the percentage related to your freelancing. This may be hard to determine if you pay just one monthly rate. But if you were to get audited by the IRS, they would ask to see some reasonable method as to how you determined how much of your cell phone use was business related. Ideally, you would want to identify each business call and deduct this amount. However, if your calls are not listed on the bill, you should try to keep some kind of log as to all of your calls and find the percentage of business calls, or you may be able to request that your cell phone company provide you with a list of calls.

**Computer:** Things like computers get a little tricky. Do you use your computer solely for your work, or is it also used for your personal e-mail and your children's homework? You should probably talk to an accountant about what you can and cannot deduct when it comes to computers, PDAs, TVs, VCRs, DVD players, stereos, and so on.

**Supplies:** Keep track of everything you buy for your office: pens, pencils, printer paper, printer cartridges, computer supplies, computer software, file folders, pencil sharpeners, stamps, everything. You can write it all off.

**Postage:** Mailing anything to an editor, client, or subject of a story can be deducted as a business expense, so keep track of any money spent on postage, FedEx, or messengers, and the like.

**Health and dental insurance:** In some cases, you can write off a portion of your health insurance premiums. Check with your accountant.

**Expenses tied to an assignment:** Any expenses that you submit to a publication and are reimbursed for cannot also be deducted from your taxes. So be sure you keep track of which expenses are covered. If the magazine didn't reimburse you for costs incurred while working on an assignment, then they're deductible business expenses on your taxes. Also, be sure to check the 1099 forms you receive at the end of the year. If the total listed there included expense reimbursements, it means you were taxed for that reimbursement as though it was income, and you can therefore write off those expenses.

**Furniture and other large items:** If you purchase large, very costly items for your business that you will continue to use for years, you generally cannot deduct the entire cost the year you buy it. Depreciation is when you spread the cost of the item out over more than one year and deduct part of it each year. Some people depreciate computers, copiers, furniture, and other big-ticket items used in their business. Talk with your accountant about what to depreciate.

**Car:** Using your car is not as simple as writing off all your gas and tolls. Instead, depending on how much you use your car for work, you can write off a percentage of all costs related to your vehicle, or write off a standard mileage rate for use related to business travel. In 2005 you could write off 44.5 cents a mile for all business miles. So keep track of how many miles you pile up driving to and from assignments, meetings with editors, and the like.

**Meals:** For the most part, meals should be paid for out of your own pocket and not deducted on your taxes; the exceptions are when you're conducting business during a meal and when you are traveling for an assignment. Basically, if you are in your own hometown, you can deduct 50 percent of a meal if it is directly related to your work; for instance, if you are interviewing a subject for a story or meeting with an editor about a possible assignment. So keep track of meals and who you ate with. If you are traveling for a story (and a publication is not paying your expenses on the trip), you can write off half your dining costs. If you don't make note of how much you spent on food on a trip, you can use a standard meal deduction set up by the government. It ranges from about $30 to $55 depending on where your travel takes you.

**Travel:** If you take a trip that results in a story, even if it wasn't with a specific assignment, you may be able to write it off so long as the costs weren't already reimbursed by the company that bought your story. So keep track of what you spend on your trips—on transportation, lodging costs, meals, telephone calls, rental cars, gas, parking. Trips to meet with editors and clients can also be deducted.

**Magazines and newspapers:** If you write for magazines and newspapers and use them for research and story ideas, you can by all means write off your subscriptions. Depending on your "beat," you may be able to also write off your cable television bill, Internet service fees, movie tickets, CD and DVD purchases, and more.

**Classes/memberships:** Memberships in professional organizations are also tax deductible. So, too, are any classes you take or seminars you attend.

**Investments:** Some contributions to retirement plans can be deducted. See Chapter 15.

**Marketing costs:** Many of the start-up costs of a freelance writing business are tax deductible. Setting up a Web site, producing business cards and stationery, sending out clips, putting together a résumé—all of these things are deductions. You can even buy your editors small gifts and write off the cost.

**Professional fees:** You may be able to deduct legal and accounting fees that result from your self-employment.

## Business Versus Hobby

Before you start deducting everything you can, you need to be sure of one thing: your writing must be a business, not just a hobby. It may seem silly, but the federal government has long had rules that do not allow individuals to deduct for losses on an activity that is a hobby.

So how is this distinction between *business* and *hobby* made? For your writing to constitute a business, you need to have made a net profit in three of the last five years. If you've just started freelancing full-time, then perhaps you'll have a loss in your first few years. But after a couple of years, don't expect to get away with it if you write off $20,000 in expenses (for your new computer, a third of your rent, and fancy pens), if you're only making $12,000 on writing gigs.

## Avoid an Audit

Unfortunately, the fact that you have a home office could be a red flag for the IRS. While there's no reason to live in fear, you should be aware. There are a few things you can do to avoid any unnecessary attention from the feds.

First, be as consistent as possible in your filing from year to year. Obviously, if you made a great deal more this year than last, terrific, don't lie about that! But continually claim the same career: don't say you're a writer one year, a bike courier the next, and a fact-checker the third. Your deductions should also not vary too much from year to year.

Be sure that your earnings reports are the same between your federal and state returns. Avoid listing lots of round numbers, especially on deductions. If you say you spent $3,000 dining with editors last year, that may be rather hard to swallow. Also, don't report huge contributions to charities when your income just wouldn't support it.

Finally, make sure you make a net profit in at least three of every five years, or the IRS may come calling.

18

# Invest More in Yourself

## Bring Your Business to the Next Level

When you're starting to feel established as a freelance writer—you're happy with the venues you're writing for, you're okay with the money you're bringing in, you have relationships with editors and sources and find you have to struggle a little less to successfully get assignments—now's the time to reinvest in your career and take things up a notch.

### First, Update Your Office

Get that great new office chair. You'll be amazed at how productive you'll be if you don't have to stand up every five minutes to stretch your aching back or adjust that pillow you're sitting on.

Splurge for the big monitor for your computer. Here's betting you'll get more done in a day when you don't have to constantly squint or stop working to rest those tired eyes.

You may even want to buy a small-business software package that will manage all of your expenses and payments. You deserve it, and it will probably pay for itself in the time you save by not having to do all those little calculations on your own.

## Additional Help

Writers have a hard time giving up control. It makes sense. Your name appears on most everything you write, and so you want to have complete say over what appears on the printed page. But that doesn't really mean you have to do everything yourself. As your freelance writing business grows, it may be time to invest in additional help. Hiring a bookkeeper or an assistant, or bringing in a college intern to help with research and organization, may be all you need to ease your workload, allowing you more time to focus on pitching stories or actually writing.

If you live near a college or university with a journalism program, you most likely will have students jumping at the chance to work with an established writer. Interns or assistants can take care of the everyday paperwork—keeping track of expenses, payments for stories, and copies of contracts as well as helping with background research for stories, setting up interviews, and even pitching markets that might be interested in reprints of your work. If you're working with college interns, consider letting them write any sidebars or boxes that will run with your piece. Check with your editor to be sure, but most will be fine giving a byline to your sidekick.

---

### FREELANCER'S HELP

"I've paid college students to transcribe interviews. I pay them well—because transcribing stinks—and it's still worth it because it takes so much time. Since I write mostly health stories and the interviews can be technical (even if the finished pieces are not), I can't trust just anyone to do this. (My helpers were majoring in nutrition and speech pathology—so they knew the lingo.) If you can find someone reliable, do it."

—*Nicci Micco, former staffer at* Self, More, *and* YM *and now a contributing editor at* Self. *She also writes for* More, All You, Cooking Light, *and* Men's Health *from her home in Burlington, Vermont.*

(continued)

"Years and years and years ago, when I was working at the *New York Times*, some college student came to interview me about being a journalist. At the end of the interview, I turned the tables on him and started asking him about j-school and what it was like. I learned that journalism schools have a great need to place their students in internships. So I started using them. Since then I always have at least one intern, and it really makes so much difference. But, the big problem with interns is that they leave. Just when you've got them trained, and they're broken in and they're on the same page as you, they leave. So at some point I was in a position where I had the money to pay them, fortunately, so I could get them to stay longer. I've been fortunate enough that I've had a couple of interns who stayed with me for a year, even a year and a half. I'm still in touch with lots of them, I consider them friends, and I'm always so excited to see them go on to get great jobs—at *Condé Nast, Fox News,* wherever. Many will stay with me throughout the course of a book project—one was just with me through the *740 Park* book, and will be staying on to help with my next book project. For the *740 Park* project, there was research I needed in Oklahoma and Texas. So I would go online and find the local j-school, and just start e-mailing professors at random until I found the one in charge of the internship program. Then I'd get a local intern to help me with the research out there—these are purely online relationships, some of them I haven't even met, but they are very helpful. At one point, there were two Arab gentlemen living in 740 Park, and so I needed someone who could read and speak Arabic. So I posted a note on the NYU listserv, and actually got hooked up with a young lady who is an opera singer. She turned out to be absolutely invaluable. Not only could she translate Arabic, but she could also find people for me to interview and make those connections and create all these relationships in a world where I was otherwise lost at sea. Whatever gene that would have somebody teaching in a j-school I've got, only I do it one-on-one."

—*Michael Gross, a contributing editor of* Travel + Leisure *and a contributing writer at* Radar. *His latest book is* 740 Park.

## Meet with Editors

You've e-mailed with them and chatted with them over the phone; now's the time to meet your editors in person. If you live nearby, ask an editor to meet for coffee, a drink, or lunch. Get to know them socially a bit—it'll give you a chance to bounce possible ideas off them and to get a better understanding of the kinds of stories they're looking for.

If the publications you write for are out of town, plan a whirlwind trip to mingle with your editors. Hey, you can write it all off. Let your editors know well in advance that you'll be in town, so you can get on their schedule. Even if they have time only for you to stop by the office for a quick hello—and be sure not to overstay your welcome—it will be well worth it. Nothing beats putting a face with a name.

### FACE-TO-FACE

"We have begun holding occasional meetings with freelancers, and hope to do that more often. It's valuable for us to see them face-to-face, to tell them what we're looking for, and for them to meet each other and talk and discuss ideas. The writers feel like the magazine is theirs if we include them in occasional lunches, and hopefully they will pitch us when they have great ideas."

—*Doug Most, editor,* Boston Globe Sunday Magazine

"If it's a writer that's demonstrated a knowledge of the material—and has good clips—I'll definitely meet face-to-face. I don't expect it to be a pitch session, but more of a feeler-outer."

—*Nina Willdorf, a senior editor at* Budget Travel *magazine and the author of* Wedding Chic: The Savvy Bride's Guide to Getting More While Spending Less *and* City Chic: An Urban Girl's Guide to Livin' Large on Less

## Bumping Up a Presence on the Web: Blogs and More

As you've probably discovered by now, having a Web site can certainly give you a leg up on the competition. While a Web site is a good tool to exhibit published clips to editors, potential sources, and PR people, it can serve many other purposes for writers as well. Your Web site might include your résumé and some testimonials from people familiar with your work. Testimonials are easy to acquire. Simply ask editors who you've worked with in the past if they are willing to write one or two sentences about your writing skills or about how it is to work with you. If you teach a writing class, ask your students to comment on your teaching skills. And, of course, ask these people if it is okay for you to post their comments on your site.

One section of your site may be for other freelance writers, including links to media organizations or journalism groups you belong to or are associated with. You can then ask for links to your site in return. Any time you do some writing for a Web site, ask if they can include a link to your site. Any new traffic could lead to more work for you.

You can even add a blog, giving people more of a reason to visit your site. Blogs are places where you can write about what you want to write about and exhibit your writing talents without having an assignment from a publisher. If you have some expertise, a blog is a great way to demonstrate it. For example, if you've desperately wanted to build a career covering the video-game business, you may want to start a blog on which you write about video games, illustrating that you are informed and articulate on the topic. If your work is well crafted and interesting, you'll start to attract more traffic and thus help promote your career.

Blogs can also be good for networking, in that they can be a means to connect with other writers and editors. You may start developing links between your sites and others, increasing traffic to your blog, and therefore increasing your visibility.

In addition, a few people out there are now getting paid for blogging. Some online magazines and Web logs have freelance contributors and editors who are paid a weekly or monthly fee to produce a number of posts each day. If your own blog gets enough traffic, you can make some real money selling advertising on it.

Another argument for blogging is that it's simply a great way to "sharpen your writing chops." The more copy you produce, the better your copy will get.

If you're really good—if you have a sharp voice and produce well-turned prose—blogs can help make your career. More than a few people have been offered paid writing gigs based upon their blog work.

19

# Boost Your Bucks

Strategies for Increasing Your Income

When a freelance writer talks about her goals, you'll hear mention of a certain publication she wants to break into, or a number of pieces she hopes to write in a month, or the number of words she hopes she can achieve in a week. But when you pin down that freelancer, ask her what she really wants to accomplish in the next year, it often comes down to nuts and bolts: she wants to increase her income. Of course, it would seem like a freelancer can always earn more by writing more, but at some point that becomes impossible. When you're working hard and efficiently but not making as much as you'd like, it's time to start working toward better pay rates.

## Know What You're Worth

Some freelancers brag that they won't accept any assignments for less than $2 per word. That sounds great, especially if they're churning out 2,000-word pieces, or bigger, on a regular basis. But ask those same writers how much they make per hour, and you're likely to get a blank look in return. Writers seldom think of their payment in terms of dollars per hour, but they should.

If that 2,000-word, $4,000 assignment takes two days of digging for backup materials, one day to track down and interview the eight

## HOW MUCH ARE WRITERS BEING PAID?

The short answer is . . . there's no one answer. Write for one publication and you may be paid 10 cents per word; another may offer up to $3 per word. A variety of factors are in play, from the publication's scale to the work involved to the kind of piece to the writer in question. Here's what a variety of publications have told mediabistro.com (in the "How to Pitch" section) they typically pay their freelancers.

SMALL-CIRCULATION NEWSPAPERS (VARIABLE—SOME PAY BY THE WORD, OTHERS JUST A PER-PIECE FEE)
- The *Queens Chronicle:* $25 per story. If you submit photos, too, you may receive an additional $5 per photo printed.
- The *Village Voice:* Varies, but new freelancers reportedly receive $175 for a quarter of a page and $500 for a full page.

LARGE-CIRCULATION NEWSPAPERS (AT BIGGER PAPERS, AS WELL, SOME PAY BY WORD AND SOME HAVE SET FEES FOR DIFFERENT TYPES OF PIECES)
- The *Boston Globe Sunday Magazine:* Varies. The starting rate for front-of-book pieces is never less than 50 cents a word and other pieces go up from there.
- *Chicago Tribune:* About $225 for a 500- to 700-word piece and anywhere from $300 to $500 for a cover story.
- The *Wall Street Journal:* About $1 per word.
- *The Washington Post Magazine:* Varies depending on the experience of the writer and the amount of reporting that goes into the piece, but never less than 50 cents a word. A cover story, on average, will get $4,500 and second features run anywhere from $1,500 to $2,500.

LARGE-CIRCULATION NATIONAL MAGAZINES (TYPICALLY $1 A WORD OR MORE)
- *Business 2.0:* Varies, but freelancers report receiving at least $1 to $2 per word.
- *Child:* $1.50 a word and up.
- *Elle:* $1.50 a word; some writers have negotiated higher rates.
- *Health:* Varies, but the minimum is $1.50 a word.
- *Mad:* $500 per page.

(continued)

- *Metropolitan Home:* Anywhere from $1 to $3 per word depending on the difficulty of the task and whether it originates with the writer or with *Met Home.*
- *Modern Bride:* $1 per word and up, depending on the amount of reporting and the experience of the writer.
- *Newsweek:* "Tip Sheet" starts writers at $150 to $300 per item; "My Turn" pays a $1,000 flat fee.
- *Outside:* About $1.50 a word.
- *Popular Mechanics:* At least $1 per word.
- *Premiere:* $1 per word.
- *Rolling Stone:* Varies, but for features and "National Affairs," $2 a word.
- *Self:* Features generally start at $2 per word for writers the magazine has worked with before; other pieces start at $1.50.
- *Shop Etc.:* $1.30 to $1.50 per word, depending on complexity and turnaround time.
- *Spin:* $1.00 per word, though the rate can be higher depending on the complexity of the assignment.
- *Teen People:* $1 per word.
- *Travel + Leisure:* Varies, but at least $1 a word.
- *Yoga Journal:* 75 cents to $1.00 per word.

SMALLER-CIRCULATION MAGAZINES AND CITY MAGAZINES
(TYPICALLY ABOUT 50 CENTS TO $1 A WORD)
- *Advocate:* The base rate is 50 cents per word, but payment is negotiated at the time of the assignment.
- *Atlanta* magazine: About $1 per word.
- *Boston* magazine: $1 per word for most features.
- *Chicago* magazine: Typically $1 per word.
- *Columbia Journalism Review:* 75 cents to $1 per word, depending on the story's difficulty and the writer's experience.
- *Girls' Life Magazine:* $350 for the front-of-book one-page pieces; the rate goes up from there for features.
- *Los Angeles:* $1 a word.
- *mental_floss:* Usually 25 cents per word for first-time contributors.
- *Portland Magazine:* About $1 a word.
- *San Francisco:* There is no set word rate, but it works out to approximately 75 cents per word. A big feature will nab $5,000, a smaller department about $2,000, and short front-of-book pieces will pay between $300 and $600.

- *Soma:* Starts at 10 cents per word, but editors are open to negotiation depending on the experience of the writer and the nature of the piece. Well-established writers have received up to $1 per word.
- *Time Out Chicago:* 50 cents per word for front-of-book pieces; $50 to $75 for reviews. Rates may vary depending on the writer's experience and the amount of reporting involved.

WEB SITES (VARIES GREATLY)
- The Nest: $1 per word.
- Salon.com: No per-word rate. Quick news hits or book reviews start at $250 to $300, but the rate can escalate quickly, depending on the experience of the writer and the amount of reporting that goes into the piece.
- Slate: "Culturebox" pays from $300 to $700; other sections offer similar rates.
- Teenpeople.com: $350 for "Tuned In" pieces. A $300 flat fee to cover an event, provided the writer comes back with five usable quotes; if the print edition also uses a quote, the writer receives an additional $75.
- Wired News: 50 cents per word and up.

experts, a day to write, a half-day to revise, and then another half-day for a last-minute sidebar, the writer is making about $100 an hour. Which ain't bad. Let's say another magazine offers $300 for a monthly gig, where you talk about the health benefits of a different vegetable each month. The editor there wants 1,000 words each month, which works out to only 30 cents per word.

What seasoned writer would take on that second project? A smart one, actually. If the piece requires no interviews, no revisions, no sidebars, and basically just a filling in the blanks of the monthly template, that's a quick and easy payday each month. If the research takes an hour and the writing another hour, that assignment works out to $150 an hour. That's even better then the first, big-bucks deal.

It's important to remember that while per-word may be how the industry looks at payment, it's not always the most useful way for a writer to think about things. Take a closer look before you pass up seemingly low-paying offers. And think twice before jumping at projects that pay well but will take weeks or even months to complete.

## Negotiate for More Money When You Can

While there are always standard practices at publications, that doesn't mean that everything is set in stone. If you feel like you're being lowballed, try to negotiate. Tell the editor that you're usually paid a better rate than what was offered. If the editor doesn't budge, you have to decide if the money offered is worth your valuable time.

If the editor wavers, or needs to get back to you, then he probably doesn't have the say over what you get paid; somebody higher up does. This is your chance to talk yourself up. If the editor has to talk someone else into paying you more, you want to be sure he has the ammunition he needs to get you that extra dough. If you've worked for him before, remind him of how you always meet your deadlines, get terrific quotes from top-notch experts, match the voice of the publication, need very little editing, and happily make revisions (if this is the case!). Hopefully he'll then be able to talk his boss into paying you better.

Most writers do advise you to wait to ask for a pay increase until after you've turned in one or two terrific pieces. That's a good idea, but it's also smart to get off on the right foot from the beginning, by letting your new editor know that you are valuable to *other* publications—and that you'll be valuable to him.

If you're offered a dollar a word, ask for $1.50 by saying, "The other publications I write for pay me $1.50 a word. Do you think you can match that?" If that doesn't fly, ask for another fifty bucks, or another $300 for that sidebar they added by saying, "Since this assignment requires quite a bit of background research, do you think you could at least tack on an additional $300?" Of course, the amount you suggest depends on the originally offered fee. If a newspaper offers you $150 for a feature story, asking for another $300 is out of the question. But if

---

---

you're talking about that $2,000 magazine feature, another couple of hundred may be looked at as a very reasonable request.

Also, take a look at the contract. If the publication is asking for all rights or even just electronic rights—and you are willing to give them those rights—then ask to be compensated for doing so by saying, "I hesitate to sign a contract that requests electronic rights. If that's all you have to offer, can you at least add another $200 to my payment?" You deserve something more if they are going to have your article posted on their Web site for years to come.

## Compromise if You Must

Nobody wants to work with a whining writer who's always haggling over nickels and dimes. If the editor is strapped for cash and really can't pay you more, try a hand at negotiating for something else— like retaining rights to the piece by saying, "I'm used to being paid more, but I'll take on the piece if all rights for the piece will revert back to me sixty days after publication." If you can immediately turn around and sell the story again, it might be worth it to write for less than usual. You may be able to make up the difference in reprints (more on doing just that to follow).

## HOW MUCH CAN YOU MAKE IN A YEAR?

Below is mediabistro.com's *Freelancer Salary Survey,* which reports on freelancers' 2004 taxable income by region, metropolitan area, expertise, industry, client type, years of experience, and annual earnings.

| Salaries by Category | 25th Percentile (25% Earn Less) | 50th Percentile (50% Earn Less) | 75th Percentile (75% Earn Less) | Number Responding |
|---|---|---|---|---|
| TOTAL | $17,400 | $35,000 | $60,000 | 3,179 |
| **Region** | | | | |
| Northeast | $20,000 | $40,000 | $65,000 | 1,613 |
| West | $18,000 | $39,000 | $60,000 | 673 |
| South | $10,000 | $28,000 | $50,000 | 457 |
| Midwest | $10,000 | $30,000 | $55,000 | 241 |
| **Metro Area** | | | | |
| New York-Newark-Edison, NY-NJ-PA | $24,000 | $40,000 | $65,000 | 1,293 |
| Los Angeles-Long Beach-Santa Ana, CA | $20,000 | $40,000 | $70,000 | 286 |
| San Francisco-Oakland-Fremont, CA | $30,000 | $40,000 | $65,000 | 124 |
| Washington-Arlington-Alexandria, DC-VA-MD-WV | $20,000 | $38,000 | $53,760 | 123 |
| Chicago-Naperville-Joliet, IL-IN-WI | $15,000 | $35,000 | $55,000 | 111 |
| Boston-Cambridge-Quincy, MA-NH | $10,000 | $30,000 | $49,000 | 89 |
| Philadelphia-Camden-Wilmington, PA-NJ-DE-MD | $14,000 | $35,000 | $70,000 | 73 |
| Seattle-Tacoma-Bellevue, WA | $16,000 | $40,000 | $54,000 | 55 |
| Atlanta-Sandy Springs-Marietta, GA | $5,000 | $22,000 | $34,000 | 43 |
| Dallas-Fort Worth-Arlington, TX | $15,000 | $35,000 | $55,000 | 39 |
| Bridgeport-Stamford-Norwalk, CT | $13,000 | $42,000 | $52,000 | 30 |
| Miami-Fort Lauderdale-Miami Beach, FL | $22,000 | $30,000 | $70,000 | 29 |
| Baltimore-Towson, MD | $5,500 | $28,000 | $50,000 | 26 |
| San Diego-Carlsbad-San Marcos, CA | $5,000 | $25,000 | $50,000 | 21 |
| Houston-Baytown-Sugar Land, TX | $9,500 | $20,000 | $34,000 | 20 |
| Denver-Aurora, CO | $18,000 | $35,000 | $56,000 | 18 |
| Portland-Vancouver-Beaverton, OR-WA | $10,000 | $20,000 | $24,000 | 16 |

| Salaries by Category | 25th Percentile (25% Earn Less) | 50th Percentile (50% Earn Less) | 75th Percentile (75% Earn Less) | Number Responding |
|---|---|---|---|---|
| Detroit-Warren-Livonia, MI | $9,000 | $43,000 | $60,000 | 15 |
| Phoenix-Mesa-Scottsdale, AZ | $10,000 | $50,000 | $76,000 | 15 |
| Orlando, FL | $20,000 | $35,000 | $60,000 | 13 |
| New Haven-Milford, CT | $10,400 | $25,000 | $42,000 | 12 |
| New Orleans-Metairie-Kenner, LA | $2,000 | $8,000 | $22,000 | 11 |
| Nashville-Davidson—Murfreesboro, TN | $2,600 | $13,000 | $20,100 | 11 |
| Las Vegas-Paradise, NV | $5,000 | $25,000 | $72,000 | 11 |
| Tampa-St. Petersburg-Clearwater, FL | $5,000 | $25,000 | $33,000 | 11 |
| Austin-Round Rock, TX | $12,000 | $25,000 | $36,000 | 11 |
| Minneapolis-St. Paul-Bloomington, MN-WI | $400 | $10,000 | $45,000 | 10 |
| Madison, WI | $2,400 | $20,500 | $50,000 | 10 |
| Boulder, CO | $6,000 | $30,000 | $55,000 | 10 |
| **Expertise** | | | | |
| Book Author | $20,000 | $40,000 | $60,000 | 73 |
| Copy Editor | $15,000 | $26,000 | $40,000 | 143 |
| Copywriter | $22,000 | $40,000 | $75,000 | 123 |
| Reporter | $11,660 | $25,000 | $45,000 | 236 |
| Researcher | $7,200 | $10,000 | $39,000 | 17 |
| Technical Writer | $20,000 | $40,000 | $78,000 | 53 |
| Writer | $10,000 | $30,000 | $50,000 | 1,032 |
| Other | $20,000 | $40,000 | $70,000 | 275 |
| **Industry** | | | | |
| Advertising: agency | $33,000 | $50,000 | $72,000 | 131 |
| Advertising: client side | $20,000 | $40,000 | $85,000 | 34 |
| Advertising: other | $25,000 | $40,000 | $60,000 | 47 |
| Association publication | $18,000 | $35,000 | $50,000 | 22 |
| Magazine: large consumer/national | $25,000 | $40,000 | $60,000 | 575 |
| Magazine: local/regional | $5,100 | $20,000 | $30,000 | 194 |
| Magazine: trade magazines/B2B pub. | $20,000 | $35,000 | $55,000 | 206 |
| Marketing (firm): Fortune 1000 clients | $7,000 | $37,000 | $75,000 | 18 |
| Marketing (firm): small/mid-sized clients | $25,000 | $38,000 | $95,000 | 25 |
| Marketing (in-house): Fortune 1000 | $31,000 | $66,000 | $80,000 | 23 |
| Marketing (in-house): small/mid-sized | $15,000 | $30,000 | $48,000 | 29 |

(continued)

| Salaries by Category | 25th Percentile (25% Earn Less) | 50th Percentile (50% Earn Less) | 75th Percentile (75% Earn Less) | Number Responding |
|---|---|---|---|---|
| Newsletter: consumer | $5,000 | $30,000 | $60,000 | 12 |
| Newsletter: trade | $9,000 | $30,000 | $36,000 | 28 |
| Newspaper: community | $2,000 | $10,000 | $20,000 | 30 |
| Newspaper: local/regional | $3,000 | $13,000 | $25,000 | 173 |
| Newspaper: national | $12,500 | $35,000 | $50,000 | 89 |
| Print: other | $18,000 | $35,000 | $55,000 | 103 |
| Online/new media | $15,000 | $35,000 | $56,000 | 219 |
| PR (firm): Fortune 1000 clients | $36,000 | $75,000 | $83,000 | 11 |
| PR (firm): small/mid-sized clients | $30,000 | $45,000 | $65,000 | 31 |
| PR (in-house): small/ mid-sized | $15,000 | $35,000 | $50,000 | 16 |
| Pr/marketing: other | $30,000 | $50,000 | $75,000 | 94 |
| Professional journal | $10,000 | $30,000 | $51,000 | 24 |
| Other | $16,000 | $40,000 | $70,000 | 245 |
| **Client Type** | | | | |
| Local/Regional | $10,000 | $24,500 | $40,000 | 982 |
| National | $25,000 | $40,000 | $65,000 | 1,742 |
| International | $25,000 | $45,000 | $70,000 | 454 |
| **Years of Experience** | | | | |
| Entry Level | $1,000 | $10,000 | $25,000 | 136 |
| 1–2 Years | $5,000 | $18,000 | $33,000 | 269 |
| 3–5 Years | $15,000 | $30,000 | $47,000 | 618 |
| 6–10 Years | $20,000 | $40,000 | $60,000 | 874 |
| 11–15 Years | $25,000 | $50,000 | $75,000 | 526 |
| 15+ Years | $25,000 | $48,000 | $75,000 | 965 |
| **Annual Earnings** | | | | |
| 2003 Earnings | $10,000 | $30,000 | $52,000 | 3,179 |
| 2004 Earnings | $17,400 | $35,000 | $60,000 | 3,179 |
| 2005 Earnings (projected), compared to 2004: | More than 2004 | | | 2,045 |
| | Less than 2004 | | | 235 |
| | Same as 2004 | | | 899 |

If all your efforts to negotiate fail, don't push it. Consider if the per-hour rate will pay you more than what you can make at Dairy Queen and how much you really want to write the piece. Will it make a nice clip? Or do you think you can get any other publication to pay you more for the same story?

## Just Say No, Nicely

Your time is money, and no matter how much you love to write, some projects just aren't worth it. It's okay to pass on an assignment that won't benefit you and will prevent you from having the time to search out more lucrative work. But always be polite when you turn down work, because that publisher or editor with little money to offer you today may be in charge of a well-endowed launch in the very near future.

---

### WRIGGLE SOME MORE

"There's a lot of wriggle room in contracts, and the moment when you have the most negotiating power is the moment when you first get the assignment. I once doubled my pay just by outlining the normal range for the bigger glossies—in contrast to the offer on the table—then waiting in silence. Remember to let your editor know when a story will require extra research or where there is a tight turnaround. It's also a good idea to take into account how much rewriting and reworking this editor or magazine usually wants. Sometimes 75 cents a word from an easier-to-work-with publication is a better deal than $2 in the long run. Right now I am timing the work I put into projects so I can see what I really am getting paid.

"If an editor genuinely can't pay more per word, and sometimes the smaller magazines can't, then think of some alternatives. One editor lowered the word count so she could pay me what I wanted yet stay within her budget. Or maybe throw in a sidebar that boosts the word count but not your workload. You can ask for a comp subscription. Or a second assignment with a better rate. And, of course, be sure you are paid for expenses. I set annual revenue goals and you can set pay rate goals as well."

—*Sally Lehrman, who writes about health, medicine, and science policy for* Scientific American, Nature, Health, *the* Washington Post, *Salon.com, the* DNA Files (distributed by NPR), and other publications and sites

---

## Easy Extra Money

Most writers work hard on developing pitches, slave over stories, hand in completed articles, and then move on to pitch another completely new idea. They may be missing out on some easy earnings. It is possible to make more money off of one idea, by either reselling the piece as is or retooling it into something new.

### Reselling stories

Let's start with reselling a piece, also known as reprinting. Let's say you're assigned an article, "How to Organize Your Kitchen," for a major women's magazine. You interview four experts and write a 1,200-word piece. You get paid $1,500, and your contract doesn't give the magazine all rights. Instead, you're merely prohibited from writing about the same topic for any other publication for ninety days. Three months after the issue with your article goes on sale, it's time to write some quick letters or e-mails to editors who might be interested in reprinting your piece.

For the most part, major national magazines are not interested in any content that has been previously published. But smaller publications such as regional magazines, newspapers, and trade publications on tighter budgets often purchase reprints. In addition, international publications (published in English), such as magazines in Australia, New Zealand, and England, often print articles that originally appeared in U.S. publications. Books and Web sites, such as *Writer's Handbook* (www.writermag.com) and *Writer's Market* (www.writersmarket.com) list thousands of venues where you can resell your article. While these smaller-circulation pubs may not be able to pay you much, you are not doing any extra work (except sending out some quick query letters), so it's just some extra cash in your pocket.

When approaching these markets, send the completed article or a small summary of the piece you are offering to them. You should also mention when and where the piece first ran. Keep in mind that if you're trying to resell the piece to a slightly different market, you may have to rewrite the introduction to fit the new audience. If some time has passed, you may need to update some of the factual information or anything else in the piece that is time sensitive. Indicate in your letter that you know these changes will be necessary and you're happy to make them.

Most publications have set amounts that they pay for reprints, while others may ask how much you want for an article. Rates vary widely: one newspaper might offer $40 for a piece, but a trade publication could pay you as much as $1,000.

Back to the kitchen story: you may be able to sell that to a few different regional magazines or newspapers (a home magazine in Atlanta, the home section of a paper in Seattle, a decorating magazine in Las Vegas) across the country. The editors will probably just want a guarantee that they are the only one in their area publishing the reprint. The same story can also be shopped around to trade magazines associated with kitchen design or food preparation.

If you don't have the time to try to sell reprint rights to your piece, there are syndication services that will do the job for you. In most cases you hand over in their entirety the articles you wish to resell and the syndicate uses its resources to sell your articles to publications all across the United States and abroad. You're paid either a percentage of what the syndicate makes from selling your piece (for example, www.featurewell.com pays contributors 60 percent of the proceeds from sales) or a set fee that the syndicate gives you for the rights to sell your work for a certain amount of time.

### Retooling a piece

Maybe you'd like to resell your work a bit more lucratively than you can by simply selling reprint rights. That's a possibility—if you're willing to do just a bit more work; you can retool, repurpose, or reslant a piece for all sorts of different markets. Let's go back to the

## RETOOLING FOR NEWSPAPERS

"There are a lot of newspapers in this country that don't directly compete. So if you write a story for a newspaper in San Francisco and a story in Portland, Maine, and it's the same story and you reuse some quotes and you don't reuse others—I mean you put in, say, 32 percent new information, I'd like to see a lawyer come to court and say, well, your story isn't 100 percent original. Well, maybe it is and maybe it isn't. So you can look at those contracts and I think you can make your own decisions about how you're going to run your business. Because reselling and repurposing is the only way to really, I've found, make a lot of dough. It's called vertical integration in the business world and you just keep reusing as much as you can. I'm doing this with a story right now where I've signed an all-rights contract. Yeah, that newspaper is going to get all rights to that story because all the sources that I've interviewed are local to that city. When I try to resell that piece to the twenty-plus newspapers that might be interested in it, I would then interview people in those cities."

—*Steve Friedman has written for* GQ, Esquire, *the* New York Times, *and many other publications and is the author of two books. Some of his work is at Stevefriedman.net.*

"How to Organize Your Kitchen" example. You probably learned a lot of details while you were reporting that never made it into the final piece. But that version, for a general-interest women's magazine, was just one way that information could have been laid out. Now's the time to explore ways to make it work for other markets. Perhaps a bridal magazine is interested in a piece about how a couple can combine two kitchens into one, with the addition of all those wedding gifts. You can include much of the material you used in the original piece, plus the same experts, to write a bridal magazine article with just a slightly different angle from the first. Or you can aim even higher and pitch a piece to an upscale food magazine on the must-have tools for reorganizing your kitchen. Sure, you might have to go back to your experts and get some new quotes, but you've got the background research done, so feed off that. The same type of piece may even work for trade publications for chefs.

When pitching an editor on a retooled piece, you don't need to mention that you wrote a similar piece for another publication; just be sure that you take a fresh angle and new quotes (even if you use the same experts).

One thing to mention: some magazines state in their contracts that you are not to write about the same topic for any of their competitors for a period of time. That's a tough one. If the topic is narrow, it's easy to abide by those instructions. But if you wrote a piece called "15 Surefire Ways to Lose Weight," does that mean you can't write about weight loss for a competing magazine? No way. Use your best judgment and be reasonable.

## THE SAME PIECE

Here are two pitch letters for the same piece. The first was sent to and accepted by the *New York Times*. Soon after, the writer successfully pitched the *Financial Times,* based in London, with a similar story idea, just retooled slightly. It's a great example of reusing your original research to get another assignment. (It's also worth mentioning that in this writer's pitch e-mails, she always includes the e-mail thread so the editor can just scroll down and see that they once saw fit to acknowledge her. Also, whenever she follows up with an editor on an article she's already sent, or with samples she sent, she always resends her original e-mail and any attachment. She tries to make life as easy as possible for the editor.)

COLD PITCH TO THE *New York Times,* SENT VIA E-MAIL

Dear Mr. [Last name of the editor of the *New York Times* City section],
My name is [Writer], and I am a freelancer living in New York. I got your

(continued)

name from an article on www.mediabistro.com, and I hope you are the person to consider this freelance pitch for the *New York Times* City Section. Please excuse me if you are not.

Like many twenty-something New Yorkers, Karyn spends beyond her means. But those Prada pumps and cute designer tops add up, and now Karyn is $20,000 in the hole to her credit-card company. Things would look pretty grim were it not for Karyn's faith in human nature and the generosity of her fellow man, for she is confident that she can get that money just by asking for it! Enter www.savekaryn.com, where viewers are invited to donate selflessly to Karyn's cause and help make her world a better place.

It's not that Karyn hasn't made sacrifices—she's stopped buying designer clothes. She's selling her copy of *Women Who Run With the Wolves.* She's grudgingly learned to let Old Navy into her heart. All she wants from us is whatever we can spare to reassure her that it's all been worthwhile. "Together," writes Karyn cheerfully, "we can make a difference!"

In the meantime, Karyn sure does her best to entertain. Her Web site keeps you amused with the sheer chutzpah of her request, and few are the surfers who can't relate to her financial woes. Highlights include her "FAQ" and "Grand Debt Tally" where she hopefully adds up "My Money," "Your Money" and "eBay Sales" and discovers that she is still significantly in the hole. With over 50,000 hits on her Web site so far (32,000 this week alone), you'd think she would have made more than $157, but hey, a girl's gotta start somewhere.

I spoke with Karyn last night and got some really lively comments from her. I think she'll make back her money; in fact, she has already been contacted by a major movie studio about the rights to her story.

For your information, I have contributed to *The Times, The Chicago Tribune,* the *National Post, The Globe & Mail, The Canadian Press* and *wallpaper\* Magazine,* as well as a number of Canadian magazines.

Thanks so much for your consideration of my pitch. I look forward to hearing from you!

Best,
[Writer]

## PITCH TO THE *Financial Times* (LONDON)

Hi [first name of the Weekend editor at the *Financial Times*], it's [Writer] writing—we corresponded about the World Cup of Lawyers last month. I write with another story idea for your consideration in the *Financial Times* weekend section.

Like many New Yorkers, Karyn spends beyond her means. But those Prada pumps and cute designer tops add up, and now Karyn is $20,000 in the hole to her credit-card company. Things would look pretty grim were it not for Karyn's faith in human nature and the generosity of her fellow man, for she is confident that she can get that money just by asking for it! That's the philosophy behind her new Web site, www.savekaryn.com, where viewers are invited to donate selflessly to Karyn's cause and help make her world a better place.

It's not that Karyn hasn't made sacrifices—she's stopped buying designer clothes. She's selling her copy of *Women Who Run With the Wolves*. She's grudgingly learned to let dime store products into her heart. All she wants from us is whatever we can spare to reassure her that it's all been worthwhile. "Together," writes Karyn cheerfully, "we can make a difference!"

In the meantime, Karyn sure does her best to entertain. Her Web site keeps you amused with the sheer chutzpah of her request, and few are the surfers who can't relate to her financial woes. Highlights include her "FAQ" and "Grand Debt Tally" where she hopefully adds up "My Money," "Your Money" and "eBay Sales" and discovers that she is still significantly in the hole. With over 21,000 hits just last week, you'd think she would have made more than $157, but hey, a girl's gotta start somewhere.

I have been in touch with Karyn and will be speaking with her this evening to discuss her strategy and the returns on her investment in her charity of one.

You can reach me by return e-mail or on my mobile phone if you wish at XXX-XXX-XXXX. I have also included the link to my recent article on the World Cup of Lawyers for your evaluation.

Thanks so much for considering this query—I look forward to hearing from you!

Best,
[Writer]

## Branching Out to Other Venues

You've got a marketable skill—writing—that's in demand far beyond the pages of magazines, newspapers, and their Web sites. Here's a brief look at other areas in which you might find some work.

### Corporate writing

Think about all the printed material you read in a day, from bill-boards on the highway to solicitations from charitable organizations to all the junk mail clogging your mailbox. Somebody writes all of it. The newsletters that accompany your credit-card bills, the updates from your stockbroker, the news from your local hospital, and the instruction booklet with any new product you purchase all are created by writers, many of them freelance.

It's always a good idea to start by writing about a subject area with which you are familiar. If you've been writing about beauty, try getting writing projects from skin-care, cosmetics, and hair-supply companies. If fitness is your thing, contact sports equipment and apparel manufacturers.

But how do you go about getting a writing gig with a corporate client? Well, it's not all that different from getting assignments from a publication. No, you don't want to send a query to a health-insurance provider pitching a story idea for its next newsletter, but go ahead and get in touch. Call and find out who at the company might hire freelancers for writing work. Chances are you'll want to talk with someone in one of the following departments: corporate communications, public affairs, public relations, public information, marketing communications, or community relations. You may have to fish around a bit, but once you find out who hires freelancers, send her your résumé and some sample clips and introduce yourself as a writer.

In your daily life, continue to network, with everyone. As a writer, every person you meet is a potential client, or may work for a potential client. You will be surprised at the number of people who will respond positively to your announcement that you are a writer, and tell you about someone or some company that needs something written. Also, start checking the classified ads and job boards on Web sites, like those on mediabistro.com, which often have postings looking for freelance writers.

Journalists sometimes shy away from corporate writing, claiming they don't really know how to do it. But in fact many companies are looking for writers who can put hard-to-understand information into easily accessible prose for the general public—exactly what a journalist does. Whether it's composing a press release, putting together a brochure, or ghostwriting speeches, letters, and articles for a corporate chief, big firms often already have all the background information handy; they need someone with a creative flare to jazz it up. In other words, the reporting's already done for you, and you just have to write (the dream of some writers!). Many corporations seeking writers simply want someone to update preexisting written material.

Think about joining a trade organization for business writers to get your name out there and to get on the pulse of this line of work. Organizations such as the International Association of Business Communicators (www.iabc.com), and the Association for Women in Communications (www.womcom.org) hold seminars and events where you can network with others in the industry.

And while corporate writing usually does not require much reporting or digging for information, it often pays better than publications, and more quickly, too! But don't expect to be offered a per-word rate from a corporation—the bosses there are probably used to paying by the hour. So you need to figure out what you're worth. This can be tough, especially if the company asks you how much you charge—you don't want to come in too high (they may give the work to someone else), and you don't want to lowball yourself either. While there are no hard and fast rules, consider a few things: the amount of time it will take you to complete the task, whether you hope to get more work from this client in the future, whether you have special expertise that makes you very valuable to the corporation, if it's a rush job, if it's a big firm, whether the company is in good financial shape, and where it's located (clients in big cities are used to paying more). A rough range for corporate-writing work is from about $30 to $100 an hour.

Once you decide on a payment, insist on some type of written contract. If hiring freelance writers is something new to the company, the manager probably won't have anything formal for you to sign. You may have to write up your own contract. At the very least, describe the work that you will complete, state the amount that you will be paid, and indicate when you will be paid. You might request a portion of your fee up front—let's say one-third of your payment before you even begin the work. And be sure your client signs the contract and returns the signed copy to you—before you start work on the project.

To help ensure that you will be paid (especially important if you're working for a small or relatively unknown company on a big project that's going to take a lot of your time), you might want to do a credit check on the business before agreeing to work with them. For around $20 you can get access to a business's credit status, see if there have been legal or collection-agency filings on them, and receive information on their payment history. Visit sites such as www.knowx.com, www.dnb.com, or the Better Business Bureau (www.bbb.org).

### Public Relations Writing

Some editors refer to writing for a PR agency as "going over to the dark side." This is probably due to the fact that there are some PR people who send inappropriate pitches to editors, then hound them mercilessly for ink about products they represent. But that's an overbroad caricature, and there are plenty of good people working in PR—and plenty of good opportunities to earn some money writing PR copy.

PR firms are often very excited about hiring a journalist to write copy that will be sent out to journalists. As a freelance writer, you can pitch yourself as a person who has a good idea of how to write for,

---

### ON GETTING PAID UP FRONT FOR CORPORATE WORK

"I have been given [up to] half the payment up front. Although I'd like to say what percentage one gets up front could/should be standard, I base it on the reputation of the company. If I've never heard of you, chances are I want half up front. But saying one-third now, one-third when it's handed in, and the last third once a final revision has been accepted is, well, an acceptable business practice. I have experienced bounced checks, even from well-intentioned clients, and have come across situations where a new director was put in place midproject and was not sure they wanted the completed project. So, one does learn the hard way. But on a brighter note, I complete between 100 and 200 freelance assignments a year (most of them paid in full upon completion or publication) and I have only come across issues with delayed or reduced payment fewer than the number of fingers I have on one hand; and total nonpayment, never. Even for those who have bounced checks, I eventually received my money. I am not averse to putting someone on a payment plan to get it."

—*Sheree R. Curry, freelance writer, has held staff positions at* Fortune *and* Advertising Age. *She has also taught page design and magazine writing at the university level.*

and connect with, other editors and writers. As long as you are sure to separate "church and state" in terms of what you write about for corporations and firms versus what you write about for publications, you will probably be in good shape.

For instance, you should probably be wary of writing about topics for firms or corporations that you might also need to write about for a consumer publication. Let's say a PR firm hires you to write a press release about a new diabetes drug, you probably shouldn't pitch a story about all types of new diabetes drugs to *Prevention* magazine. That's a conflict of interest.

All companies need good PR, even the little guys. So, apart from writing for a big public relations firm, consider approaching smaller locally or independently owned operations and offering up your services to put together a flyer or brochure for them. Many small companies and nonprofits need marketing collateral and publicity but just don't have the time or the staff to put written material together. You can do that for them. This is an area where you might need to do some work pro bono, just long enough to acquire some samples of your work to offer to the big guys with the big bucks.

### Writing for trade publications

In general, trade publications are intended for people associated with a specific industry or business. For instance, there's the *Service Industry News* for pool and spa service professionals and *Funeral Service Journal* for funeral directors. They're not for the average newsstand reader. But they might be markets for your writing. As mentioned earlier, when just starting out, trade publications may be a good place to get an "in" and acquire some much-needed clips, and they are also a great way for

---

### MATCH THE TONE

"I do assign stories to writers who I have not worked with before. I look first at their résumé and clips to see if they have the tone that fits our publication's as well as evidence of quality reporting. Then I like to talk to them about what they like to write about and brainstorm. Then I give them a trial run, and if they produce quality copy ON TIME, then I'll continue to work with them in the future."

—*Rebecca Goldberg, managing editor, Sipco Publications. Sipco produces trade publications (both magazines and newspapers), including* Fabrics & Furnishings International, Contract/Hospitality News, Decosit News, Heimtextil News, Evteks News, *and* boutique DESIGN.

more established writers to supplement their income. (FYI, "trade" in the magazine industry means the exact opposite of what it does in the book publishing industry. Trade book publishing means fiction or nonfiction aimed at the general public and sold in bookstores.)

In some ways, trade publications are an untapped market. Writers shy away from them, thinking that they don't pay well or just are not as glamorous as consumer magazines. The glamour part is probably true, but, ignoring that, many trades pay a lot better than you might think. While some might pay as little as $50 a piece, some now pay $1 a word and more. In addition, if you start writing for some trades frequently, they may set you up with a regular gig that provides you with a steady check and does not require you to do any pitching—the editor just calls you with your assignment for that week or month.

In addition, if you have a special area of expertise, you're likely to find a number of trade publications that cater to an audience related to that specialty. For instance, if you want to write about interior decorating, or have done so for a consumer magazine, there are countless trade publications you can target: *Window Fashions, Fine Furnishings International, Interiors and Sources, Furniture Design Management, Period Homes, Upholstery Design & Management,* and on and on. As well as supplementing your income by writing for these trades, you will also get your name in front of the movers and shakers in that particular industry. So if you're seeking corporate writing gigs with, let's say, major furniture makers, start writing for the trades that the executives of those companies read. This model can work in any type of industry or area of interest.

These are just a few ideas for alternate ways to earn money as a freelance writer. Many writers teach writing to all those aspiring to see their names in print. Others ghostwrite for those dreaming of telling their life stories but lacking the skills to do so. Continually keep your eye out for any opportunity to put your talents to work. And as we keep saying, let everyone know that you're a writer. One

## ON WRITING FOR A TRADE MAGAZINE

*Below is a pitch letter one writer used to respond to a freelance posting on a Web site requesting a writer for a golf-related article. Nothing fancy, but it earned him a $7,500 job and a pay rate of $1 a word in a trade magazine. Note that in his pitch letter, he said 25 cents a word would do the trick. Once he met with the client and found out the scope and scale of the job, he renegotiated the rate for the actual contract.*

I am responding to your request for a freelance article about the 2005 PGA Championship at Baltusrol. My writing credentials include several articles for the *San Francisco Chronicle* wine section, including a cover story (see links below). In addition to earning a B.A. in English and Creative Writing from Middlebury College, I received an M.F.A. in Creative Nonfiction from Goucher College in Baltimore and attended the Breadloaf Writer's Conference. On the freelancing front, I have recently had golf travel article queries accepted at *Yankee* and *Golf Illustrated*. An avid golfer, I play to an 8 handicap.

My résumé is attached as a Word document and I've included links to my clippings below. Although much of my writing work so far has been wine-related, golf is a passion of mine and I'm looking to branch out and establish myself as a golf writer. My desired pay rate is $.25 per word plus any travel-related expenses. Please feel free to contact me with any further questions.

Thanks in advance for your consideration,
James Meyer

New York City–based magazine writer is now at work on her first book—a flashy style guide for a major publisher. Why? Because she once mentioned to her hip hairdresser that she's a writer. So when the hairdresser was ready to move forward on his second book, who did he tap? That's right—one of his favorite clients.

Keep spreading the word about yourself! Your next assignment could be right around the corner, with your next phone call, or from the next person you meet.

# Conclusion

You'll note that nowhere in this book did it ever say freelancing is easy. Some days, weeks, and months can be hard to endure if your query letters are being ignored and the assignments are not coming in. But keep at it. Maybe you are shooting for the stars a little too soon. Lower your horizon and pitch to some smaller publications. Build your portfolio confidently.

Step-by-step you will make your way closer to your goal. The nice thing about being a writer is that on every day of your journey you can discover something new and then you can sit down and write about it—and share that something new with others. What could be better or more rewarding?

# Resources

## News About the Publishing World

### Media News

Mediabistro.com's daily "Morning Newsfeed"—a roundup of all the day's news about the media business—can be accessed on our site or sent directly to your in-box. The mediabistro.com site also offers tons of information for writers, including original media reporting, word of job changes in the business, and seven fun, opinionated blogs about different aspects of the industry.

www.mediabistro.com

### The Columbia Journalism Review

Part of the Columbia University Graduate School of Journalism, *CJR* follows the press, including newspapers and magazines, radio, television, and cable, as well as the wire services and the Web. Cjrdaily is a blog commenting on news coverage on a more immediate basis.

www.cjr.org
www.cjrdaily.org

### Editor & Publisher

The oldest journal covering the newspaper industry runs a continually updated Web site with breaking news about the newspaper business specifically and the media world more broadly.

http://www.editorandpublisher.com

### Mediaweek

Breaking news in the media business, with analysis and commentary.

www.mediaweek.com

### "Off the Record"

The *New York Observer*'s media column. The *Observer* has recently added a daily blog version of the column, called the Media Mob.

http://www.observer.com

## Potential Markets for Your Work

### How to Pitch

Mediabistro.com's tip sheets, straight from the editors, on how to pitch big-name publications including *Rolling Stone* and *Glamour*.

www.mediabistro.com/content/archives/howtopitch.asp

### Featurewell.com

Markets previously published articles to newspapers, magazines, and Web sites throughout the world.

www.featurewell.com

### Freelance Marketplace

A forum for talented freelancers to showcase their work and a quick way for editors and other media managers to find quality people who match their needs.

http://www.mediabistro.com/fm/

### The Writer's Handbook
Guide to more than 3,000 magazines and book publishers, explaining what they buy and how to contact them.

www.writermag.com

### Writer's Market
Continuously updated information on editors and agents to pitch.

www.writersmarket.com

## Jobs in Journalism

### Mediabistro Job Listings
Continuously updated extensive media job listings. Nearly 1,000 media-related openings across the country are posted to mediabistro.com's job board every month. The site attracts the most desirable jobs in the industry, from positions at small PR firms to jobs at Condé Nast.

http://www.mediabistro.com/joblistings/

### Editor & Publisher Classifieds
Classifieds from *Editor & Publisher* magazine.

http://www.editorandpublisher.com/eandp/classifieds/index.jsp

### Journalism Job Bank
A listing from UC Berkeley Graduate School of Journalism.

http://www.journalism.berkeley.edu/jobs/

### JournalismJobs.com
Jobs in journalism, mainly in newspapers, operated in partnership with *Columbia Journalism Review* magazine.

http://www.journalismjobs.com/

## Insurance for Freelancers

### mb Health Center

Mediabistro.com's health insurance and dental discounts.

http://www.mediabistro.com/insurance

### eHealthInsurance

A resource for individual health insurance plans.

www.ehealthinsurance.com

### Working Today

A national nonprofit that represents the needs and concerns of the independent workforce.

www.workingtoday.org

## Associations for Journalists

### American Society of Journalists and Authors

A trade association of freelance writers.

www.asja.org

### Asian American Journalists Association (AAJA)

An association of Asian Americans and Pacific Islanders who work in journalism.

www.aaja.org

### Association of Food Journalists (AFJ)

A networking system created especially for journalists who devote most of their working time to planning and writing food copy for news media worldwide.

www.afjonline.com

### The Authors Guild
A society of published book authors and freelance journalists.

www.authorsguild.org

### Investigative Reporters and Editors (IRE)
Provides educational services to reporters, editors, and others interested in investigative journalism.

www.ire.org

### National Association of Black Journalists (NABJ)
Has a mission to strengthen ties among African-American journalists, promote diversity in newsrooms, and honor excellence in the media industry.

www.nabj.org

### National Association of Hispanic Journalists (NAHJ)
An association dedicated to the recognition and professional advancement of Hispanics in the news industry.

www.nahj.org

### National Association of Science Writers (NASW)
An association for freelance science writers.

http://nasw.org

### National Lesbian and Gay Journalists Association (NLGJA)
An organization of journalists, media professionals, educators, and students who work within the news industry to foster fair and accurate coverage of lesbian, gay, bisexual, and transgender issues.

www.nlgja.org

### National Writers Union
A labor union for freelance writers.

www.nwu.org

### Native American Journalists Association (NAJA)

Serves and empowers Native American communicators through programs and activities.

www.naja.com

### Outdoor Writers Association of America (OWAA)

A nonprofit, international organization that represents those who write about the outdoors.

http://owaa.org

### Society of American Business Editors and Writers

A not-for-profit organization made up of business journalists in North America.

http://www.sabew.org

### Society of American Travel Writers

A professional association for travel writers and photographers.

http://www.satw.org

### Society of Environmental Journalists (SEJ)

An organization of journalists who cover the environment.

www.sej.org

### The Society of Professional Journalists (SPJ)

A society dedicated to the perpetuation of a free press as the cornerstone of our nation and our liberty.

http://www.spj.org

### South Asian Journalists Association (SAJA)

An organization that provides a networking and resource forum for journalists of South Asian origin.

http://www.saja.org

## Lingo

Publishing is a jargon-intense business. "Stet those changes, and finish the heds and deks quick, because we've got to flow this tonight to make ship!" If you've never worked on the staff of a publication, that sentence probably makes little sense. So here's a mini glossary of some everyday publishing terminology you may encounter as you become an established freelancer.

### ABOVE THE FOLD

A newspaper term, *above the fold* refers to the articles that appear on the top portion of a page (usually the front page) and are therefore still visible once the paper is folded in half. Writers strive to have their articles printed above the fold. The term is also used by some Web sites to indicate what you see on a page (typically the home page), without having to scroll down.

### ADVERTORIAL

Ads that look and read a lot like real editorial copy are called advertorials. Most editors require those placing advertorials in their publications to print the word *advertisement* across the top of each page or somehow indicate that the ad is not editorial content, so that readers do not confuse it with the publication's actual content.

### ANNOTATED COPY

When you hand in an assignment, many editors will ask you to also submit an annotated copy of the piece. This is a hard copy (printed out) of the piece marked up with names, phone numbers, and publication references that provide sourcing for all the factual information and quotes in the piece. A researcher/fact-checker will use this information to verify the information in the article.

## ART DIRECTOR/CREATIVE DIRECTOR/DESIGN DIRECTOR/GRAPHICS EDITOR

The art director, creative director, or design director oversees everything from the cover image and cover text to the illustrations, photos, and designs for each article. Art directors have a staff that may include an associate or assistant art director, photo researchers, perhaps some photographers, and a number of designers. Art directors are not involved with designing advertisements that appear in their publication. Newspapers sometimes simply have what they call a graphics editor.

## BACK OF BOOK

A magazine term, back of book, or BOB, for short, is the last third or so of the publication. The articles found here are often shorter than those in the feature well but longer than those found in the front of the book, often about one or two pages long. The pieces may be service oriented, such as reviews of all sorts of things—books, TV shows, movies, music, food, restaurants, electronics, gadgets, whatever. Many magazines use the last page of the pub, before the back cover, for an essay, some humor, or a full-page photograph.

## BEAT

Reporters for newspapers, magazines, Web sites, and even television news are often said to have a "beat." A beat is a subject, an area, or an industry that the reporter is responsible for covering at all times. City hall, higher education, health, or the beauty industry might be a beat. A specific company might be considered a beat if you're writing for an industry publication. Sometimes a writer will cover more than one beat.

### BIMONTHLY/BIWEEKLY/DAILY/WEEKLY

A publication that comes out every other month—six times per year—is considered bimonthly. Biweeklies are publications that come out every two weeks, or twice a month. Dailies are papers that come out just about every day of the week. (Some dailies no longer publish Saturday editions.) Weeklies are publications that come out once a week, and usually on the same day each week.

### BOOK

A magazine.

### CAPTION

Below or beside a photograph you'll find a caption that describes what's in the photo or that identifies the people in the photograph.

### CITY EDITOR

Edits copy, as well as manages assignments and oversees scheduling at newspapers. A newspaper may employ several city editors and assistant city editors. They work on stories in the news section of the paper, and both their workspace and team of editors and writers is often called the city desk.

### CLIP/TEAR SHEET

Also known as writing samples, clips and tear sheets are examples of what you have written in the past. Photocopies of published articles are usually referred to as clips. When an editor sends you copies of your article on the actual paper the publication is printed on, they are called tear sheets.

### CLOSE/CLOSING/SHIP

When articles or pages of a publication are almost complete and are about to be sent off to the printer (shipping), they are said to be *closing*. It's common for editors to say, "I'm so busy. We are in the middle of closing." Or "I'm crazed, it's ship." All last-minute changes to articles are made during closing, so it can be a very hectic time. At some publications (typically weeklies) a close of an issue can occur in one night; monthlies usually have a closing week. Daily newspapers usually close at the same time every night and may be said to be "going to press." The phrase "putting an issue to bed" means the same thing as closing or shipping.

### COPY

The words printed in a publication are called the copy. Editors often refer to copy in terms of one article at a time. For instance, when assigning you a story, an editor may say, "How soon can you get me the copy?" He is asking when you will hand in your completed article. Editors may also use the term when referring to small bits of text. For instance, an editor may say, "We need some copy to go under this picture." He is requesting a caption.

### COVERLINES

Not the same as headlines, coverlines are catchy phrases that appear on the cover of publications, in an attempt to draw in the reader. Coverlines are, for the most part, directed at newsstand readers. Editors work hard to create coverlines so enticing that a browser feels he needs to purchase a copy of the publication.

### CREDIT LINE

Credit lines often appear in the gutter (inside) of a page. They include a list of the photographers or illustrators who created the photos or illustrations appearing on that page. Credits also sometimes include the names of the model in the picture, the modeling agency, the stylist who set up the photo shoot, and the makeup artist and hairstylist who made the model look beautiful. The credit lines usually appear in small type.

### DEADLINE

The date or time your assignment is due is your deadline. At a monthly magazine, your deadline is a certain day; at a daily newspaper, your deadline may be a certain time of day, such as 6 p.m. for the morning edition. Meet all your deadlines and your editors will love you.

### DISPLAY TYPE

Any type that is pulled out of the running text (the main text of a piece) can be considered display type. Display type, such as a hed, dek, or pull quote, is usually printed in a larger font or different color than the rest of the copy in an article. This treatment is intended to help grab the reader's attention.

### EDITOR AT LARGE

The responsibility of an editor at large varies from magazine to magazine. Some are full-time staff members, who have an office at the publication and write and assign like any other editor on staff. Other editors at large are freelancers who function more like contributing editors. And still others are staff editors who live and work elsewhere, but contribute regularly.

### EDITOR/EDITOR-IN-CHIEF

Although usually called the editor-in-chief, some of those whose names grace the top of the masthead simply go by editor. The final say on everything that appears in a publication resides with the EIC. Before any article gets assigned it probably needs the editor's approval, just as she needs to sign off on every page before it's sent to the printer. The EIC may oversee the publication's budget and entire staff. Some EICs get very involved in the design of the publication, especially the cover. In addition, the EIC holds the position of figurehead for the publication, and may keep a busy social schedule. Editors also work closely with the publisher on advertising issues.

### EDITORIAL ADVISORY BOARD

Experts from many areas of expertise who assist the publication's staff. For instance, magazines that cover health, nutrition, and fitness have advisory boards made up of prominent doctors, nutritionists, and personal trainers. Advisors are sometimes consulted when editors are considering topics to cover in their publications, or may be interviewed as sources in articles, and sometimes even write regular articles or columns for the book.

### EDITORIAL CALENDAR

An editorial calendar maps out the upcoming issues of a publication. A calendar may merely list the themes or major topic areas of the issues, or it may be more detailed, describing actual scheduled articles. Some editorial calendars are available to freelance writers, while others are intended just for advertising purposes or for the staff of the publication.

### EVERGREEN

An *evergreen article* is one that can be printed at any time. It typically has no news peg that would require it to appear at a certain time of year or around a specific event. For instance, men's fitness magazines seem to print the same story, "How to Get Great Abs," every few months, all year long. That's an evergreen.

### EXECUTIVE EDITOR

Typically the number two spot (and the right hand of the editor-in-chief) on the editorial staff of a publication. The executive editor usually approves all assignments and all editorial copy before print (and before the editor-in-chief lays eyes on it). The executive editor may be more involved in hiring editors than the editor-in-chief. At some magazines, the executive editor looks after all of the copy, while the editor-in-chief acts simply as the face of the magazine.

### FEATURES EDITOR

At both newspapers and magazines, features editors edit feature stories. But they may be your ticket to getting into a newspaper. Newspaper feature editors are more apt to buy from a freelancer—more so than, let's say, a city editor.

### FILLER

Content that is used to fill holes (or blank space) in a publication.

### FRONT OF BOOK

Also called FOB by editors, the front of the book is usually comprised of short, quick, usually newsy articles intended to draw the reader into the magazine and leave them wanting to read more. Many magazines encourage new freelancers who pitch items for the FOB before attempting to write for other departments or longer features.

### HARD COPY

If an editor requests that you send along a hard copy of the article you write, this means she wants to see a printed version of the piece. During the editing process, an editor may also inform you that she will be sending you a hard copy of your piece with comments on it—in most cases she is probably asking you for a rewrite based on those comments.

### INFO BOX

If you're writing about an event for a newspaper, your editor most likely wants you to include an info box. This will include everything a reader needs to know to act on the event you just described—the hours of the event, the Web site, the ticket cost, the phone number, etc.

### INVENTORY

Articles that are ready to go—and usually paid for—but as yet unscheduled are considered part of the publication's inventory. Most publications try to eventually publish everything they have in inventory, but that does not always occur.

### LAYOUT

Graphic designers and art directors lay out stories, meaning they plan and arrange where the text, headlines, pictures, and captions will go on the page or pages of the publication. Used as a noun, the *layout* is the finished product the designer has created when he is done laying out the pages.

### LEAD TIME

*Webster's* defines *lead time* as "the time interval between the initiation and the completion of a production process." In publishing, the lead times can be long or very short. For instance, an article that appears in the September issue of a monthly magazine may need to be completed and sent to the printer by July. The art and editorial departments of the magazine may need at least a month or two to get it edited and designed for publication. That means the writer needs to submit it in May. That means it needs to be assigned in April. So a freelancer interested in getting a piece published in a September issue probably needs to pitch the idea by March. At a daily newspaper, a piece assigned to a reporter at 8 a.m. may be due to the editor by 3 p.m. and sent to the printer by 6 p.m.

### LINEUP/BUDGET

The lineup is the list of articles planned for a specific issue of a magazine. Most monthly magazines have prepared a tentative lineup for any particular issue many months in advance. Upon assigning you a story, an editor may tell you that it is not yet on the lineup, which means it is not yet scheduled for a specific issue. At a newspaper, the lineup is typically called a *budget*—it is a list of the stories running that day. A newspaper editor may ask, "Is this story on today's budget?"

### MANAGING EDITOR

Maintains law and order at a publication. Managing editors (MEs) often rule with an iron fist. At a newspaper, the managing editor is often the liaison between the newsroom and upper management, paying close attention to the publication's budget. At a magazine, most MEs map out the production schedule and all deadlines of a publication—and then make sure editors adhere to those deadlines. The managing editor's main responsibility: getting the magazine to the printer on time. MEs may be in charge of hiring and vacation time for staff members. They typically manage the copy editors. The managing editor often works closely with the EIC and publisher on the layout of the magazine, determining where editorial and where advertisements will appear. Many MEs also help with the budget, keeping track of expenditures for art and editorial. Some even do some writing and editing. Just to confuse things, the top editorial position (usually called the editor-in-chief) goes by the title managing editor at some publications. For example, managing editors run the show at Time Inc.'s magazines, including *People*, *InStyle*, *Sports Illustrated*, and *Real Simple*.

### MASTHEAD

Not just a nautical term, the word *masthead* has two meanings in publishing. Appearing most often within the first few pages of a magazine, the masthead is the official list of names, along with job titles, of the people who put the publication together. Mastheads are harder to find in newspapers, as they are often buried somewhere in the publication (sometimes on the editorial page), if they exist at all. The masthead is a good place to check on the spelling of an editor's name. Interestingly, the term also refers to the title of a newspaper or publication that appears across the top of the first page (it is also called a nameplate).

### MULTIPLE SUBMISSION

A *multiple submission* is an idea that has been pitched to more than one magazine simultaneously. In general, this is considered a bad idea. Not only can you get yourself into trouble if more than one publication is interested in your idea, but a good pitch letter should be specifically tailored for one publication, which would make a multiple submission impossible.

### PUBLISHER

The top advertising person at a magazine; the top dog overall at a newspaper. At many publications, the publisher reigns as the ultimate authority. In the newspaper world, he often owns the entire paper. At today's larger corporate-owned papers, he usually at least oversees the entire budget of the pub—on both the editorial and advertising sides—and may have final say on editorials. At many magazines, the editor-in-chief and publisher are on equal footing, with the publisher overseeing the advertising department and the EIC overseeing editorial, and both reporting to the president of the company. In some situations, the EIC reports to the publisher.

### PULL QUOTE

A pull quote is an eye-catching sentence or two that is "pulled" from the running text of an article and featured as display type. Also referred to as a "call out" or "teaser," a pull quote is meant to draw in the reader. Pull quotes are also used to break up text-heavy articles.

### QUERY

The terms *query* and *pitch letter* are used interchangeably. Both refer to letters or e-mails from freelance writers to assigning editors describing a possible story idea. To confuse matters, editors will often use the term *query* when requesting more information from a writer. For example, they might say, "I have a few queries about the content in the first half of your article." In addition, the word is also used as a verb. A writer may say, "I queried that editor six times and never heard back about any of my ideas."

### RUNNING TEXT

Used to describe just the body of an article (also called the main bar), *running text* refers to all the text of a piece, apart from the sidebars, boxes, charts, and hed and dek. Editors, when assigning you a piece, may say, "I see this piece as all running text." Or, "Let's have two pages of running text, along with a sidebar at the end of the second page."

### SCHEDULED/UNSCHEDULED

Scheduled articles are those that have been put on a lineup and are set to appear in a particular upcoming issue. Unscheduled articles, on the other hand, are those pieces that have been assigned but have not yet been planned for a certain issue. (If the piece is complete, but not-yet scheduled, it is said to be in "inventory.")

### SEVEN SISTERS

The original seven magazines that targeted women readers are referred to as the Seven Sisters. They are *Family Circle, Woman's Day, McCall's* (no longer in existence), *Better Homes and Gardens, Good Housekeeping, Ladies' Home Journal,* and *Redbook.*

### SHELTER MAGAZINES

Magazines that focus on the home, decorating, gardening, and food are referred to as shelter magazines.

### SIP (SPECIAL INTEREST PUBLICATION)

Some national magazines also put out SIPs, an acronym for special interest publications. A SIP is a spin-off of an established magazine. It is either produced by the staff of the mother magazine or developed by an entirely new (or freelance) staff that is brought in just for the SIP. A SIP may come out just one time, or once every year, or four times a year, and SIPs sometimes end up launching into their own regularly published magazines. A good example is *InStyle* magazine's *InStyle Weddings*. You will hear these publications referred to as either SIPs (where every letter is enunciated) or as one word: *sips*.

### SLUG

The titles of regularly appearing columns or sections of a publication are called slugs. The slug is often found on the top of a page, above the title. You may also hear the term *slug* applied to a working headline for a piece. In this case, the slug is simply used when editors are referring to the piece in the early stages of editing, before the official headline is written.

### SLUSH PILE

When freelancers send in pitch letters or unsolicited manuscripts and they are not read right away (that's most of them), they may be tossed into a pile on an editor's desk or in the corner of the office. This is called the slush pile. So you may hear an editor say, "I haven't seen your story idea, but I haven't been through my slush pile in weeks." Freelancers are in luck when editors suddenly need to fill some holes in the magazine and they turn to the slush pile.

### SPREAD/DOUBLE-TRUCK

A spread is what you call an article that runs across two facing pages of a magazine. In newspapers it is called a double-truck.

### STAFF WRITER/REPORTER

A freelancer's "in-house" competition. Common to newspapers and weekly magazines, staff writers and reporters are typically full-timers who get paychecks on a regular basis and actually go out and report and write articles for their publications. They seldom have editing responsibilities. Most have desks, or a cubicle or office, at the publication.

### STET

If an editor returns a hard copy of your manuscript to you with comments on it, you may see the word *stet* next to some crossed-out text. This means to ignore the crossed-out markings or changes and consider the text back in its original form.

### STRINGER

Although not as common as they used to be in magazines, stringers are freelance reporters who provide national publications with story ideas based on what's going on in their area of the country. They'll also help with small bits of local reporting for stories pulled together from around the country—an L.A. stringer, for example, might provide a few quotes for a celebrity piece that's being reported and written by a staff writer in New York. Stringers still are fairly common in newspapers, reporting news from outlying areas where the publication may not have regular staff writers working. Stringers may cover City Hall in a small town or report high school football scores to a sports section. While the pay is usually not good, working as a stringer may be a good way for a freelance writer to get noticed by a newspaper or magazine.

### SUBHEAD

Subheads break up a long article into sections. They are mini chapter markers within the running text of a piece.

### TK

If a magazine editor sends a piece back to you for a revise or for changes, you will probably find many TKs scattered throughout. Basically, the letters *TK* are placed anywhere where information is missing. TK is a place marker used in drafts and is short for *tokum,* which is the intentional misspelling of "to come," as in "more info to come." The term is also used in conversation. An editor may call you and say, "I'm e-mailing your story back to you. Can you fill in all the TKs?" Within your copy you may find sentences like the following: "The couple was married in front of a crowd of TK (how many?) happy guests." Or "TK percent of the U.S. population is now considered obese."

### TRADE (MAGAZINE or PUBLICATION)

A publication that is intended just for workers in a specific industry or business is called a trade.

### WELL

The center of a magazine is called its well or feature well. This is the meat of the magazine and is, for the most part, comprised of feature stories. Most of these stories run two to three pages or more. The well is also the place where you'll find pieces that require two-page spreads, such as fashion and beauty features. Articles announced in the coverlines often appear in the well. Most magazines keep advertisements out of (or to a minimum in) the well.

## Acknowledgments

One of my very first clips appeared in the Japanese newspaper *Yomiuri Shimbun.* I was dumbfounded when my mentor, Larry Richardson, at the *Syracuse Herald Journal* told me that the *Yomiuri* was the largest paper in the world, with a daily circulation of more than 10 million. Did those millions of people on the other side of the world really care what a teenager in upstate New York had to say? I am still amazed daily by the power of the written word. And through the process of writing this book, I've again been awestruck— this time by the talent and dedication of people who have made writing or editing the focus of their lives. All of those who contributed to this publication did so without hesitation and revealed a real love for the journalism profession. I, indeed, have many people to thank.

First to Shana Drehs, my editor at Crown, who, like the manager of a winning baseball team, swiftly and smoothly kept this project moving in the right direction. She did so by asking the right questions, providing motivation when necessary, and in the end making this manuscript shine. To my top editor, Jesse Oxfeld, who, as my first-base coach, talked me into stepping up to the plate in the first place and then coached me on when to hold back and when to push it to the next level. And to Kyle Crafton, the publisher and CFO of mediabistro.com, who calmly acted as the umpire, being sure that everyone played fair and that everyone was happy with the final results. Special thanks to Greg Bloom, also at mediabistro.com, who was basically my clean-up batter, making sure this project made it home. And, of course, thanks to Laurel Touby, founder and cyberhostess of mediabistro.com, and owner of this "team," whose extraordinary understanding of and love for the "game of publishing" made this book a reality.

The following writers, editors, and experts all generously gave of their time and offered their knowledge for the benefit of the reader. Thank you: Omer Algar, Kim Atkinson, Richard Baimbridge, Julie Bain, Greg Beaubien, Trisha Calvo, Sheree Curry, L. Divona, Robin Donovan, Daryn Eller, Steve Friedman, Elina Furman, Aileen Gallagher, Adam Gnade, Rebecca Goldberg, Lawrence Grobel, Kendall Hamilton, Terrence G. Harper (Society of Professional Journalists), Amy Hauck, David Hochman, Douglas Imbrogno, Sebastian Junger, Kristin Kemp, Sally Lehrman, Jillian Lewis, John Loecke, Don MacLeod, Ruth Manuel-Logan, Julia Maranan, Tracy Mayor, James Meyer, Nicci Micco, Celeste Mitchell, Doug Most, Amanda Pressner, Tracy Propora, Larry Richardson, Teri Rogers, Howard Samuels, Rebecca Shotwell (*Sierra Club* magazine), Laura Siciliano, Rachel Sklar, Miranda Spencer, Elizabeth Spiers, Nell Stundell, James Sturz, Jennifer Tanaka, Duy Linh Tu, Ellen Ullman, Alex Waterfield, Alison Wellner, Nina Willdorf, and Claire Zulkey.

Special thanks to the authors of mediabistro.com's "How to Pitch" columns, whose talent as writers contributed immensely to this book: Taffy Akner, Nilsa Alston, Claire Atkinson, Nicole Beland, Joshua M. Bernstein, Jamila M. Bey, Greg Bloom, Caroline Callahan, Jackie Cohen, Adrienne Crew, Aaron Dalton, Jennifer Doerr, Rossiter Drake, Dan Dupont, Kristen Elde, Phyllis Fine, Shannon Firth, Emily Fromm, Adriana Gardella, Carlos Greer, Kristine Hansen, Carrie Havranek, David S. Hirschman, Heather Kelly, Caroline Keough, Stephanie Kuenn, Sunny Lee, Jessica Marmour, Melissa Marshall, Gina Masullo, Celeste Mitchell, Matthew L. Nestel, Rebecca Onion, Iva-Marie Palmer, Sabrina M. Parker,

Rebecca Ruiz, Tracy Saelinger, Jamie Allison Sanders, Maria Santos, Darby Saxbe, Erin Schulte, Jonathan Schultz, Jill Singer, Rachel Sklar, Simone Swink, Paula Szuchman, Melissa Walker, Hannah Wallace, Adam Wasserman, Alex Waterfield, Laurie Wiegler, Emily Wojcik, Chrys Wu, and Claire Zulkey.

# Index

## About the Authors

For more than a decade, **Margit Feury Ragland** has worked on both sides of the editorial fence. She began her career as an editor, holding positions at *Family Circle, Woman's Day, Walking,* and *Natural Health* magazines. Acquiring a firm grasp of what happens *inside* a magazine's front door, she took a step *outside* and began freelance writing. Her work has appeared in a wide variety of magazines and newspapers, including *Self, Fitness, Health, Glamour, More, Marie Claire, Redbook, Parenting, Child, American Baby, Boston Magazine, Concierge, Ladies' Home Journal, Cornell Magazine,* and the *Boston Globe Sunday Magazine.* She has also worked on a variety of book projects.

Ragland's connection with mediabistro.com goes back to her early days as an editorial assistant in New York City, when she attended some of Laurel Touby's first mixers for the media. She teaches mediabistro.com classes in Boston, including "Introduction to Magazine Writing" and "Stiletto Boot Camp: Writing for Women's Magazines." In addition, she provides intensive one-on-one instruction by way of mediabistro.com's "E-Boot Camp for Journalists." And for the past three years she has served as hostess for the mediabistro.com mixers in Boston.

**Laurel Touby** started her career at *Working Woman,* moved on to *Business Week* as a staff editor, and in 1993 began editing and writing a column on workplace issues for *Glamour.* She has covered everything from travel to business to breast cancer for a variety of publications, including *New York, Travel + Leisure, Self, Redbook, McCall's,*

*Family Circle, Good Housekeeping, Working Mother,* and the *New York Daily News.*

The original idea for mediabistro.com was cooked up in 1993, when Laurel—who was contributing to *Glamour* magazine at the time—and a friend decided to host a mixer for media people. About ten editors, writers, and other content creators came to that original cocktail party at Jules Bistro in the East Village. Attendees bought their own drinks and enjoyed casual after-work bonding in the company of like-minded people. The parties quickly grew, and soon Laurel had 4,000 of New York's top media talent on her e-mail list. After creating a Web site in 1997 and adding features such as job listings, bulletin boards, classes, e-classes, and a freelance marketplace, Touby's business began to take off. Today, 450,000 media professionals have registered for various mediabistro.com services around the world.

Born in Oahu, Hawaii, Laurel grew up in Miami (before South Beach existed) and graduated from Smith College with a degree in economics. She lives in Williamsburg, Brooklyn, with her husband, Jonathan Fine, the mediacentric columnist at *Business Week.*

## Mediabistro.com Special Offer

Reading this book is a great first (or second or third) step toward enjoying a long and successful freelance-writing career. Taking advantage of the mediabistro.com site is the ideal next move!

To thank you for buying this book, mediabistro.com is offering discounts to readers on all of its products and services. Check out this page:

*http://www.mediabistro.com/insideguide/*

to get information and to access the special deals, which include:

* Premium content access
  —All How to Pitch articles and much more are included!

* Freelance Marketplace discounts
  —Create a listing featuring your work samples and start getting some freelance assignments (the editors will come to you!)

* Class, Seminar, and eClass discounts
  —Take our courses designed for professional writers at all levels, online as well as offline!